Tangible Strategies for Intangible Assets

How to Manage and Measure Your Company's Brand, Patents, Intellectual Property, and Other Sources of Value

JOHN BERRY

McGraw·Hill

New York   Chicago   San Francisco   Lisbon   London   Madrid   Mexico City
Milan   New Delhi   San Juan   Seoul   Singapore   Sydney   Toronto

658.15
B534 Z

Library of Congress Cataloging-in-Publication Data

Berry, John, 1960–
    Tangible strategies for intangible assets : managing and measuring intellectual
property, intellectual capital, and other critical sources of value / by John Berry.
        p.   cm.
    Includes bibliographical references.
    ISBN 0-07-141286-7 (hardcover : alk. paper)
    1. Intangible property—Management.   2. Intangible property—Valuation.
I. Title.

HD53.B468   2004
658.15—dc22   2004012351

MIL

1 2 3 4 5 6 7 8 9 0   FGR/FGR   3 2 1 0 9 8 7 6 5 4

ISBN 0-07-141286-7

McGraw-Hill books are available at special quantity discounts to use as premiums and
sales promotions, or for use in corporate training programs. For more information, please
write to the Director of Special Sales, Professional Publishing, McGraw-Hill, Two Penn
Plaza, New York, NY 10121-2298. Or contact your local bookstore.

This book is printed on acid-free paper.

For my mother and father, without whom I would not be much

CONTENTS

ACKNOWLEDGMENTS

Although the acknowledgments page is often the first passage of a book read, it is certainly the last written. It, therefore, holds a special place in the hearts of authors for a couple of reasons. The acknowledgments symbolize implicitly the profound relief that the work of writing the book is actually done. This realization brings a singular kind of joy that authors cannot be reminded of often enough. More important, the acknowledgments recognize explicitly the contributions of experts without whose guidance and insight the finished work would be impossible to deliver. The saying goes that in a knowledge economy one of the scarcest resources is time. The investment certain people made in this resource to illuminate the many concepts and subject matter explicated in this text, coupled with the fact that a few people who committed to providing information and who agreed to interviews walked away at the last minute with no explanation (and they know who they are), makes the contributions of those who did share their expertise and wisdom all the more generous. For this reason, they deserve a place in the acknowledgments.

Wholehearted thanks to Tim Bernstein of QED and yet2.com, who spent countless hours explaining the company's business model and how it fits into open-market innovation practices today, as well as illustrating how specific companies are leveraging OMI precepts in their intellectual property/asset management. Also, thanks to Phil Stern at QED, who reviewed the OMI chapter, and to Darrell Rigby of Bain, who elaborated his insights on the subject, which originally appeared in a *Har-*

vard Business Review article. Likewise, a special thanks to Gregory Watts, a valuation expert at CBIZ Valuation Group, who revealed his talents as a teacher in explaining the byzantine workings of accounting as they relate to goodwill and intangible asset valuation. His good humor and patience were in high demand as the chapter covering the subject was being written. David Bowerman, also of CBIZ, set the direction early on for my discussion with Watts.

Jay Doherty of Mercer was especially helpful in pointing out resources on human capital management. Human capital—employees—is arguably the most valuable and important intangible asset in an organization's arsenal and is not managed as effectively as it could be. Mercer's work here is groundbreaking and the book is better for inclusion of its thinking. Jeremy Gump, a manager with Ernst & Young's human capital practice, also provided valuable insights into how organizations can better manage their human capital expenditures. Gump's explanations of human capital ROI are highly appreciated. I would also be remiss if I did not thank E&Y partner Bill Leisy for providing me important human capital background information that set the stage for subsequent discussions with Jeremy.

The chapter on knowledge required the input of several people, including Nathaniel Palmer, a chief analyst with Delphi Group, with whom I have had several fruitful conversations on various management subjects over the years. Palmer injected his explanations of the problems with knowledge management as currently practiced with generous doses of dry humor, which kept our discussions lively and thought-provoking. Ted Graham of Hill & Knowlton is a big champion of knowledge management and its usefulness in an organization such as H&K, which relies so heavily on ideas to succeed. Graham's early KM strategies, demonstrated in this text, were quite innovative, and for this I am indebted. Also, thanks to Michael Cahill, the creator of Knowledge Object Theory, for the time he invested to explain the methodology and theory behind it.

Last but not least, the reservoir of appreciation must be big enough to apportion the proper amount of thanks to my editor at McGraw-

Hill, Kelli Christiansen. Her patience was of biblical proportions as she waited for delivery of a final manuscript. As hard as writing a book is, the process is made slightly less maddening in the presence of an editor who knows when to and when not to ask how the book is coming along. Discretion is the better part of valor, and for Kelli's valorous performance, I am very grateful.

CHAPTER 1

INTRODUCTION
BASIC QUESTIONS ABOUT THE NATURE OF INTANGIBLES

What is an intangible asset? The best way to define the term might be to define its component parts first. A dictionary definition of the word *intangible* is "incapable of being felt by touch" or "not readily discerned by the mind." An *asset* is an item of value or a source of wealth. Thus, an intangible asset is an item of value or source of wealth that cannot be felt by touch or is not readily discerned by the mind.

The Brookings Institution mobilized a working group to delve into the subject of intangible assets as they pertain to businesses. The group arrived at a working definition explicated in *Unseen Wealth: Report of the Brookings Task Force on Intangibles*: "intangibles are nonphysical factors that contribute to, or are used in, the production of goods or the provision of services or that are expected to generate future productive benefits to the individuals or firms that control their use."[1] The key elements of this definition include the fact that these assets are nonphysical and are, rather, conceptual and intellectual in nature, as well as the fact that these factors do provide present and future economic value to the organization, which can extract value out of them. An organization that can extract and assign value to intangible assets can, therefore, manage those assets.

The Brookings definition seems like a good baseline upon which to build a deeper analysis because it is one of the few recent, formal efforts to tackle the subject. We will, therefore, use these definitions of *value* and *intangible assets* throughout this book.

Brookings took a crack at classifying intangible assets around the definition it constructed, concluding that intangible assets fall into one of

three strata depending upon whether the particular asset can be measured.[2] According to Brookings, the three classifications are:

1. **Assets that can be owned and sold:** These assets have property
   rights associated with them and include patents, brands, trademarks,
   and copyrights. *Property rights* means that protections from theft or
   appropriation for these intangibles are hard coded in our legal system. These assets are so well defined that they can be bought and
   sold and often are in the context of different kinds of business activities such as mergers and acquisitions. The fact that these types of
   intangibles can be bought and sold does not, however, mean that
   they are valued accurately. A company often overpays for intangibles when it acquires these assets from another company.
2. **Assets that can be controlled but not sold:** These assets are not
   discretely autonomous and therefore cannot be sold or given away
   as an asset. These include in-process research and development
   (R&D) or unique business processes or management techniques.
   R&D represents a well-defined collection of critical elements, such
   as people—research scientists—as well as information technology
   (IT), which supports employees in their work. Yet all the elements
   that constitute a world-class R&D capability might be unique to the
   organization that built them and therefore impossible to simply forklift as an autonomous entity to another company even if an acquirer
   offers a fair price for them.
3. **Assets that may not be wholly controlled by the company:**
   The primary example of this kind of intangible asset is people.
   Employees are the source of many other intangible assets that are
   controlled by the firm—brands, patents, trade secrets, know-how—
   yet they are not owned by the organization (as much as some managers might believe they are). Employees can leave the firm and take
   their expertise with them. They are assets but very mobile ones.

At a high level of abstraction, success in deepening our understanding about intangible assets and their contribution to value creation

means exploring issues from three broad perspectives. One is the internal valuation issue: can we use tried-and-true assessment tools to understand how a certain intangible asset will perform? Two, how does the business community report on financial statements the economic value of intangible assets? And three, and most important, as new thinking around issues 1 and 2 emerges, are there management techniques available for managers to obtain clarity about how best to manage these assets for value?

Answering the last question is the primary focus of this book. Let's probe deeper into intangible asset discussion from the three sets of issues raised by the Brookings work.

Issue 1: Internal Measurement and Valuation

The reason why Brookings brought to our attention intangible asset characteristics in the context of measurement is the belief that the beginning of good asset management begins with valuation. By valuation, we mean the assignment of a dollar value for that asset against which managers can assess the returns or the lack of returns the asset delivers over time. Elementary finance and accounting provided those assessment tools many years ago. The issue is as simple as this basic formula:

$$\frac{\textbf{Profit}}{\textbf{Investment}} = \textbf{Return on Investment}$$

This is the classic elemental measurement tool that managers will use to assess the viability of a capital allocation, whether it be for a new x-ray machine, a drill press, a metal lathe, HR and payroll software, a truck fleet . . . the list goes on. If a $100 investment in an asset returns $20 in profits through cost savings or profit, the return on investment (ROI) is 20 percent. Now consider this:

$$\frac{\text{Profit}}{\text{Intangible Investment}} = \textbf{Return on Investment}$$

Supposing the same manager wants to make a $100 investment in an intangible asset—say, a patent someone wants to sell or license him. If the company can generate a $20 profit through the creation of a product reflecting the secret know-how in the patent, the manager will be congratulated on the 20 percent ROI the intangible asset returns. Level 1 intangible assets allow for the reasonable assessment of future economic benefits because valuation techniques exist.

However, the calculation is complicated by the fact that the very nature of intangible assets is that they are complementary with other assets, which, in sum, deliver the economic benefit. In this case, the investment includes not only the dollar cost of the patent but the product development and marketing strategy that convinces the public that the product is an innovation worth buying. These are critical complementary drivers of value extraction from the patent.

We can add up the costs of all these inputs, which constitute the denominator of the ROI calculation. The patent, the product development capability, and the marketing expertise are all assets factored into ROI. How does a manager apportion the revenue or net income generated from the new product to all the inputs that went into its sale by customers? Which asset gets what weighting? How much more important is the patent than marketing, or is product development execution equally important as the patent in driving the financial impact? A patent is not much use unless managers have a firm grasp of the potential market receptivity to the innovation and can execute effectively.

With level 2 intangibles, the valuation can be even more problematic for the same reason—whether they are complementary. If a manager makes a $100 investment in resources that create a competitively differentiating business process, he or she might be able to calculate its ROI. But the calculation is not so cut-and-dried. Supposing a manufacturer wants to improve its service parts management operation to reduce delivery times to customers. It builds proprietary logistics software and undergoes data cleaning, classification efforts, and the reorganizational design of service parts personnel for improved planning across its service network. All these efforts require resource investment, chiefly people and money. What is the investment base a manager would use to assess the viability of embarking on this project?

It wouldn't be hard to calculate the resource commitment in labor and technology to reengineer the parts-selling organization so you would have a handle on the investment, or denominator of the ROI calculation. The results might be fairly easy to quantify, too, such as improvements in working capital efficiency.

The result of this investment effort is a new intangible asset (the combination of technology, procedural steps, and people), which provides the organization unique efficiencies in the delivery of service parts to customers—and that's not an insignificant achievement, considering that aftermarket service and parts account for 20 to 30 percent of revenues and about 40 percent of profits for most manufacturers.[3] If the company wants to monitor or measure the performance of this "asset" over time, what would it be measuring? How much weight should be given IT's contribution as opposed to the organizational design and procedural arrangements, which the technology supports but which together constitute this asset? Suppose this asset could be improved upon in some way to extend the efficiencies throughout the supply chain, from manufacturer's floor to customer plant. How has the asset appreciated in value? How would a manager calculate the ROI of the incremental investment needed to extend the original, intangible benefit for additional economic value?

Measurement in level 3 becomes quite difficult. Today, people are paid at least the lip service of being an organization's most important asset. Companies spend enormous sums on workforce training. What's the organization's ROI for an advanced degree invested in a middle manager? What's the payback period? Does an ROI calculation take into account the risk factor of the middle manager's departure from the firm a week after receiving a diploma, essentially wiping out any potential asset investment gains? If we choose not to use the tried-and-true historical methods of economic assessment like ROI, what metrics take their place?

These hypotheticals show that because the business community rightfully believes these intangible capabilities are truly assets, problems emerge in quantifying them for their proper management using assessment methods meant for buildings and machinery. This is the internal measurement challenge posed by intangible assets. The traditional tools of accounting and finance, such as ROI, are difficult to apply to intangible assets because intangibles are not traditional and do not conform to the historical understanding we have of that concept called assets. Yet if intangible assets are truly assets, then empirically tested techniques for value extraction must be developed, or in the end these assets will lie fallow or huge opportunity costs will be incurred because capital was not invested in other value-producing assets. Assets must be managed if full value can be realized from them. This book explores some of those techniques.

Issue 2: External Measurement and Valuation

This is where the ride gets wild. The accounting profession is in a funk because not only are the economic assessment tools used internally somewhat ill suited to the task, but the entire function of reporting the financial health of an organization fails miserably in telling stakeholders how much a driver of growth and profit performance all those intangible assets really are. As far as how accounting treats them, intangible assets are assets only to the extent that managers believe they are because they have proven their ability to deliver value to the organization. These "assets" are not assets at all on financial statements. One of the loudest examples of this disconnect is the accounting treatment of research and development.

R&D is a critical resource, considered by many to be a highly valuable intangible asset, maybe one of the top three in an organization. Not the intellectual property (IP), which is the ultimate outcome of R&D, but the organizational, people, and know-how components that constitute the R&D function itself. A company invests in R&D capability, and its managers wholeheartedly believe this capability is an asset that will deliver future economic rewards in the form of other kinds of intangible assets—trade secrets and patents, which are direct sources of revenue and cash flow. Yet R&D is treated as an expense in financial reporting. The investment is not capitalized on the company balance sheet as would be an investment in a new building or piece of machinery. The amount of the investment is expensed at the time of investment.

The punishment is a double whammy. Not only do financial reports not recognize investments in R&D as an asset, but the investment is actually punished because the amount of that allocation into R&D is expensed at the time of the expenditure, becoming a hit to earnings.

This example is not meant to expose the weaknesses of accounting so much as to demonstrate the disconnect between what managers in the U.S. economy believe are assets and how financial reporting standards treat business activities around the cultivation of those assets. This tension can be described as the external measurement and valuation problem. This disconnect between investments in and cultivation of intangible assets and their portrayal on balance sheets and income statements is larger in some industries than others depending upon how important intangibles are in influencing the delivery of value to customers and ultimately profit growth. Entertainment, pharmaceuticals, technology companies, and some consumer goods manufacturers own and rely upon a high amount of intangible assets for their success. Retail less so. Yet even in industries where the aggregate quantity and intensity of intangible asset ownership and influence are seemingly low, their importance to the success of the business might be quite high.

For example, consider the local Thai restaurant that makes unique and excellent food because of the skill and recipes of the chef. The restaurant managers and owners know full well the quality of the food is the primary driver of its success because enough customers have raved about it, and, as a result, the operation is highly profitable. The restaurant owns a valuable intangible asset even if its managers do not conceive of the unique recipes of Thai cuisine in this way.

The external valuation tension, the disconnect between how accounting rules portray intangibles versus how managers' imagination and gut instinct portray them, is a key reason why the intangible asset phenomenon is attracting increasing attention from business leaders. If managers did not stand up and declare that some capability or some entity in the corporation was an asset worth leveraging for its value, there would be far less discussion about the subject. Yet managers have stood up and declared that people, organizational capabilities, brands, and other phenomena are indeed assets and worth managing for value even if the internal and external measurement solution is incomplete.

One caveat. Experts in the profession point out that the science of accounting does not value anything but merely reports. It is true that the dollar figures that appear on balance sheets are derived from assignment of dollar values conducted elsewhere. Yet reporting and valuation are closely linked to the extent that managers would like to report the contribution of some intangible assets, but current accounting does not allow it and, therefore, does not reflect their full financial potential. Financial reporting, in fact, requires the assignment of a dollar value first, so although valuation is not reporting, one is contingent upon the other.

Issue 3: Valuation Versus Management

The oldest saw in management is "If you can't measure it, you can't manage it." This is perhaps true in the ideal; however, managers do not have complete, locked-down measurement systems for the scientific quantification of all intangible assets, and yet they have moved beyond the struggle accounting has with the topic. They are managing intangible assets for contribution to financial performance even though in some instances a direct causal linkage between an intangible asset and the actual financial performance is, at best, tenuous. Likewise, valuation of some intangible assets is pointless; for example, what's the dollar value of a piece of knowledge? Maybe it would be interesting to know, but it does little to extend our comprehension of what intangible assets are and how they are managed.

In defense of the assertion that valuation is not management, consider this exercise to compute the value of a brand. The following simple but illustrative example (Table 1.1) is adapted from a *Harvard Business Review* article.[4]

This brand methodology is the result of two numerical values: the net after-tax profits excluding the earnings of an unbranded equivalent product and the brand strength multiple. The multiple scores a company brand along the following dimensions:

Table 1.1   Computing the Value of a Brand

Company X annual operating income for the year XXXX (in billions)	$1.000
Minus operating income of an unbranded equivalent product	.055
Company adjusted operating income for the year XXXX	.945
Company adjusted operating income for the previous year	.892
Weighted two-year operating income average (year XXXX weighted two times the previous year)	.927
Minus U.S. tax rate of 34%	.315
Company X two-year weighted, after-tax net income	.612
Company brand strength multiple 19.04	
Company X two-year weighted, after-tax net income	.612
Times company brand strength multiple	11.6
Company X estimated brand value for the year XXXX	11.6

- ability to influence the market
- ability to maintain a consumer franchise
- vulnerability of market demand because of shifting tastes or technology
- ability to build a market internationally
- long-term appeal
- communications effectiveness
- strength of owner's property rights over the brand

The higher the multiple, the higher a company's brand strength. In this valuation method, multiples range from 6 to 20.[5]

In the example above, this brand is worth a little more than $11.6 billion in year X. For argument's sake we'll say that the next year's brand value is $11.7 billion. Brand value has appreciated $100 million. Do managers know with any degree of certainty what strategies and tactics caused this to happen? Were managers able to isolate and weigh the relevant importance of communications effectiveness, which might have caused the brand to increase in value domestically, versus its growing popularity overseas? How much influence did a Six Sigma quality improvement effort have on the incremental increase in brand value? How about a new product design or a redesign of the company's website? In the absence of any deep understanding of all the levers that influenced a rise in brand value, what future course of action are managers supposed to take should they be required to boost that value on a consistent quarter-in, quarter-out basis?

Unless managers can decompose the complementary elements that constitute improvements in a brand, knowing how much the brand is worth at any given time has limited value.

Put another way, if senior management set a 10 percent increase in brand value for the next quarter, would brand managers have any confidence in their understanding of the levers that drive its value—which go way beyond advertising and PR—to manage for that 10 percent increase?

Don't Just Value Intangible Assets—Manage Them

So this book is not simply about valuation. What this book concerns itself with is capturing the latest thinking and innovations in how managers are managing discrete intangible assets for value even if pure measurement systems do not yet exist. Throughout the pages, which explore these techniques, it is shown conclusively that new management and measurement systems exist; they just are not exact replicas of ROI tools used historically to assess physical assets. And the good news is that these techniques are not beyond the comprehension of everyday walking-around managers.

The book is designed to explore several classes of intangible assets. They are:

- information technology
- intellectual property/intellectual assets
- knowledge
- customers
- brand
- employees

Each of these classes, with the exception of brand, receives its own chapter. A discussion of brand is covered late in the book in the context of organizational issues around effective intangible asset management. In deciding which intangible asset classes to explore for new value creation techniques, we used the Financial Accounting Standards Board laundry list of commonly understood and identifiable intangible assets as a kind of baseline.[6] Table 1.2 shows this inventory.

As you can see, most of the intangible assets in the FASB's list are not dealt with directly in this book. While all the intangible assets in this list are important sources of value, they are not necessarily applicable to the everyday concerns of managers. Or they are derivative of more important intangible assets. This idea is worth exploring for a moment.

Take a customer list. This is an asset managers can do many things with, but a customer list is a kind of residual benefit from managing a much more important intangible asset—the customers themselves. The customer list is the result of successfully leveraging customer relationships for profits. What is more important to manage, a list or the assets that the list comprises?

Now consider rights-of-way, a contract-based intangible asset delineated in Table 1.2. This is a kind of strange intangible asset that many readers might not be familiar with. Rural municipalities are keen on building the proper economic and regulatory environment that encour-

Table 1.2   FASB Intangible Assets

Intangible Asset Type	Comprises
Marketing-related	Trademarks, trade names, service marks, trade dress (package design), newspaper mastheads, Internet domain names, noncompete agreements
Customer-related	Customer lists, order backlogs, customer contracts, noncontractual customer relationships
Artistic-related	Plays, operas, ballets, books, magazines, newspapers, musical works (e.g., compositions, song and advertising lyrics)
Contract-based	Licensing, royalty agreements, service contracts, lease and franchise agreements, construction permits, use rights (e.g., utility, telephony rights-of-way, water, air, timber cutting rights), employment contracts
Technology-based	Patents, software, unpatented technology, databases, trade secrets (e.g., recipes, formulas)

ages infrastructure upgrades from telecommunication carriers who have little economic incentive to make capital investments because rural areas are much more expensive to serve and therefore provide an uncertain payback or ROI for those capital investments. Resistance by carriers to investment in advanced telecommunications leaves rural communities economically disadvantaged, so they seek strategies and tactics that would at least improve the environment of incentives that might attract the investment these officials seek.

A right-of-way in which a municipality provides a contractual permission for a carrier to trench streets and other public land within its local domain is a necessary step for a carrier to provision telecommunications services in a community. A right-of-way is a hugely important asset having a precise cost associated with it in cases where local jurisdictions are asking for compensation from the carrier in exchange for permission to provision service. It is a cost that has actually risen as communities have caught on to the revenue-generating potential of charging fees for rights-of-way. This kind of intangible asset is very well defined economically. A carrier could conceivably sell this option to provision service to another carrier if it was not prohibited contractually from doing so. The valuation is well defined in terms of the purchase price carriers pay to obtain the right-of-way.

From a management perspective, however, is a right-of-way an intangible asset that can be leveraged for value like other intangible assets? Once the right-of-way is obtained, it does not require a whole lot of management, and in and of itself it offers no incremental economic benefit. The real benefit derives from winning customers through the availability of advanced voice and data services. The right-of-way itself is not an ongoing source of increasing value but a stable option that enables the delivery of value in the marketplace through the provisioning of advanced services. Management of this critical intangible asset will turn on compliance issues with the terms of the contract. Unlike other intangibles, a right-of-way does not lend itself to forward-going management techniques for continuous value extraction once the permission has been obtained.

The point is that while some intangible asset classes do not require the intensity of management, others obviously do, even though they are considered assets. This book is confined to those intangible assets that require an enormous intensity of focus and effort. If organizations can successfully manage the intangible assets defined in the book's chapters, the other intangible assets will take care of themselves.

You might also have noticed that two classes of intangibles tackled in this book fail to make the FASB list: employees and customers. This standards body's orientation and concern are around financial reporting, and these two categories are not considered assets that require capitalization for reporting purposes. (You could argue that customers' participation on a balance sheet would be redundant because their contribution to financial performance is already well represented on the income statement.)

Customers differ from all other intangibles in one critical aspect: the firm has little or no control over them. Nevertheless, as an intangible class, it is included in this book because, first, the rhetorical fishing net has caught the concept of "the customer" along with all the other intangibles that swim in the media and business press ocean. You don't have to troll long before reading some executive's pronouncement that a company's customers are one of its greatest "assets." And two, a certain aspect of the customer profile remains intangible because businesses do not bother to quantify it. That is the customer's profitability to the firm with whom he or she does business. For many businesses, this dimension of the customer is quite measurable and can have significant impact on customer-oriented strategy. So even though "the customer" fails one of Brookings/the FASB's definitions, it is included in this text as a class of intangible asset in which techniques exist for their management.

Conclusions

If intangible assets are to be managed for value, they have to be defined clearly in contrast to what we have historically considered assets. Ridiculously commonsensical perhaps, yet the work by Brookings is a long-overdue analysis of the basics—the fundamental nature of intangible assets. The application of sophisticated management techniques can bear no fruit unless the simple questions are first asked. It is likely that the history of the science and art of management will view its task force work kindly.

Logic of Book Structure

Before readers embark on learning the specific techniques for improved intangible asset management, the book begins with a chapter outlining the fog the experts find themselves in when defining intangible assets, as well as providing some definitional clarity missing from the analysis. Brookings argues that definitional clarity and a commonly accepted taxonomy of all intangible assets are essential for universal comprehension and improved management. One manager's "intellectual capital" is another's "knowledge capital" and yet another's "structural capital." The difference might seem trivial, but it isn't when the business community is attempting to build a common language and universal understanding around intangible assets.

Another chapter provides some historical backdrop of the challenges the accounting profession faces. Again, the valuation and financial quantification issue surrounding intangible assets is distinct from their management. Yet both are inextricably linked to the extent that if accounting could devise new ways to portray the financial implications of intangible assets, managers would have no choice but to fold them into asset management strategies. The profit and loss (P&L) statement still reigns supreme as an indicator of managerial performance. A deeper understanding of the nature of intangible assets requires a basic understanding of the reporting challenges corporate America faces.

In the end, there was one key question when deciding whether to include a class of intangible asset in this book: are there new or innovative approaches for the extraction of value from intangible assets that at least infer some strategic impact to the organization? Hopefully, in asking this question themselves, managers can legitimize some managerial actions and delegitimize others, while gaining an intellectual backdrop upon which they make more informed day-to-day decisions in their organizations.

CHAPTER 2

TOWARD DEFINITIONAL CLARITY

The twentieth-century philosopher Ludwig Wittgenstein said that the limits of language are the limits of reality; if we can't ascribe a commonly understood and agreed-upon term to describe a phenomenon, then it eludes our ability for comprehension—we are unable to make it a commonly accepted part of our reality. There can be little argument that the concept of intangible assets has an unreal, otherworldly quality to it. A lot of ink has been spilled discussing the growing intangibility of the sources of wealth inside a company, but these assets have been treated haphazardly in rhetorical terms and have therefore defied neat categorizations.

The definitions of intangible assets can be understood in the shifting perceptions of managers. As the American economy has evolved, the sources of value creation have simply shifted. In a cookie-cutter, mass-production, industrial economy, labor supported capital-intensive output. Workers were interchangeable, they were subservient to capital (to machines), and their mental contributions were not sought or needed. How could a company view employees as an asset? Contrast that with the high level of mental output necessary to run businesses today. Intellectual contributions in whatever form—ideas, strategies, plans, blueprints, technical specifications, patents, trademarks, and so on—are at the core of a company's success. Employees take on the quality of an asset because they are a fundamentally more important source of value creation than machines. The related intangible asset, knowledge, is also perceived as an asset. Knowledge is the manifestation of the mental effort human capital makes for the business to succeed. This manifestation of that effort must itself be managed for value.

Information technology has undergone a similar transformation. By the 1960s and '70s, companies could not survive without mainframes to organize operational information as businesses scaled to ever larger sizes. Yet once everyone automated critical business processes, there was little strategic value in IT. This was the age of green screens and dumb terminals.

As IT evolved into distributing computing arrangements with the emergence of client/server architectures, we began to see packaged application vendors come out of the woodwork with software that allowed companies to not only cut costs through automation but gain a competitive edge (however short-lived) through the tweaking of business processes. The same shift in attitude occurred with internally built software. Ironically, a shift in managerial attitude, which acknowledged IT's potential strategic value, was arguably less radical than the shift had been regarding employees, for the simple reason that IT was treated as an asset on the company's books. IT had already been conceived as an asset, only now more so.

In some experts' estimation, customers are an asset today, too—they are part of a company's "relational capital." Customers fail almost every definition of what an asset is, but it hasn't stopped them from being cast in this way. Much of the reason why customers are thought of as assets is not that they are suddenly a source of value—they have always been a source of value, the ultimate arbiter of a company's financial performance. What they are today is scarce. There is so much competition for people's money, so much competition for people's time, so much competition for repeat business that managers have fenced customers into the intangible asset corral because there is so much urgency around acquiring and keeping them. Companies don't just want customers— they are (in many businesses) desperate for customers. As much as some may find it a stretch in calling customers an asset, those who do find that customers are worth managing for value.

The Nature of Intangible Assets

Brookings has an easily understandable definition of an intangible asset, as we saw in Chapter 1. The Financial Accounting Standards Board provides guidance for reporting purposes as to what are commonly possessed intangible assets. Any investigation into emerging techniques, methods, or practices around the better management of intangible assets must not just know what intangible assets are but also must examine their nature. The purpose of this chapter is to explore the nature of intangible assets, to discern patterns in their behavior that might help us classify them and so deepen our understanding of them.

The approaches to intangible asset classification include contrasting the attributes of intangible assets versus the attributes of physical assets, defining intangible assets in terms of causality and complementarity (that is, how other intangibles influence their creation, value, and management), and analyzing the unique economic attributes of intangible assets. Every classification exercise reveals something unique about intangible assets, yet no single exercise provides a universal definition into which every intangible asset fits neatly.

Intangibles Are Not Physical Assets

As Brookings has already pointed out, intangible assets, broadly understood, are defined as assets that cannot be touched, have no independent market value (as opposed to physical hard assets, like a building or a tractor, which do have value), and are not treated as assets at all on financial statements. (The exception is IT.) Most assets deemed intangible find their way onto a company's income statement, where they are expensed, as opposed to being placed on a balance sheet, where they would be capitalized. (More on this in subsequent chapters.) We know that these assets include but are not limited to company culture, innovation, brands, market position, intellectual property, leadership, knowledge capital, human capital, organizational agility, and loyal customers. Because intangible assets have come to mean any perceived or real source of value creation other than the assets documented by accounting (in its bookkeeping logic), the seeds of confusion are sown.

Another way to define intangible assets is to understand what they are not. The Financial Accounting Standards Board (FASB), a financial reporting and accounting standards body, has established clear rules as to what an asset is for reporting purposes, including the following:[1]

- They must be well defined and distinct from other assets.
- The organization must have effective control over them.
- Future economic benefits from their exploitation and use must be measurable.
- It must be possible to determine economic impairment—assets become obsolete and wear out and therefore depreciate.

As a consequence of this set of definitional parameters, assets have traditionally meant equipment, plant, and other physical capital, as well as financial capital (bonds, stocks, cash, etc.). How do intangible assets delineated in this book fit into this construct? Table 2.1 demonstrates that some intangible asset classes satisfy some of the criteria around the definition of an asset. It depends upon the intangible asset itself.

Table 2.1 Are Intangible Assets Really Assets in the Formal Sense?

	Information Technology	Intellectual Property/Assets	Knowledge	Customers	Brand	Human Capital
Well defined, discrete	Maybe	Yes	Maybe	Yes	Yes	Yes
Organizational control and ownership	Yes	Yes	Maybe	No	Yes	No
Predicted economic impacts	Yes	Yes	Very indirect	Yes	Yes	Yes
Obsolescence factor—determination of economic impairment, loss of value	Yes	Yes	Maybe	Yes	Yes	No

Table 2.1 shows that there are no absolutes in the world of intangible assets when defined in contrast to old-world assets. Let's explore each category.

Information Technology

IT passes the FASB's litmus test along every dimension . . . sometimes. Technologies are well defined and often discrete. Think of IT hardware—servers, mainframes, etc. Software, however, loses its discreteness once it is integrated with an array of other software out of which a particular application's total value is realized. A new customer relationship management application might be integrated with a company's old billing system. A new supply chain software package might be integrated downstream with either a supplier or a vendor. In both cases, a company records the new software on its books as an asset, yet each application's maximum value is defined by its interoperability with other systems. The borders that define a software investment as a discrete, well-defined asset become blurred in terms of its total value as it complements other software assets over time.

As mentioned, IT shares one attribute with traditional assets. Both hardware and software are booked as assets on financial statements, and IT's value is drawn down over time because it obsolesces (newer improved versions are released). Its future economic value can be predicted, and it is under an organization's control (unless the company outsources the functionality—in which case, there is no asset to own).

Intellectual Property/Intellectual Assets

Intellectual property (IP) and intellectual assets (IA) also pass the FASB's definition. Patents, copyrights, and trade secrets are very well defined. Their economic impact can be forecast using established valuation methods employed by experts in the field. Mergers and acquisitions and asset-backed financing are a common context around which these valuation activities will take place. Although IP and IA are probably the best-known and oldest intangible asset, their intangibility speaks more to the fact that they can't be touched physically rather than to any challenge in measuring and managing them.

Knowledge

This is a strange one. Knowledge is not well defined. One person's knowledge might be another's data. The company that creates knowledge might control it, or knowledge might be under the control of the employee who has neither the opportunity nor the inclination to share it. It resides in his or her noggin. The economic impacts from knowledge value extraction—knowledge management—might have some operational impacts if deployed correctly, but the direct relationship of knowledge with improvements in earnings is tenuous at best. Does knowledge obsolesce? Sometimes. Employees get a lot of mileage out of insightful market analysis for about six months, but the pace of market conditions changes rapidly and its contents lose some of their saliency. However, the collective knowledge of the organization increases in value because someone offers new insight that replaces the old. Is there a way to determine its loss of value? No, because there is no way to determine a dollar value from a piece of knowledge in the first place. Knowledge often fails every definition of a traditional asset. Nevertheless, the chapter on knowledge will hopefully demonstrate that while the concept of it is often foggy and almost impossible to measure, this has not stopped managers from managing knowledge for value.

Customers

Companies wish they had effective control over their customers. Wouldn't sales meetings be much more pleasant if that were so? Despite the absence of ownership (which is a core attribute of an asset), managers insist customers are assets to the company. In fact, predicting the economic impacts of customers is one dimension of their performance profiles either ignored by many businesses today or not attempted because they lack the capability to make these calculations. The ability to quantify customer profitability is core to advanced management of this intangible asset class.

Brand

A company's brands satisfy every dimension of an asset. They are well defined: Procter & Gamble and Unilever can distinguish between every brand in their consumer products lineup. They are also discrete: valuation techniques exist to assess the future income potential from a brand, and brands are bought and sold all the time. Valuation techniques also provide the ability to determine whether a brand has diminished in economic value over time. Despite maturity in valuation and a long history of the purchase and sale of a brand, this intangible asset is not capitalized on a balance sheet. Yet a brand's accounting treatment has not diminished the belief that it is a vital asset in the organization's portfolio.

Human Capital

Employees are arguably the most intangible of intangible assets. They certainly have a physical presence in the world, so this class fails the touch test. Yet the intangibility of employees—human capital—derives mainly from their treatment on financial statements; they are expensed rather than capitalized. Formal financial reporting denies that employees are assets, yet no company could argue that they are not. Because of this reporting treatment, economic impairment of human capital is impossible to determine since employees are not considered an asset in the first place, even if an employee's departure, retirement, or death has a palpable impact on the operations or value-creating capacity of a business. In fact, the opposite holds. Releasing this asset from the company's "ownership" improves its economic conditions because it is no longer an expense and, therefore, a drag on earnings.

The fact that some dimensions of intangible assets fail the FASB definition does not mean they are not assets. The comparative exercise was meant to illustrate the points of divergence between the definition of an asset rooted in accounting and what managers know to be the truth. Understanding this difference is a necessary first step in defining what intangible assets are.

Causality and Complementarity

Let's return to the Brookings definition, now organized in the form of a chart (see Table 2.2).

Table 2.2 Intangible Assets

Intangible Class	What It Includes
Level 1: assets that can be owned and sold	Intellectual property, such as patents, copyrights, and brands (brands are often bought and sold through mergers and acquisitions)
Level 2: assets that can be controlled but cannot be made discrete and sold as autonomous entities	R&D, unique business processes, and good management systems*
Level 3: assets not wholly owned or controlled by one firm	People, stakeholder relationships (R&D partnerships, supply chain, or product design collaborations), and network effects

*Brookings, p. 54. Brookings argues that level 2 intangibles demand a consistent vocabulary, and we are far from having one.

The Brookings approach is really classifying intangibles in terms of salability. That is, can the asset be sold as a discrete good? If yes, then this means that the particular asset has to be well defined and discrete in order for its ownership to transfer to the buyer.

Another way to think about intangible assets is around complementarity and causality. That is, the value of any intangible asset is tied up in its interplay with other intangible assets. We have already seen this phenomenon at work, such as with IT. In conceiving of intangible assets around complementarity, we see that these assets possess both root and derived properties. Root properties mean any intangible asset class can be managed as a distinct, discrete entity without regard for how it is influenced by other assets. For instance, a company brand has meant managing product categories through advertising, promotion, package design, and other marketing activities. Yet the power of a brand is influenced by many other company assets and processes, both tangible and intangible, such as manufacturing quality control, information technology, and collaborative product design with partners and customers. The creation of full value of a brand includes the derived properties of success in these other areas. Should brand management include a voice and involvement in the utilization of any of these other assets and capabilities given the inherent complementarity embedded in a brand? And if not direct involvement, should brand managers at least increase their literacy of how these other elements drive brand as a way to inspire deeper thinking about more effective ways to exploit a brand for value creation?

Employees are another example. There is a growing body of thought that argues that if employees are going to be managed for their fullest value potential, they must be viewed as part of a larger system of recruitment, retention, and training—a system of policies, procedures, and strategies aligned with the business objectives of the firm. The company workforce is often managed in a vacuum that is completely blind to the larger human system that influences financial performance. This is because managers have a difficult time linking any decisions around human capital management with their effects on the bottom line. There is simply too much causal ambiguity between the performance of individual workers and financial results of the company. If this were not true, companies would, for example, make much shrewder and subtler decisions about who gets laid off when.

And often they are not motivated to calculate those causal linkages, if they exist at all, for the very fact that employees are an expense and not an asset in the traditional sense. Yet employees cannot be leveraged as human capital assets for their full value-creating potential unless they are conceived within this larger interdependent system. One consulting firm's work proves this.

Figure 2.1 illustrates the complementarity and causation in the creation of intangible assets, revealing the root causation and derived properties for each class. The illustration simply reinforces two ideas. First, many but not all intangible assets in the organization are created rather than acquired. This means they are customized to the unique needs and goals of a particular organization and offer a potential competitive advantage. And second, any intangible owes its existence to other intangibles that precede it—they have derived properties. Any intangible is also complementary with other intangible assets, which might cause managers to manage them more holistically than has been the case.

Consider the causality and complementarity of each intangible asset.

Figure 2.1 Causation and Complementarity of Intangible Assets

System of hiring = Human capital

Human capital sharing their expertise + IT to share and access knowledge = Knowledge

Programmers and project managers + Knowledge—unique business process design = IT

Talented engineers + Technical knowledge + IT-supported R&D capacity = IP/IA

Marketing employees + Knowledge about products and customers + IT for man. quality/customer service + Production innovation through IP/IA = Brand

All employees + Domain expertise + IT running the entire enterprise + Product/service innovation + Great products/brand equity = Customers

Human Capital

Human capital, the intangible asset buzzword for employees, is the root of all other intangible assets. All intangible asset creation begins with employees. There are no other intangible assets without people. Does human capital have a derived component?

Companies do not create employees in the strictest sense. Yet the acquisition of the right employees who serve company objectives means the organization needs to have a well-conceived hiring process in place. Bad hiring decisions result in human capital that is misaligned with the goals of the organization, and this capital input, conceptually speaking, delivers less than optimal returns. In this sense, good hiring practices are a necessary input to the "creation" of employees. New techniques that consider hiring practices as just one component of a multifaceted system for value creation out of human capital reflect this.

Knowledge

Fill a room with knowledge management practitioners, and you are bound to get as many definitions of knowledge management.[2] There is much confusion around the management of knowledge precisely because it does have root properties. Knowledge management is defined by some to mean the archiving and labeling of information for easy access and retrieval, with the goal of helping employees do their jobs more effectively. Getting people to willingly part with their hard-won experiential expertise is often overlooked. The chapters on knowledge demonstrate that although it can be managed as a stand-alone kind of intangible asset class, the contributions of employees influence the degree to which value is extracted out of the management of knowledge. In this light, the derived property of knowledge, chiefly the processes and dynamics of the creation and sharing of knowledge by employees, is a necessary input and a critical success factor in knowledge management that creates value. A view of knowledge management confined to the archiving and labeling of information for easy retrieval is a limited view.

The other challenge is defining what knowledge is. It has been referred to as anything from opinions and observations captured in e-mail to news reports of a competitor's actions, pieces of a sales proposal, a JPEG of an organizational reengineering effort—in fact, almost any information bounded by the limits of a software program required for its access and deemed useful by the knowledge consumer. A definition of something that is so open-ended runs the risk of meaning nothing, and this is one of the greatest weaknesses of knowledge management today.

Conceptually, knowledge is a kind of raw material intangible asset, and there is no company on the planet that can succeed without it. A necessary condition for its creation, of course, is the people who produce it. Managing knowledge means managing in specific ways the input to its creation—people. Therefore, knowledge has a single yet important derived property—human capital.

Information Technology

Much IT is bought from vendors, yet for some companies, competitive differentiation can be found in architecting unique processes built around homegrown code. Where no competitive differentiation exists, many companies still opt to build in-house; vendor software simply won't do the job the way the company wants it. At the root are the talents of programmers, business analysts, and project managers who bring the software design to finished product.

A great example of a company creating a valuable intangible asset in software is Amazon.com, with its uniquely designed platform, which supports both the purchase of goods at its website and the back-office workflow and business processes that make its e-commerce site possible. Just about all of Amazon's e-commerce Web interface is tied into all the supporting activities, which enable people to easily browse the merchandise, make a selection, choose a payment method, and hit the purchase button with the expectation that the goods will arrive on time. This browsing, selecting, and buying environment was built from scratch. What intangible assets went into the creation of perhaps the most important intangible asset the company now owns (second only to the talents of the people who built and support it)? (This environment is far more valuable than the brand, which is a derivative intangible from the functionality of the easy-to-use online shopping environment. The uniqueness of the IT platform drawing in and pleasing customers drives the brand, not the other way around, a point explained in more detail later.) The unique IT platform derives its value from the human capital who tackled the complexity of building a workable system that serves many constituencies simultaneously.

Intellectual Property/Intellectual Assets

Innovation-intensive companies have understood for some time the powerful complementarity between people, R&D, and intellectual property. Skilled engineers placed into the proper research environment create the patents, trade secrets, or other know-how that has the potential to be the next great product. Managing IP itself as a discrete asset also has a long lineage. Management activities include prioritizing the portfolio and then licensing, selling, donating, or relinquishing ownership. Intellectual property management is quite sophisticated today and well covered in valuation literature.

What is less understood is how companies can better balance resource investment in R&D with know-how acquisition from the outside when the complementary assets of skilled researchers and R&D practices fail to produce the ingredients for the next innovation. Innovation is so important today that if new ideas are not produced from the sweat of its own R&D organization, a company better have an efficient way to find new ideas from somewhere else.

Solutions have emerged that help companies greatly ramp up the acquisition of IP/IA intangible assets when internal efforts fail to create them. Known as open-market innovation (OMI), this IP management trend calls for a wholesale reassessment of the capabilities found in all the intangible assets, which, when taken together, are supposed to deliver the innovations that feed growth and earnings performance. They include human capital, the human capital compensation and incentive reward system, R&D, and any other unique organizational elements. OMI demands an understanding of intangible asset complementarity less for how it creates IP/IA and more for how it fails to do so. Companies that operationalize the acquisition of IP/IA will likely deemphasize or cut back investment in certain intangible assets established for their creation. The sellers of IP/IA who sit on the other side of this market exchange will also renew their interest in understanding the collection of intangible assets that create IP/IA because of their potential to generate revenue through licensing, an opportunity organizations may not have had in the absence of an OMI vehicle through which innovations are rented out.

Brand

A company's brand is the outcome of superior performance along a number of dimensions: quality, price, product design, customer service, etc. A brand is a promise delivered. Historically, brand management really meant product marketing. The brand was the product—a car, a box of cereal, or whatever. A manager would reach for market share increases of a specific product through the interplay of advertising, product promotion, and pricing.

The Brookings Institution contends that the value of an intangible asset derives from its interplay with other assets and that it is a waste of time to attempt valuing it on a stand-alone basis.[3] A brand is dependent upon "product quality, price, distribution channels, dealer relationships, and other factors."[4] The sentiment is that attempts to value a brand separate from its component parts are pointless. Perhaps that is so, with respect to assigning a financial value to a brand (despite the fact that many valuation techniques exist). But valuation is not management, and companies, for better or worse, do manage their brands. The real question is that if brand is truly a critical intangible asset, does this mean brand managers will be asked to manage brands for value in such a way as to understand and influence the inputs that went into a brand's creation? Will brands be managed with complementarity in mind? As stated earlier, acknowledging a brand as a critical intangible asset must also mean acknowledging the causal and interdependent elements that went into its creation. Perhaps a clearer understanding of the centrality of complementarity might drive fundamental changes in what brand management means, a subject that will be revisited in later pages.

Customers

Likewise, when we speak of loyal customers as an intangible class, we realize that loyal customers are the output of many input factors—some of which are intangible and some that are not. These inputs include smart employees, great products and services, the capacity to innovate in the creation of those products and services, price leadership, effective marketing and promotion, and so on. The customer is the hard-won "creation" of all these interdependent elements. It is the endgame intangible; winning the customer is the purpose of creating all these other intangible assets, or else what's the point?

The sum of all the complementary assets when working effectively and in unison to create customers is reflected in revenue the company earns. It is also reflected in the profitability score of each customer. Not all customers are made the same. A higher-revenue customer might actually cost far more to serve than a lower-revenue customer and therefore is a lower-profitability customer. The contribution margin and lifetime value of customers is not a new idea, but it is growing in importance as a dimension used to manage customer relationships. For example, I called my cell phone carrier recently and during the call was informed by the rep that the company treated all customers equally. She said this as if it were a badge of honor. Equality is essential under the law. But under the law of the jungle, in the estimation of some business experts, this is exactly the wrong customer strategy, and more companies are realizing this.

By scoring customers based on their profit contribution, companies are completely rethinking how they categorize customer classes and, perhaps more important, how they allocate labor and capital—the fundamental job of a manager—in service of customer-directed business goals. Customers are no longer measured by just demographic group, income level, or some other psychodemographic or historical purchasing data point. In itself this might not seem radical, but it reflects a new way of thinking about customers, and this kind of measurement can have profound effects on a company's daily business practices. A company committed to a differentiated approach to customer management will almost organically begin thinking about the complementarity of at least some of the assets and resources that went into earning the business of a customer because it will allocate these internal resources with more efficiency now that it understands the profitability the customer represents to the organization.

Each intangible class derives its existence from other intangibles, which must come into being before it can be created. Some intangibles, like management processes and organizational arrangements, are so indiscrete that managers might have a tough time defining what the boundaries of these assets really are. The inherent complementarity of intangible assets means managers must explore whether they require different management approaches if they are to be leveraged for full value.

Economic Attributes

Baruch Lev, a finance and accounting professor at New York University, has been studying the subject of intangible assets extensively and is considered an expert on the subject. His research has found that the following economic attributes of intangible assets distinguish them in fundamental ways from physical assets.[5] Understanding the economic levers behind these assets can only add clarity to our complete understanding of them.

Intangibles Have a Multiplicity of Simultaneous Uses

The economic term for this is *nonrivalry*. Physical assets inherently possess an opportunity cost because if they are used in one way, they are precluded from being used in another way simultaneously. Think of an airplane assigned to one route, which automatically precludes its use on another route at the same time. Think also of a grain thresher. Farmer Bob is using the grain thresher on the far western end of the farm. Business partner farmer Pete would like to use the grain thresher at the same time to thresh the wheat at the eastern end of the field. The laws of physics to which physical assets are chained say that Pete's wish is impossible. Also, part of the cost of the thresher is the opportunity foregone in not investing in another asset that might have proven just as valuable—say, new irrigation and sprinkling equipment.

Conversely, intangible assets are nonrival. They can be deployed in a multiplicity of contexts and needs. Therefore, many intangible assets have zero opportunity costs after the initial investment.[6] The airline's jet can only be pressed in value-creating service in one manner, while the airline's reservation system, another example of an intangible asset, can be used thousands of times simultaneously.[7] The limit to its use is the scalability of the software and hardware upon which the system resides.

The reason why some intangible assets are nonrival is the fact that they are subject to high up-front costs but negligible marginal costs. Software and pharmaceuticals are the two most common and vivid examples. Siebel Systems spends gobs of money in human capital and R&D making its customer relationship management software. Same goes for Pfizer in regard to Viagra. The company invested significant financial capital in development of this blockbuster drug. The cost of making the first pill was in the billions. The cost of making the second through the millionth pill was mere pennies.

Contrast these economics with those of airplane manufacturing subject to marginal returns as increasing amounts of physical capital can only help produce so many more aircraft. Nonrivalry is a central attribute of some intangible assets.

Intangibles Are Subject to Network Effects

Network effects describe how individual members of a network gain incremental benefit when the size of the network increases.[8] Networks, in this sense, do not have to be physical, like a phone network. They could be virtual, like the number of people who use the Windows operating system. A good example of the economics of networks actually does come from telephony.

When phone service emerged early in the twentieth century, a number of carriers competed with each other, and many of these networks were not interoperable. They did not connect. Therefore, the value of phone service for Aunt May is confined only to others on the same network with whom she can communicate. As it happens, her niece June lives hundreds of miles away and gets her phone service from a rival carrier. No interconnection agreement exists like they do today. The value of the respective networks to which May and June belong would increase were they interoperable.

A more recent example is AOL Instant Messenger versus Microsoft's messaging service. When their respective software did not interoperate, the value of each network to its members was limited to the size of the universe of others on the same network with whom they could communicate. Greater benefit would accrue to all users if the network were expanded to include the interoperable communication between users from both platforms. Arguably, the benefit to Microsoft users would be disproportionate because the size of AOL's market was so much bigger to begin with.

A fundamental aspect of network effects is that the size of the benefit goes up as new members are added to it. This creates positive feedback; that is, the participation of additional members feeds on itself as more and more people want to be part of the popular network. A great example of this is eBay. Before it became arguably the greatest success story arising out of the Internet, many auctions competed for buyers and sellers. eBay grew astronomically because there was additional value to be gained for new participants to join it as opposed to other auction markets. Each side of the market exchange was drawn to eBay in ever-increasing numbers. Sellers were attracted in the belief that more buyers meant higher prices for merchandise they wanted to auction. Buyers were attracted in the belief that there would be a wider selection of goods on which to bid if more and more sellers offered their wares on the site. Positive feedback fueled the participation on each side of the auction block and increased the overall value of the network.

The relevance of network effects to understanding the economic forces of certain intangible assets is Lev's assertion that at the center of newly created networks is an intangible asset participants were attracted to in the first place.[9] For example, eBay's buying and selling environment is a mammoth intangible asset that a network exploits. A complementary asset is its brand, which springs into existence out of the media attention, satisfied customers, and cottage businesses it has spawned.

Visa is another example of a company in which network effects are central to its business model. "It's Everywhere You Want To Be" is a powerful brand-building idea and a classic reminder that the company's core value as a clearinghouse for credit card transactions is the fact that consumers can have high expectation that if a merchant accepts credit cards, it will probably accept Visa. There is increasing value in additional merchants' participation in its network, which sends positive feedback to consumers that Visa-sponsored credit cards are the cards to own. Visa reminds everyone of its network effects power when it points out that many merchants do not accept American Express.

Alas, if intangible assets are such a powerful driver of value, why are so many businesses intangible-poor? Why aren't organizations expending effort in creating and managing them? There are several inherent economic reasons why, as discussed in the following sections.

Potential market size. Some industry markets are not large enough to benefit from the scalability factor and network effects that intangible assets attract. The growth potential of eBay was enormous. Sabre's growth potential was equally large because of the size of the travel and related services market. Not so in apparel or home appliances, to name two relative failures in this area.[10]

Ownership risk. The ownership of physical assets is clear. Steal someone's energy turbine, and you go to jail. Copycat the concept of a new auction marketplace, and it is not so clear-cut that anything was actually stolen. Patents and copyrights are supposed to protect the ownership of someone's ideas, but many powerful ideas are not codified as either copyrights or patents. Often a competitor who figures out a way to reengineer the basic idea of the innovation will steer clear of intellectual property infringement. Airlines are less worried that their airplanes will be pilfered than they are worried that someone might start an online reservation system to compete with Orbitz.[11] Imitation is the sincerest form of flattery but little comfort to a pioneer.

Challenges to asset optimization. Asset optimization means extracting maximum value from an asset. A hospitality company like Marriott, which wants to improve asset utilization—room occupancy—can lower prices or promote specials. How does a software vendor optimize network effects when this phenomenon defies top-down control? It is a daunting challenge.

Payoff risk. The goal of any asset is to obtain a substantial return on investment. Intangible assets have the potential of returning substantially more value than do physical assets, yet at far greater risk. Lev cites a study by some researchers that analyzed the value creation from a collection of German and U.S. patents, as well as the capital market performance of U.S. start-up companies.

A small percentage of patents and start-ups constituted the bulk of the innovation value derived from these sources. The top 10 percent of patents accounted for 80 to 90 percent of total patent value. Essentially, many patents were busts. The study also found that the 10 percent of start-ups accounted for 60 percent of the market values of all the companies surveyed. Innovation, comprising many interdependent intangible assets, is quite risky. In another study, it was shown that the earnings volatility from R&D is three times riskier than investment from physical assets.[12] Many intangible assets have a winner-take-all quality to them. The payoffs are huge but concentrated.

Conclusions

Intangible assets defy easy classification because there is no universal definition of what an intangible asset is. Some intangible assets are so because they are naked to the eye. Some intangible assets are so because they are not treated as assets on financial statements. Yet these attributes are not universal across all intangible asset classes. Information technology cannot be felt by touch, but it is treated as an asset for reporting purposes. Human capital can be physically touched, but it is not treated as an asset for reporting purposes.

However, all intangible assets are so because managers declare that they are assets in the sense that they contribute to value creation even if these assertions are born more out of gut instinct than empirical analysis. Good managers know what drives their business, and if those sources of value can be identified and defined, then they have embarked on the path of managing them for value extraction. In the end, this might be the only definition that matters: intangible assets are newly discovered sources of manageable value creation an organization has some relationship to.

CHAPTER 3

REPORTING GAAP

H ere is the crux of the financial reporting challenge as it relates to intangible assets. It is the story of Microsoft.

The company's market capitalization is a moving target but comes in around $250 billion, while the financial value of its property and equipment totals only a couple billion dollars. The difference between what the equity market values the company at and the measurable value of its physical assets (buildings, PCs, and other equipment) is a crude but telling proxy for all other assets of the company—assets that are difficult to quantify yet are crucial factors of production contributing to Microsoft's breathtaking wealth.

What would these assets consist of? We have an idea. The talent of Microsoft's code jocks and marketing executives, its brand, and the brainpower of its operations executives, who time and time again shrewdly figure out new tactics to leverage the company's de facto monopoly in the operating system market in order to enter new markets. We would throw in its portfolio of intellectual property and certainly the network effects that accrue through such high adoption of its desktop software; the more people who use it, the more useful it becomes because of its inherent interoperability with other people who use it. People can collaborate and share.

Some might argue that Microsoft's organizational agility, which arises out of a unique company culture, also is an asset not to be overlooked. When Netscape released the Navigator browser in the mid-1990s, Microsoft immediately grasped the true significance of the introduction of software to view Web pages on this new network called the Internet. An army of employees were told to drop everything they were working on and get to work building its own viewer software. Despite its visionary leadership—an asset itself—and great product, Netscape today is a logo and a website, while up on Mount Olympus, Bill Gates et al. smile down on PC land, where nearly every desktop contains that little blue *e* for Microsoft's Internet Explorer program.

Many pundits and business gurus were astonished that a company as large as Microsoft could pirouette so gracefully around the reallocation of internal resources to enter a new market with the focus, speed, and drive it demonstrated. Microsoft destroyed the competition.

It is not too far an exaggeration to say that Microsoft could detonate its buildings and have its employees work under circus tents on its campus in Redmond, Washington, and it wouldn't materially affect its value to the investing public (although productivity might decline, what with bugs in the summer and the cold in the winter). This isn't the case with some companies. Dismantle the planes owned by an airline or level the real estate owned by McDonald's, and see what would happen to its stock. Although McDonald's possesses some intangible assets, such as a powerful brand, a lot of its wealth is tied up in the real estate it manages.

Microsoft and many companies in other industries are the poster children for the fact that current financial reporting standards fail to completely communicate the value drivers of a company. In the case of Microsoft, we know that it owns several billion dollars' worth of assets because the company's financial reports say so. We also know that Microsoft has at its disposal an array of other capabilities that are not depicted as value-creating assets in these reports but which investors believe are a powerful proxy for the future growth expectations of a company.[1] The difference in these two financial values—assets versus market cap—is a proxy for the value of a company's intangible assets. The difference is also the symptom, rather than the cause, of limitations in current financial reporting. The search for more complete reporting techniques that reflect the contributions of intangible assets has commanded the attention of researchers for many years, and there is no reason to believe the exploration will not continue, as these assets have only grown in importance.

Joining Brookings and the FASB, the Council on Competitiveness has created an Innovation Index, which serves as a kind of scorecard to assess America's competitiveness based upon benchmark criteria around research and development and intellectual property creation activity.

In one of the most recent and ambitious undertakings, MIT launched the New Economy Value Research Lab, with the mission to apply the tools of economics in assigning financial values to intangible assets. Arthur Andersen funded the effort, which unfortunately blew up when the Enron mess emerged and Andersen ceased as a business. Clearly, however, MIT recognized the need for the application of intellectual firepower toward this subject.

Why Intangibles Are a Big Deal

Consider that the assets of a corporation historically have comprised equipment, real estate, and inventories. In 1950 almost 80 percent of what a company owned consisted of these types of assets. Today that proportion is about 50 percent. The other half of the average consists of intangible assets.[2]

One way to understand intangible assets within history is to understand the bias against them. Our early economy was mostly goods based. People bought and sold things. Goods were physical and could be stored, while services were transitory. Their transitory nature argued that they should not be treated as assets.[3] The logic of this reasoning is that only those things that were tangible—goods—should be counted as investments. The result was that nonmaterial entities, such as patents, goodwill, or a brand, were overlooked as sources of value creation. The famous Yale economics professor Irving Fisher (known best for excessive stock market enthusiasm before the 1929 crash in spite of his training and academic pedigree) defined economics as the science of wealth, and wealth meant ownership of material objects. This definition informs national income accounting techniques used to determine asset values as well as profit and investment—which explains why national accounts measurement fails to include R&D as an investment.

Another way to view the growing proportion of intangible sources of wealth is to simply look at the companies that dominate the economy. In 1917 the largest companies included United States Steel, Standard Oil, International Harvester, and Phelps Dodge—all industrial or natural resource–based companies possessing high levels of physical capital.[4] Today, look at the Dow Jones average. It includes natural resource companies such as Exxon Mobil, but it also includes Intel, Microsoft, Hewlett-Packard (HP), and Disney. The change in the complexion of businesses that constitute the Dow reflects an inexorable evolution toward the reliance upon intangible assets to drive wealth creation. It is a vivid depiction of how intangible assets dictate whether a modern company succeeds or not.

Perhaps the significance of this shift is most deeply reflected in the fact that the laws and precepts of economics are being rewritten. Scarcity of resources and its interplay with supply and demand have occupied the center of everything this discipline has sought to explain about a world dominated by companies such as Standard Oil and Phelps Dodge. The scarcity assumption worked well in a world of natural resource extraction and subsequent manipulation into products. In fact, economics got its name "the dismal science" not, as is popularly thought, because it is boring but because economists hundreds of years ago observed the diminishing returns from exploiting land in the face of ever-increasing population growth. Economics demonstrated quite effectively that the peasant's life was condemned to one of meanness and want because fixed amounts of land faced production limits in the crops it could yield.

Classical economics animated by scarcity does a poor job of explaining increasing marginal returns of today; the content of resources is increasingly intellectual and less physical and therefore runs little risk of depletion. In fact, intellectual assets can increase in value from the "standing on the shoulder of giants" phenomenon. Simply put, existing ideas and intellectual constructs inspire new ones, and their production potential is virtually limitless. The only scarce resource producers of ideas face is time—the race to get all the good ideas out before a shift in market condition makes them irrelevant or because of organizational or human mortality the producer's own demise makes them nonexistent. (Most companies occupy a position in the spectrum between the extremes of limitless marginal returns, such as software, and pure diminishing marginal returns, such as mining.[5])

Let's look at a specific example of how companies are challenged to reconcile the economic realities of information, ideas, and knowledge— their lack of scarcity—with an optimal management and organizational arrangement.

The new manager of the market research division of a company decides that its operational model is inefficient. Historically, the division would receive a large budget and do research into any area it wished, and its efforts were often misaligned with the information needs of an operating unit. The new manager decides to spread the budgeting funds amongst the operating units, telling them they could buy any necessary research from the researchers so that marketing research projects were focused on problems that business units needed solutions to.

Business unit A commissions some research around a particular problem. Business unit B commissions the researchers around a similar problem. Unit A's research meets much of unit B's needs. But B cannot receive the original study without permission from A, and the two get bogged down in protracted negotiation about how much B should pay A for portions of the research now that A has asserted a property right over it.[6]

There are many morals to this story. One, pricing a knowledge good internally will restrict demand and therefore the flow of knowledge and ideas within the organization—a bad idea in light of information's increasing returns. The more information and knowledge are shared, the more value to business goals they deliver. Two, information and knowledge possess perfect marginal returns. The cost of these kinds of products is all up front in creating the first iteration; copies have negligible costs. Charging multiple times for the same information is a terrific business model when applied to external customers but a sizable cost drag internally when the whole idea of establishing internal market mechanisms is to infuse the company with fiscal discipline. Three, given the reality of the second point, organizations are still figuring out optimal institutional arrangements where the assets that managers are attempting to leverage are fundamentally intangible. In this case, the inherent economic nature of this kind of asset runs up against received wisdom of how to organize internal functions for maximum efficiency.

So here we are, well into the new millennium, in a time of medical breakthroughs (using genetics for the treatment of disease) and technological breakthroughs (the miniaturization of electronics) and, on a more mundane level, a time of continuous advances in management: Six Sigma, business process reengineering, and total quality management. Yet we grope in the dark when intangible assets are discussed. We know they exist, we know that the sources of corporate wealth increasingly reside in them, but we don't have any formal, systematic, repeatable, and consistent methodologies or best practices to manage them as we have to manage a company's portfolio of machinery, information technology, financial instruments, or real estate. However, they are starting to emerge.

Booking the Right Values

Executives interested in pursuing a better management regime for the exploitation of the component intangible assets that drive company performance will gain some valuable perspective by understanding the roots of the intangible challenge. The bean counters have yet to construct a workable financial vehicle through which to view the financial conditions of a company, as those conditions are influenced comprehensively by *all* the asset drivers in the company.

Is Luca Pacioli turning in his grave? The father of double-entry booking invented a systematic way to account for assets and liabilities as well as profit and loss. A Franciscan monk born in the fifteenth century, Pacioli taught mathematics in pre-Renaissance Italy. How ironic would it have been had he considered the intangible phenomenon, a not-so-silly idea given the intellectual ferment that bubbled from the cobblestone streets of Florence a hundred years hence. As it was, Pacioli's contribution to modern life is undeniable. He invented a language for the expression of phenomena occurring in private enterprise, as important an invention as the creation of a programming language to express the functionality of software. James Buchan, the author of a history of money called *Frozen Desire* (1997), said that Pacioli gave the modern world a conception of profit that was mathematically sound, empirically verifiable, and, therefore, tangible.[7]

Perhaps our inventive cleric would have trouble explaining the Microsoft conundrum, the discrepancy between the book value of a company's assets and the financial claims made on a company in the form of both equity and debt. This discrepancy is a rough proxy for the existence, importance, and value of intangible assets. The reason is that while people continue to invest in companies, the book value—the historical cost of a company's tangible assets—has not in aggregate appreciated proportionately. That is, book values or the physical capital of corporations in the aggregate have not appreciated significantly, even after adjusting for inflation, while the amount of money people have plowed into these companies has taken a kind of hockey stick path.[8]

Consider Table 3.1, from a detailed study by the Federal Reserve Bank. In it you see that research and development more than doubled, from 1.3 percent to 2.9 percent, while investment in fixed tangible assets remained flat, at about 12.6 percent.[9]

If people are pouring money into stocks and bonds at a far greater rate than the rise in aggregate book value, what are they investing in? Certainly not real estate, machine tools, warehouses, or a portfolio of stocks and bonds. They are investing in the brand of the company because they believe a powerful brand makes money for a company. They are investing in the CEO and her management team because she has a track record of delivering profit growth quarter over quarter. They are investing in the company's capacity for regularly turning out new stuff that proves a big hit with the public. They are investing in the intangible worth of a company because they believe this is the driver of the company's future wealth, even though dollar amounts have not been assigned to component intangible assets.

Investors understand the intangible sources of future wealth at Microsoft—its monopoly power, its shrewd ability to execute when entering new markets. They understand Disney—the power of its brand, its consistent delivery of quality family entertainment, its raw

Table 3.1 R&D, Tangible Investment, and Advertising of Nonfinancial Corporations

(as a proportion of nonfinancial corporate gross domestic product)*

Period	Research and Development (Percentage)	Fixed Tangible Investment (Percentage)	R&D and Tangible Investment (Percentage)	Advertising Expenditures (Percentage)
1953–59	1.3	12.6	13.9	4.2
1960–69	1.7	12.7	14.4	3.9
1970–79	1.8	13.9	15.7	3.4
1980–89	2.3	14.1	16.4	3.9
1990–97	2.9	12.6	15.5	4.1

Source: Flow of Funds, National Science Foundation, and McCann-Erickson.

*The gross domestic product originated by a firm is its revenues less purchases from other firms. Nonfinancial gross domestic product can be thought of as total nonfinancial domestic corporate revenues after eliminating double counting due to interfirm transactions. An advantage of using this measure over total revenues as a basis for comparison is that changes in corporate structure—mergers and spinoffs, for example— can affect the amount of interfirm transactions and thus change the amount of total corporate revenues even though final production is unchanged.

creativity. But these are conclusions that come from intuition and qualitative assessments rather than purely objective calculation based on what is gleaned from balance sheets or income statements.

Economists argue that if intangible wealth were more accurately reported, perhaps equity and debt markets would be more efficient. Certainly, the almost maniacal focus on quarter-by-quarter earnings growth blinds people to the more nuanced and equally legitimate narratives inside companies, which might go something like this: "Yes, we have taken a hit the past year, but we have increased R&D expenditures 20 percent, have filed two new exciting patents around a core product, and have two new exciting products in development."

Investors will fold these realities into their decision making but will pound the stock down nonetheless if the company doesn't hit its numbers. Might the punishment we've seen in the equity markets since March 2000—the drop in earnings—have been less severe had there been a reliable and agreed-upon way to calculate the beneficial impact of an intangible asset for the same reporting period?

This is the kind of question being explored by the best minds in the business, and it is not a new one. That we don't have an answer yet, however, is a signal of how hugely challenging the subject is. And while this text is not explicitly about how to improve financial reporting, again the gap between what financial statements communicate about the value of a company and the drivers that influence those values is large. This is not only a profound development in accounting and finance but a vivid reflection of the challenges at a management level in utilizing and exploiting those sources of intangible wealth.

It's as if a boat's navigator were steering his boat to the safety of an island beginning to loom large in his eyepiece, not noticing a gigantic rock sitting just to the port side of the field of view and behind that someone in another boat sending a warning signal and suggesting an alternative course around which to navigate the impending danger. The navigator keeps his attention transfixed on the safe harbor getting closer only to miss all that is happening in his midst because of his reliance on what is viewable through the spyglass. Financial statements are a kind of spyglass whose focus is getting narrower because of increases in intangible phenomena happening outside the field of view. The result is unparalleled myopia. Perhaps Baruch Lev, an NYU accounting professor and pioneer in the subject of intangible assets, puts it best: "It's really mind-boggling when you think about this whole accounting machinery that ends up with a balance sheet that explains less than one-sixth of a company's real value."[10]

Reporting: A Crisis in Confidence?

The breadth of the split between realities portrayed in financial reports and the realities of the activity engaged in by business surrounding their intangible assets is nothing short of astounding when you consider that executives are fully aware of the extent of the disconnect and view generally accepted accounting principles (GAAP) with a wink and a smile.

PricewaterhouseCoopers conducted a survey of high-tech executives in which they were asked to rank the top ten performance measures reflecting corporate performance in order of importance; only three were quantifiably financial in nature, which could be gleaned from financial statements: earnings, cash flow, and gross margins.[11] Fully seven measures were nonfinancial, and a couple had intangible qualities associated with them: quality and experience of the management team and strategic direction.

PwC also found in its survey work that only 38 percent of executives overall thought that their financial statements communicated effectively the value of their companies. In the high-tech industry, the figure was an appalling 13 percent.[12] Consequently, executives report financial conditions in such a way because it's the law—or at least a standard. But they know better. The real story is found under the covers.

Hints of the Future

What would financial reporting that included more information about intangibles look like? PwC is pushing its ValueReporting model, comprising the following four interrelated reporting criteria:

1. **Market overview**, which consists of the company's regulatory as well as macroeconomic environment
2. **Value strategy**, which consists of an explanation of company goals and objectives, its organizational design, and its governance structure
3. **Activities that drive value creation**, including intangible drivers, such as brand, customers, supply chain relationships, and corporate reputation
4. **Financial performance information**, including the company's financial position broken down by operational segment and its risk management strategy[13]

The idea is for companies to provide as much performance transparency as possible. Transparency traditionally is lacking in balance sheets, income statements, and cash flow positions because the intangible asset story is left out. PwC's approach calls for the communication of intangible asset contribution to overall performance.

An Attempt at Value Reporting: The Skandia Experience

Skandia has heeded that call for at least eight years, having recognized as far back as the mid-1990s that traditional financial reporting standards were deeply flawed. The Sweden-based global financial services company has embarked on a financial reporting effort that communicates intangible asset contribution to overall performance. Its efforts are well known.

For instance, in a supplement to the company's 1996 annual report, Skandia outlined a number of customer-focused initiatives expected to ultimately drive financial performance. In the United States, that ultimate financial goal is defined as a minimum after-tax return equal to the ten-year government bond rate plus 8 percentage points.[14]

One of those initiatives was DIAL Forsakring, a service operation supporting personal insurance lines established in 1991.[15] Skandia essentially outlined a strategy in which the company aligned call center customer service around customer profiles; it was not uncommon in the insurance industry that if a customer had a claim, she called one number, then for a policy question, another number, and for inquiries around other products, yet another number. Skandia's program integrated all the contexts that instigated customer contacts so that the customer dealt with one company representative only.

This strategy is no longer a service innovation in the financial services industry. But it was in 1996, and the company's explication of this strategy and the elements it built in support of that strategy must have been quite a revelation for both investors following the company and its clueless competitors ten miles back.

While this value-reporting effort can't precisely quantify the effort's contribution to the bottom line, the company did deconstruct for public consumption the elements driving this customer strategy. In response to those skeptical of this effort, would you be *more* likely to buy the stock of this company in the absence of this intangible asset-reporting exercise? In a refutation of the famous words of Ludwig Mies van der Rohe that in architecture "less is more," for reporting purposes in a world of intangible assets and their large influence on financial performance, more is more. Table 3.2 gives an example of Skandia's advanced reporting technique taken from a supplement to one of its annual reports.[16]

Table 3.2 A Snapshot of Skandia's Value-Reporting Technique

	1996	1995	1994
Financial Focus			
Gross premiums written (MSEK)	935	880	667
Gross premiums written/employee (SEK 000s)	3,832	3,592	3,586
Customer Focus			
Telephone accessibility (%)	95.8	92.5	90.0
Number of individual policies	320,139	275,231	234,741
Satisfied customer index (max. value = 5)	4.36	4.32	4.15
Sweden's Customer Barometer (max. value = 100)	65	69	n.a.
Human Focus			
Average age	40	40	37
Number of employees	244	245	186
Time in training (days/years)	7	6	3.5
Process Focus			
IT employed/total number of employees (%)	7.4	7.3	8.1
Renewal and Development Focus			
Increase in gross premiums written	6.3	31.9	28.5
Share of values in claims assessment system (%)	20.5	9	n.a.
Number of ideas filed with Idea Group	175	n.a.	n.a.

The Skandia experience raises several important issues that should inform the debate around value reporting and the financial reporting reformist movement. First, in order to avoid sowing any confusion, it is important to understand that the crusade for better reporting does not necessarily mean new techniques will suddenly emerge that can magically assign a dollar value to a company's capacity for innovation, to the company's employees, or to the value of the company's brand. Although valuation and reporting are inextricably related, accounting is not the science of measuring the value of anything. It is the science of reporting and informing about financial and economic activity.[17] In other words, reporting is not valuation (although we have seen the important codependent relationship of the two). What better reporting does constitute is the release of more relevant information about the contribution of intangible assets to company performance, even if the information takes the form of text and charts outside the narrow, structured confines of an income statement or a balance sheet. It's an acknowledgment of the importance of intangible asset influence that it be documented in some form as an adjunct to standardized financial statements. We have some distance to travel, however, in having the ability to assign dollar signs with any confidence to these drivers of corporate performance.

Second, standard setting will be crucial if improved financial reporting is to occur with the breadth and sweep that reformists would like. Consultants like PricewaterhouseCoopers and others evangelizing their own flavors of value reporting have a vested interest in advocating their approach as the magic bullet to the current reporting crisis. As valuable as their ideas are, acceptance and systematic use of a value-reporting regime must emerge out of standards bodies such as the Financial Accounting Standards Board, even if elements of consultants' intellectual property are adopted. There can be no proprietary approach to the transparency movement, for we would sacrifice consistency, repeatability, and shared understanding of what value is being added to financial statements. The fact that PwC has trademarked two common words when joined together—ValueReporting—indicates the market opportunity consultants have identified out of a fragmented and nascent movement. This is one case in which intangible assets—trademarks, methodologies, techniques—will need to be sacrificed if improved financial reporting across all publicly traded companies is to win.

Third, the reformist movement is predicated upon a huge assumption that companies will enthusiastically reveal more about the strategic and intangible levers moving their organizations. In fact, many of these intangibles may be sources of competitive advantage. Although the FASB and some academics are pushing for more transparency and maturity in the presentation of assets hidden in the logic of today's financial reports, business executives might very well resist the efforts. How enthused will management be in publicizing its future goals and all of the interesting internal tactical efforts launched to support it? It is not hard to imagine executives at other insurers going stiff with the suggestion that they report the details Skandia has willingly reported. The idea that some companies will balk at new levels of transparency while others embrace it goes to show you how intangible itself is the risk associated with revealing intangibles.

Fourth, the reformist movement is predicated upon another large assumption that, by virtue of increased disclosure of nonfinancial but important related information, the company will become more attractive to investors. In the case of Skandia, this isn't necessarily so. Its stock vaulted in value from approximately 50 Swedish kronur in 1998 to a high of 250 SEK in 2000, only to descend the roller coaster with considerable g-force to a price of 18.50 SEK early in 2003.[18] Does any of the meteoric rise of the stock equate with a series of detailed intangible asset disclosures and explanations from 1994 through 1998? Does its fall equate with the absence of these disclosures from 1999 through 2001? If any causality exists at all, how much of the stock's behavior has a first-order link to value reporting or its absence? The contention that consistent reporting of intangible assets provides a fuller, more textured profile of the company—and therefore, an invitation for investment that otherwise might not have existed—is untested. The Skandia experience does not mean that there is no causation but that because we're so early in the reformist movement, empirical studies will be called upon to test this hypothesis.

Fundamentally, the financial reporting reformist movement will need to change the bias of accountants in how they treat the behavior of assets in a business because this bias exacerbates the disconnect between today's financial statements and the intangible phenomenon. Remember Chapter 2, in which we saw the rhetorical and conceptualization challenge in defining the nature of intangible assets. As we saw, the accounting industry has a long-accepted definition of what an asset actually is, and this definition today has little room for intangible assets. These criteria are easily applied to plant, equipment, buildings, manufacturing machinery, etc. The job becomes manifestly more difficult if not impossible when the assets under analysis are knowledge, employees, customer loyalty, and intellectual property.

The creation of such a definition occurs against a backdrop of deep conservatism in the accounting profession. The rationale is that statements should generally fall on the side of understating rather than overstating financial performance. There is a commendable habit of mind, which minimizes risks associated with wild overstatements of financial performance—chiefly the burning of the investing public and the other actors who have a financial stake in the company. Consider that research and development expenditures are considered an asset if acquired but a pure expense if the capability is generated internally.[19] One perspective is that this bias derives from a key constituency for whom financial reports are prepared: creditors. Banks tend to lend against tangible assets only to protect their interests, and accountants are happy to accommodate them. There's a thinking that if we're not sure about the worth of one of these strange kinds of new economic assets, we should just expense it and understate earnings.[20]

The Knowledge Capital Scorecard

Another approach to reporting that raises the visibility of intangible asset value creation is the Knowledge Capital Scorecard (KCS), created by Baruch Lev and Marc Bothwell, a portfolio manager at Credit Suisse Asset Management. The idea behind the scorecard is to acknowledge that intangibles such as customer and supplier relationships and workforce quality (human capital) are collectively called knowledge capital, and knowledge capital explains why a company is able to earn above average returns on its asset base.[21]

Calculating the KCS begins with three years' worth of normalized earnings for the company in question. Normalized earnings are the combination of three years of historical earnings and three years of consensus analyst estimates, which considers empirically proven past performance as well as forward-looking value-creation potential. These normalized earnings are then compared to the rates of return on the organization's physical capital reflected on the balance sheet.

Because balance sheet assets are mostly commodities, the rates of return used in the calculation are 7 percent for physical assets and 4.5 percent for financial assets. Any normalized annual earnings that exceed the expected returns on these balance sheet assets are considered knowledge earnings and a telling indicator of a company's capacity to drive value out of its intangible assets (even if we do not know which intangibles are producing how much). Knowledge capital is calculated as the net present value (NPV) of all future knowledge earnings. Lev used a 10.5 percent discount rate to calculate this knowledge capital NPV, derived from the after-tax return of three intangible asset-intensive industries: software, biotechnology, and pharmaceuticals.[22]

The scorecard for 2000 (the third annual Knowledge Capital Scorecard was the last Lev published[23]) confirms that companies with higher investments in the processes of intangible asset creation, particularly R&D (intellectual property/intellectual assets) and advertising (brands), have proportionately higher knowledge earnings—and better stock performance.[24]

The KCS is also a useful comparative gauge to measure the relative intangible asset management effectiveness between competitors. The analysis found, for instance, that although Ford Motor Company's third-quarter 2000 book value was 60 percent that of General Motors, it posted 50 percent greater knowledge earnings than GM. This says that at least at the time, Ford was demonstrably more effective in extracting value from its intangible assets than was GM.[25] Table 3.3 gives a breakdown of knowledge earnings and knowledge capital of major American industries from the KCS.[26]

Could the KCS be adopted as an adjunct to traditional reporting? (Lev holds patents to the methodology, so this is unclear.) Whether it

Table 3.3 KCS Results

Industry	Knowledge Capital (in millions of dollars)	Knowledge Earnings 1999 (in millions of dollars)	Change in Knowledge Earnings 1998–99 (in millions of dollars)	Knowledge Capital/ Book Value
Aerospace and defense	23,447	1,417	65	3.58
Airlines	7,949	399	22	2.12
Biotech	4,393	171	40	5.18
Chemicals	9,948	632	42	3.08
Computer hardware	49,857	2,490	389	6.69
Computer software	38,908	1,782	279	5.68
Electrical	7,690	450	29	3.70
Electric utilities	10,351	691	177	1.11
Food and beverages	18,565	1,306	67	7.48
Forest products	8,884	854	285	0.87
Home products	19,296	1,097	109	8.10
Industrial	23,132	1,166	113	3.65
Media	16,759	646	119	0.94
Motor vehicles	13,413	962	97	3.50
Newspapers	5,619	336	44	3.77
Oil	24,559	2,210	585	1.71
Pharmaceuticals	75,224	4,295	621	8.44
Retail	15,406	885	115	2.89
Semiconductors	42,029	1,859	1,051	6.23
Specialty retail	10,320	512	84	2.62
Telecom	81,221	4,851	660	3.26
Telecom equipment	26,947	1,684	615	3.25

is KCS or some other technique, this is a flavor of the kind of additional financial reporting techniques that could be yoked to traditional accounting in furtherance of a keen desire to better document the intangible drivers of financial performance.

Chicken and the Egg: Forces of Change

What are the practical implications for managers from reporting techniques that more fully explicate the intangible drivers moving the organization? Ironically, perhaps very few. Put another way, what will come first—a value-reporting regime or management practices for the improved management of intangibles? (Which is the chicken and which is the egg?)

In fact, innovations in the management of intangibles might do more to influence reporting techniques in the end than vice versa; after all, aggregate financial reporting is a roll-up of all activity below the top level. If senior management wishes to more fully understand and analyze the intangible-oriented activities of the business, the content being reported as well as the specific technique used to calculate or assess that content will emerge from operational domains with the most direct control over the particular intangible: knowledge, customers, brand, etc.

The very need management has for better techniques to manage intangible assets over which they have direct control might very well spur the creation of key performance indicators, benchmarking processes, and data collection activities that would be distilled into a summary and sent up the line to the chief financial officer (CFO) for dissemination to investors and other stakeholders. It seems difficult to imagine the opposite scenario being the most likely; senior management mandates qualitative information supplements to balance sheets and income statements, and suddenly managers are inspired to embark on an intangible treasure hunt simply because the boardroom demands more information for reporting purposes.

A vivid example of modern performance pressures affecting management is the shift in customer strategy. Traditional accounting has a decidedly product-oriented focus. As we saw in the last chapter, management, on the other hand, is beginning to think more strategically about customers as an asset class; let's shift our efforts to selling around customer classes instead of product classes, the traditional orientation of companies. While academics acknowledge that financial reporting of customer-oriented goals is a necessary addition to some value-reporting schemes,[27] a good case can be made that the imperative to apply better techniques and tools to the active management of customers arose completely independently of the reporting reformist movement. In fact, line managers using sophisticated techniques that score customers around their contribution margin might listen to the sudden reformist cry of the CEO demanding the roll-up of value-based information for financial reporting and respond, "Where have you been?"

Consider the example of labor as expense. Labor—or some labor— is the root intangible asset of all intangibles. When business conditions go south, the first plan of action is layoffs. This happens almost reflexively and is an immediate boost to company earnings because it has just knocked out a big expense—often the single biggest operating expense. Now supposing techniques emerged to better score employees' value to a company in acknowledgment of a cruel truth: not all employees are the same in their ability to contribute to the company. As much as we would like to believe that, just like in Lake Wobegon, everybody is above average, this of course isn't so. Employees have different strengths and weaknesses, but some have more strengths than their peers. Some are simply better at their jobs than others are. In some cases, it is rather easy to identify the star. You're not going to lay off your top sales gal— she's the best closer in the company. That's obvious. But there might be more subtle dimensions to an employee profile worth managing and weighing: the guy who quietly leads and persuades and is, therefore, very effective in motivating and directing people has a huge skill. How do you capture and objectively quantify these intangible attributes? So instead of the crude hatchet job done at layoff time, in which this fella might have been turned loose, the cuts are perhaps conducted with more surgical precision and sophistication. The manager is managing the intangibility of his human capital assets.

Suspend your disbelief for a moment as to what the specific measurements are that drive this kind of management decision making. The important idea here is to see that because these human capital management techniques are emerging, the manager—and the CFO—now has a "value story" to tell the investing public. The company uses some management techniques to better assess employee contribution to the performance of the whole organization. So instead of the company simply managing its earnings through layoffs, it also conveys, through value reporting, a more nuanced set of circumstances, giving a more comprehensive picture of what is going on. In this case, the company demonstrates its superior employee assessment techniques—an intangible asset itself—its ability to keep the best and the brightest, which portends favorably for the company's future; and productivity improvements in doing more with less. Are people going to lay down hard-earned cash for the company stock in possession of this information? Maybe not. The point is that this story can be told if the company chooses to because management saw the need to embed these practices in daily operations.

So the manager's willingness and ability to operationalize a human capital management program with software, data collection, and measurement functions will be the source information used by senior executives in the new financial reporting schemes at reform-minded companies. While the need for reporting changes will transform the content of what is contained in financial statements, the creation of that content will derive from new operational functions that satisfy a very different need: better management of the intangible drivers of wealth in a company. It just so happens these needs are complementary.

The question then is this: can we really expect that senior management's desire to divulge more about company performance—much of it involving intangibles—will be the catalyst for innovations in management techniques to better manage sources of intangible wealth? Maybe. However, senior management can demand all the value reporting it wants. If the company does not deploy intangible asset management techniques, audiences might ask how substantive this new information really is.

Which is the chicken and which is the egg is a question of causality important for managers serious about better management of intangible wealth to be aware of. An attitudinal shift from senior management acknowledging the benefits of value reporting and demanding value reporting depends upon some activity involving intangibles that is worth telling the public. Likewise, a manager who feels strongly about asking for money, people, technology, and time investments to operationalize techniques for better intangibles management might find a more receptive audience in an environment that recognizes the importance of better reporting. Both sides of the intangibles management agenda are mutually reinforcing.

. . . and Goodwill to All Managers

While the accounting industry and the standards-setting bodies that support it appear hidebound to tradition, one change to financial reporting procedures as they relate to intangibles occurred in 2001.

Goodwill is a term in finance that defines the excess over the fair market value of the target company's assets—both tangible and intangible— the acquiring company pays. The amount of goodwill in acquisitions is also considered another kind of proxy for the value of *unidentifiable* intangible assets. When a company pays $1 million for a company and $400,000 reflects the fair market value of the assets being acquired— both tangible and identifiable intangible assets—the remaining $600,000 is considered goodwill, a reflection of what the acquiring organization is willing to pay over the market price, grounded in the belief that the intangible synergies created out of the marriage will generate exponentially more wealth for the new company.

Historically, accounting has required that the acquiring company automatically expense or draw down this excess value on a regular basis over a fixed period of time. The goodwill or intangible assets were capitalized on the acquiring company's balance sheet, and then over the economic life of the asset (say, a period of twenty years), a portion of this value was annually subtracted from the total dollar value of the goodwill—amortized—and this dollar amount was expensed on the income statement.

The wasting of goodwill over time was done on autopilot—no one gave the value of goodwill a second thought because reporting procedures simply required shrinking the dollar value of goodwill at a regular percentage and on a regular basis.[28] Savvy professionals following the performance of a company have been able to distinguish between earnings from operations and this kind of automatic charge against profitability.

In 2001 the FASB instituted a change in its rules, known as SFAS (Statement of Financial Accounting Standards) 142, which demands companies now to test the value of goodwill yearly to determine if there has been any impairment or damage to the intangibles. If so, the decrease in intangible value is again moved over to the income statement and drawn against earnings. The impairment or decreasing value of those intangibles is not a fixed percentage. The impairment might be less than what had to have been amortized in the past, or the impairment might be more—quite a bit more.

Consider that in Chapter 1, we explored the conceptual challenge in defining some commonly identified intangible assets based upon inherent cause-and-effect and ability-to-manage properties. As it happens, the FASB has some clear definitions and categories of intangibles that require explanation now so that the impacts of rule 142 can be clearly understood. According to the FASB, there are three categories of intangible assets: amortizable, nonamortizable, and goodwill.[29]

Amortizable intangibles are those assets that have a fairly well-defined life to them. The time period over which these intangibles deliver benefits is measurable. Amortizable intangibles would include customer contracts, lease agreements, and water and land use rights. Nonamortizable intangibles are assets that are longer lasting and whose economic life and benefit to its owner are indefinite. Nonamortizable intangibles might include trademarks, service marks, and artistic assets, such as movies, plays, ballets, or works of literature.[30] Again, goodwill is the difference between the dollar premium price an acquirer pays for a target company and what the fair market value of all tangible and identifiable intangible assets of that target company is actually worth at the time of acquisition. By definition, goodwill represents unidentifiable intangible assets—everything left over after all the amortizable and nonamortizable intangible assets (as defined by the FASB) have been flagged in the acquisition. It is not important that a distinction be made between amortizable and nonamortizable intangibles to understand the larger points being attempted here but rather that readers understand that these two types of intangibles are well defined by the FASB and are assigned a dollar value by valuation experts (often using a discounted cash flow method).

Following is a simple example of how goodwill is now treated for reporting purposes. Comprehension of this reporting policy change is an important development in the treatment of intangible assets and perhaps in our ability to clearly identify them when goodwill describes unidentifiable intangible assets.

Life with Mama

Suppose Mama's Ice Cream Company wishes to acquire Papa Softee Ice Cream Company. Table 3.4 illustrates the balance sheet of Mama's Ice Cream at the time of acquisition, as well as the results of the goodwill impairment test. All numbers are expressed in dollars.

Column A represents the dollar value at which Mama's books the acquisition on its financial ledgers. The total asset value of the acquisition is $300. At the time of acquisition, Mama's has not identified any identifiable intangible assets as outlined by the FASB but pays a premium for Papa Softee over the value of its physical assets. Mama has acquired $100 in goodwill.

Now a year has gone by, and the ice cream market proves to be a difficult one. Summer was unusually cold, so there was less demand for ice

Table 3.4 Mama's Ice Cream Balance Sheet

	A	B	C	D
	Original Book Value	New Book Value	Fictional Step I "Fair Value" Balance Sheet	Fictional Step 2 "Fair Value" Balance Sheet	New Financial Accounting Balance Sheet
Current assets	$100	$100	$100	$100	$100
Tangible assets	125	100	100	100	100
Intangible assets	—	—	—	25	0
Goodwill	—	100	50	25	25
Total assets	225	300	250	250	225
Liabilities	200	200	200	200	200
Equity	25	100	50	50	25

Source: CBIZ Valuation Group, Inc.

cream, and the economy was lousy just in general. At the end of the year, the stock market and management determine that the total assets of Mama's are $250. Was there impairment to goodwill? Maybe. We know that total assets have decreased by $50.

It turns out that goodwill might be impaired by $50. For purposes of illustration, assuming the values of the current assets and tangible assets remain constant, this value is determined through the following calculation:[31]

Total assets of $250 − current assets of $100 (receivables, cash) − tangible assets of $100 (plant, equipment, real estate) − identifiable intangible assets of $0 = goodwill of $50

This is reflected in column B.

Goodwill is calculated residually through the process of subtraction after all other assets have been accounted for. The determination of the value of goodwill is a residual one. It is residual because by definition we do not know exactly what the goodwill consists of. It simply defines a premium paid over the value of physical and identifiable intangible assets at the time of acquisition. Because goodwill might have been impaired, a step 2 test is called for.

During the company's step 2 test, it discovers the presence of a new identifiable intangible asset that valuation experts believe to be worth $25. What could this new identifiable intangible be?

In this example, we will say it is the recipe for a new flavor of ice cream, Turkey Surprise, which was acquired as a trade secret in the purchase of Papa Softee.[32] Mama's launched it, and it turned out to be a huge hit despite a bad economy and a weak market for ice cream in general. A trade secret was turned into value creation for Mama's. Here's where things get quite interesting.

Step 2 impairment in this example reveals that goodwill impairment is not $50 but worse than originally thought. By virtue of creation of an identifiable intangible asset of $25 discovered in the impairment test process (column C), subtraction tells us that goodwill is really only worth $25 now:

$250 − $100 − $100 − $25 = goodwill of $25

The total goodwill impairment for purposes of reporting on the income statement is then $75, the difference between what goodwill was worth at the time of the acquisition ($100) and what it is worth now ($25). This $25 of goodwill is put back into Mama's balance sheet, shown in column D. The $75 impairment is taken out of the hide of earnings.

Again, the logic of financial reporting today tells us that the value of goodwill is a residual one after all identifiable intangible assets have been accounted for on the financial statement. Had Turkey Surprise already existed as a recipe and been booked as an identifiable intangible asset at the time of acquisition, goodwill originally would have been $75 instead of $100 because Mama's accountants would have documented Turkey Surprise for $25 on the balance sheet. By the time of a step 2 impairment test, goodwill would not have been impaired as deeply because Turkey Surprise already would have been documented. The original $75 value of goodwill drops to $50 as in the original example but is not impaired beyond this because there is no discovery of a new intangible. Impairment, therefore, is only $25, a far less dramatic hit to earnings.

Notice in column D that $25 of goodwill survives and is placed back on the balance sheet. But what happens to the newly created intangible that helped the company's financial performance? Exactly nothing because the bias of accounting will not allow the appreciation in asset values of intangibles. Turkey Surprise ice cream is a big revenue generator for Mama's Ice Cream Company, not the least of which because it took the talents of managers to leverage the combined advantages unique to each company. For internal purposes, the company knows a new intangible has been created. But this asset is given no standing on the balance sheet, while a large goodwill impairment charge—made larger by the introduction of an identifiable intangible asset—is fully reflected on Mama's income statement. True, the creation of the new intangible is communicated in many other, more powerful ways—increased sales, brand building, etc. Yet the disconnect between palpable value-creation activities in the company and what certain elements of accounting standards require seems to continue apace.

The Moral of Mama's Story

This simplified example of a change in policy in the treatment of goodwill touches a number of dimensions of intangible assets and their management.

Intangible Assets Do Not Automatically Decrease in Value

To nonexperts, the FASB's change in goodwill reporting practices seemed to signal an acknowledgment that intangible assets do not automatically waste in value and in many cases actually increase in value. Although the policy change does not allow balance sheet changes to reflect any increases in value, the fact that goodwill is no longer amortized on autopilot seems to be at least a tacit or an indirect acknowledgment of the laws of increasing marginal utility, a concept coined by economist Paul Romer at Stanford University; they increase in value the more they are shared. The policy change simply reminds us of the unique economic behavior of intangible assets even if this attribute had nothing to do with the FASB's policy changes.

Additional Rigor in Identifying Intangibles Is Required

In the estimation of Greg Watts, a managing director at CBIZ Valuation Group, a leading consulting firm in the art of valuation, the FASB policy change is a clarifying event in our understanding of intangible assets. The analysts involved in assessing asset value after an acquisition might be motivated to look much more deeply into the price premiums an acquiring company paid in order to flag all identifiable intangible assets before the acquisition, to account for them right up front. Previous to the rules change, there was less motivation to probe in any detail what intangible assets were being acquired because they would be amortized on a regular schedule. Today, however, the more that identifiable intangibles can accurately become part of the company book value at the time of acquisition means the less that goodwill impairment might suffer. Additional analytic rigor injected into the process of intangible asset identification and valuation at the time of acquisition was an important part of the FASB's motivation for the rule change. Despite gaps in reporting of intangible assets, the FASB is demanding that greater scrutiny be applied to the subject of goodwill. Could this provide managers with any greater clarity about what those assets might be?

Not All Intangibles Are Easily Identifiable

In this example, a trade secret that delivered value to Mama's Ice Cream Company caused the recalculation of the value of goodwill. Some intangibles, however, are not so easily identifiable. Unique organizational arrangements that Brookings and others have argued are true, value-driving intangible assets (which are explored later in the book) might be very difficult to identify—let alone assign a dollar value to. The process of elimination of all identifiable intangibles during an impairment test might leave a company with a goodwill value that represents some other intangible category that is not on the FASB's radar screen yet is understood by managers. And if managers can get a handle on what intangible asset is buried in goodwill, they can at least attempt to manage it for value creation. For reporting purposes, however, it will remain goodwill because it is not an identifiable, defined intangible asset per the FASB's list.

Another question out of the FASB rule change arises: will earnings generally improve, deteriorate, or neither for a company with goodwill on its books, now that automatic wasting through amortization is not required? Consider Table 3.5.

This chart was published when the rule change first went into effect. In the case of AOL Time Warner listed here, the poster child for busted mergers, the company took a $54 billion goodwill write-down in the first quarter of 2002.[33] Qwest Communications took a $41 billion goodwill impairment charge in 2002 as well.[34] Rare as the circumstance of these two might be, the numbers are nevertheless breathtaking.

Put another way, what's worse (or better) for a company's earnings: a complete and deep impairment hit early in the life of an acquisition or a percentage autopilot amortization scheme? A related question arises: if impairment testing gets the pain of goodwill off the books early in the life of the acquisition, could the accretion of any identifiable intangible assets and their contribution to wealth creation going forward make up for any early losses arising out of large goodwill impairments? Will Mama's recover from its $75 goodwill impairment

Table 3.5 Goodwill Amortization as a Percentage of Net Income for Selected Companies

Company	Goodwill (in billions of dollars)	Annual Goodwill Amortization as a % of Net Income (over 30 years)
General Electric	23.1	6
Berkshire Hathaway	18.3	27
AOL Time Warner	15.5	57
Raytheon	12.0	123
Infinity Broadcasting	11.8	98
Allied Waste	8.2	207
RJ Reynolds Tobacco Holdings	7.6	72
Ingersoll Rand	3.7	23
Northrop Grumman	3.5	18.5
Tenet Healthcare	3.2	26.6

Source: U.S. Bancorp Piper Jaffray, with permission from Piper Jaffray.

hit and subsequent earnings dilution because additional cool identifiable intangible assets other than a new ice cream flavor are sure to emerge out of the marriage?

Lastly, how should the performance of managers who champion and influence acquisition decisions be treated when the results, such as the case of Mama's Ice Cream, are not so cut-and-dried? Would shareholders see an acquisition with a large impairment write-down as justification for shooting the managers at dawn even though this is only part of the story? Mama's has assets that might deliver big returns in the future—one already has.

If the valuation experts and finance executives are motivated to rigorously account for all possible intangible assets at the time of acquisition, might this mean companies pay less of a premium above and beyond the discounted future income streams for those assets both physical and intangible that are clearly identified going into the acquisition?

CBIZ's Watts argues that under the old goodwill regime, acquirers were less motivated to document and assign a financial value to all intangibles and would instead toss these assets into the goodwill pile, so to speak, knowing that their reduction in value was predictable and automatic. That goodwill premium defines unidentifiable intangible assets; why bother expending energy to figure out what they are exactly? Have companies overpaid for these unidentifiable sources of future value in the mistaken belief that synergies might grow organically out of the fusion of two cultures, two sets of human capital, two stores of captured knowledge? Consider the merger of Time Warner and AOL. The much-anticipated synergies that were expected to emerge out of Time's vast entertainment library in film and music and AOL's new distribution channel (the Internet) and viewing platform (PC plus AOL software) never materialized. Instead, their two very different cultures clashed bitterly, and the marriage has resulted in a colossal destruction of value.

The reporting challenge is an important chapter in the overall intangible asset management narrative. Specifically, the FASB's rule change in the treatment of goodwill is a potentially powerful force for greater understanding of intangible assets. Yet the accounting issues run along a parallel track to the more urgent need, which is that managers have tools, techniques, and frameworks to more effectively extract value out of the intangible assets in their midst. So we will leave the reporting debate and its little tortures to the academics, accountants, and finance experts and move on to the heart of the subject, the advancements in intangible asset management, which happen to be the focus of the next five chapters and the bulk of this text.

Conclusions

Financial statements are a kind of narrative that tells the story of how well a company is making its way in the American economy. Income statements and balance sheets are not complicated documents and deliberately so; the language of numbers is precise and clean (assuming the numbers are accurate to begin with). Yet the narrative power of financial statements is limited because they hide a couple of important things. For one, hidden is much of the drama behind how an organization got where it is financially—the thousand decisions of strategy and tactics that dictated the deployment of labor and capital. Second, but more important for our purposes, hidden is the influence of intangible assets on the very financial performance these documents are designed to reflect. The simplicity of current financial statements in a world populated by important intangible assets suggests there is as much to learn between the line items as on them.

The FASB's policy change concerning the treatment of goodwill demonstrates a sustained effort to include, at least minimally, the behavior of intangible assets in reporting standards. The debate over the reporting treatment of intangible assets is not a new one. It has drawn the attention of rules setters for at least thirty years and will continue to do so for the foreseeable future, as long as a growing proportion of the private sector's wealth-creating capacity is sourced from intangible assets as opposed to traditionally understood assets. While the oil companies remain a powerful force in the economy arising from our insatiable appetite for fossil fuels, just as many companies prosper from the creation and leverage of assets that are not extracted out of the ground but from the imaginations of people. How these companies seek this prosperity concerns the rest of this book.

CHAPTER 4

"IT" STANDS FOR INTANGIBLE TECHNOLOGY

Information technology is maybe one of the least intangible of all intangible assets. As an asset class, it is treated for reporting purposes much the same way as a traditional tangible asset.[1] Its investment is capitalized and depreciated over its useful life. As an asset class, its most intangible characteristic might be that you cannot see or touch it.

While IT's treatment on financial statements is tangible, what managers find highly intangible is many of its impacts—the benefits it delivers the organization. These benefits seem intangible by virtue of the fact that they are devilishly tough to quantify financially. Managers feel the impact that IT delivers in their jobs. They are convinced that some application has delivered productivity improvements, better decision-making capabilities, a sense of shared purpose, and clearer communication amongst operational functions inside the enterprise, but they are hard pressed to articulate some of those impacts in a return on investment model that might have been constructed as a decision framework to go ahead with the investment. Intangible benefits are, in fact, proliferating as the technology being invested in has less to do with running infrastructure or even cost savings and more to do with strategic goals and business process reengineering required by IT to realize these goals.

At the macro level, the literature is fairly extensive about IT's economic impact in the enterprise.

The sense of urgency around the entire economic value depiction imperative of information technology has many varied and interrelated reasons. They include:

- **IT is the business:** No longer can IT be regarded as a set of discrete services. Technology is now woven into the fabric of companies and touches most if not all the value-driving activities a company engages in to succeed in the marketplace. This includes but is not limited to financials, customer-facing applications including marketing automation and sales force automation, product design collaboration, HR self-service, supply chain partnering—the list is as long as the number of critical business operations. In fact, MIT research in the mid-1990s found that investors value technology investment at ten times what they value conventional capital investment.[2] This is because IT invites improvements in the performance of people as well as with internal and customer-facing processes supporting business goals—all intangible assets.

- **The changing role of the IT organization:** Historically, an IT/IS organization was regarded as a utility services organization, a group that delivered uptime capability, a help desk, troubleshooting, and software and hardware installation. The IT/IS organization was akin to facilities management—the mandate was to keep the lights on and the boilers running. Very important but hardly partners in delivering value to the company. As the kinds of IT available to companies have evolved from simply supporting strategic goals into delivering them, demands have been put upon information systems personnel to consider alignment of technology with business need. This has proven to be a sizable cultural shift.

- **Technology failure rates:** Although the aggregate failure rate for IT investment might be more than slightly inaccurate given the possibility that no single company that is in the business of reporting failures has access to a statistically valid sampling, the anecdotal evidence is vivid and not a little horrifying. I know for a fact, for instance, that a major U.S. insurance company was into one customer relationship management (CRM) vendor for $10 million before the carrier walked away, defeated in the conclusion that the software was simply uncustomizable for its needs. In other words, it cost the insurance company $10 million just to learn that the application under consideration was ill suited to its business goals, a colossal failure on many levels. Other statistics abound. Half of all IT projects come in late and over budget.[3] This kind of reckless legacy is ripe for an injection of fiscal sobriety. And it goes to show how, suddenly, everyone is conscious of the need for IT to receive the same kind of financial scrutiny as any other capital investment.

- **The CFO has skin in the game:** Because IT holds the promise of delivering performance value to the organization—revenue and market share increases, faster product development cycles, reinforcement of brand value, etc.—the CFO increasingly is entering the IT investment narrative. Insofar as this is so, the language and habit of mind of finance are being superimposed upon the language of technology. For more strategic kinds of IT investments, the conversation is directed by concepts such as internal rate of return, cash flow, and return on invested capital, as much as it is by MIPS (millions of instructions per second), FLOPS (floating-point operations per second), batch-processing speeds, and network throughput.

Other reasons for increased interest in technology ROI are complementary to these major trends, including the fact that, increasingly, budgets for technology investment to support business goals in operational areas—whether the investment is a packaged application or an in-house custom program—are being funded out of the line of business rather than through the technology organization.[4] The result is that managers are being held accountable for these expenditures; suddenly, the act of conducting a cost-benefit analysis to depict all the impacts and cost drivers of the project becomes a management imperative because the act of depicting economic value infuses investment decision making with additional clarity and provides some additional foreseeability to the risks associated with it. In light of the heightened accountability for investments that managers seek, the emerging abiding principle surrounding strategic kinds of IT investment is that you should be careful of what you wish for.

Executives with long experience in modeling the economic impacts of capital investments—plant, equipment, or real estate—might view the frenetic buzz surrounding the theme of IT's economic value with bemusement or shock. Should we not be startled at least slightly that well into the millennium we're only now having our collective consciousness raised about the need and value in at least attempting to quantify the returns to information technology? For as many companies as there are with long histories in conducting financial assessments to any investments including IT, there are as many organizations that have only embarked on these activities within the past few years. In many cases, it's as if an ROI analysis of a software package is a concept born from the loins of the software itself rather than being the child of the science of finance that it is. With rapid awareness of the value in quantifying the economic value of IT has also come the realization that some of the impacts are difficult to measure.

Factors of IT Intangibility

People, or human capital, are an intangible because, amongst other reasons, they are not categorized as an asset on a company's balance sheet. Intangibility arises out of a conceptual shift; from a value-creation perspective, people are an asset and not a pure cost. Yet, as we've seen in previous chapters, financial statements treat them as an expense. The disconnect creates intangibility. This is clearly not the case with technology.

Rather, IT's intangibility arises from the fact that many of its benefits are difficult to measure in such a way that those benefits can be assigned a hard, numerical financial value. And as we know from Finance 101, return on investment for any investment is expressed as follows:

$$\frac{\textbf{Profit}}{\textbf{Investment}}$$

A profit of $20 on an investment of $100 equals a 20 percent ROI. Often, managers will use permanent cost reductions in the numerator as a proxy for "profit"; that is, the cost savings are substituted for after-tax earnings because the IT investment is not designed to deliver profit. The exception, of course, is those technology investments that generate revenue, yet these are rare. A cost savings of $20 on a $100 investment represents a 20 percent ROI. This assumes that all cost savings find their way to the bottom line of an income statement—that the 20 percent cost savings means a direct 20 percent increase in profitability. The calculation also assumes that both costs and profits are held constant so a meaningful comparison before investment and after investment can be made. How often does this occur? Never. Yet the arithmetic is a rough proxy for the cost-driving improvements a technology can deliver.

When pure profit is not applicable, some companies will use the payback method, which measures how long it takes an investment to pay for itself out of the cash flows it generates.[5] The shorter the payback, the better. This is for two reasons. First, a shorter payback period means less risk from investment in the project. And second, the quicker a break-even point is reached, the quicker that amount of capital is freed up for other projects. Rare is the organization whose IT capital investment choices mean only such straightforward and unambiguous calculations.

Many more companies live with a series of IT capital investment choices, which presents a mix of hard-coded, easily quantifiable financial benefits and harder-to-calculate yet equally as important intangible benefits. Again, IT benefit intangibility does not mean the impacts aren't palpable and felt; rather, they are difficult to hang a number on when an ROI model is presented to senior management as part of a persuasive business case to move ahead with the investment. This quandary is often most keenly felt when an ROI exercise is used as a decision-making framework to determine the choice of capital investment when many are competing for selection.

For instance, let's suppose a bank analyzes both a loan-processing software application and a suite of applications designed for banking customers to pay their bills online. The return on investment is nearly identical. Each is expected to deliver either measurable cost savings or incremental revenue. Upon deeper analysis, however, the bank discovers that the online billing portal strategy for banking customers offers some longer-term but more intangible benefits, chiefly the ability for the bank to solidify and extend its relationship with banking customers. The bank has a strategic business goal of keeping customers through the deployment of value-added online services. Providing a one-stop portal where customers can manage not only their checking, savings, mortgage, home equity, and investment accounts (we'll assume the bank is already offering these services online) but also all of their recurring arrangements for the payment of utilities, phone bills, cell phone bills, car payments, etc., clearly helps the bank in this goal. The low monthly fee the customer pays for this service will justify the IT investment on a payback or break-even basis. Yet a deeper multidimensional financial relationship with customers through the Web is the real source of value for the bank even if it does not have a firm handle on the precise future revenue implications of the relationship. The identified benefit "deeper relationship with customers from this value-added service" is intangible because there is no reliable way to quantify the net present value of the future income stream from a deeper relationship—at least not yet because the bank might not have developed the service—but given the high-level goals of the bank, it chose the online billing project over a loan-processing application.

The chief driver of IT's intangibility arises out of causal ambiguity that comes in a couple of flavors. One is the inability to link outcomes to the business that can be isolated to the specific technology investment, called *isolation ambiguity*. The second variety arises when a clear cause-and-effect relationship between the investment and the outcomes can be established, but the relationship is indirect and several steps removed, involving intermediate steps between the technology cause and business effect and contributions from other factors. How much impact should the manager realistically assign to the technology as opposed to the other contributors of value that the impact delivers? This is categorized as *weighting ambiguity*. Examples of both follow.

Isolation Ambiguity

Supposing a retailer invests in improved call center infrastructure hardware and software, a discretely defined category of application within the larger category of customer relationship management. No class of software has broken more chief information officers' hearts than CRM because the vendor overpromised and underdelivered and also because companies did not adequately respond to the organizational challenges this class of software instigates. Nevertheless, call center applications as a subset of CRM contain powerful functionality to help businesses better match internal resources to the calls coming into its contact center and generally handle call volume more efficiently.

Let's say a company is convinced that a 30 percent drop in the average hold time of inbound callers will not only save on telecommunications costs but improve customer satisfaction. It invests in a collection of software and hardware that allows the organization to better balance staffing with inbound call loads. Hold times decrease a whopping 50 percent over the first three months the IT is in use. The company is ecstatic, and sales are up 10 percent for the first half of the year. How much of the improved revenue can realistically be attributed to the IT investment? To hear vendors, the answer is all of it. Lift in customer satisfaction resulting from a much better call center experience is a key pivot point of their sales pitch.

No doubt, a better call center experience can influence customers' opinions of the company and their desire to do future business with the company (especially in businesses where there is a heavy call center element to the relationship, e.g., in the field of technology, such as with vendors of PCs and other high-tech gadgets, as well as financial services). Yet even if the bump in revenue was solely due to improvements in customer satisfaction—unlikely as it is—how could the organization prove the direct causation between the two events, IT investment and revenue increases? Could the organization isolate even 5 percent of the revenue growth distinctly to customer satisfaction improvements as opposed to a better economy, a major advertising campaign, or some product innovation popular with the public?

Take the bank's online billing IT investment, for example. Six months after the bank introduced this service, three thousand banking customers have signed up for it. The bank learns that investment services revenue has increased a small but noticeable amount from customers who have signed up for online billing services. In the absence of survey data, which requires bank investment sales employees to capture data confirming that online billing capability is driving investment services sign-ups from the same customers, we do not realistically know if the bump in revenue is directly linked to online billing, a friend's recommendation, dissatisfaction with another broker, all of the above, or none of the above. Is the search for causation even worth exploring? One would think so if the bank is minimally interested in confirming its instincts that an online billing portal is an important element in its customer relationship–building agenda. A person's finances are one of the most powerful and important facets of her life. The addition of online billing is just more glue in the bond the bank hopes to build with customers who take advantage of the service.

Weighting Ambiguity

Perhaps a more common challenge managers face is assigning a valid contribution from information technology investment when other elements were required ingredients in the recipe used to create value. We know that IT drove the positive economic outcome, but how much driving did the technology do, independent from the other important contributory elements identified along the way?

Consider the experience of Dreyfus, a very large mutual fund company. Its desire to conceptualize how it would approach a serious asset attrition problem leveraging customer data with the assistance of technology actually reveals the challenge in giving that IT investment its proper recognition and no more or no less.

At the time Executive Vice President Prasanna Dhore joined the company, the attrition rate was around the industry average, and techniques attempted to staunch the flow of money out of the company's family of mutual funds were not working. The imperative was clear: figure out customer-centric strategies and tactics to keep people from moving their money elsewhere. In the end, asset attrition is the result of poor fund investment performance. But the reality for Dreyfus was more nuanced and subtle, as Dhore and colleagues learned.

Dhore knew that all tactical and strategic decision making begins with information—in this case, information about customers—and the financial services industry has mountains of it. The key was sifting through all this information in such a way for meaningful patterns to emerge that might help explain the attrition problem and also identify the characteristics of investors who had large asset totals with the company. Dhore invested in data-mining tools from SAS to help in this job of data analysis. Data-mining software happens to be an excellent example of the weighting ambiguity problem that managers discover when hunting for an ROI from the software because so many elements participate in delivering that return.

One way to isolate all the sources that contribute to the total value of data-mining software, and which illustrate the challenges of weighting ambiguity and the vexation it causes managers in determining hard returns for a particular IT investment, is to use a technique called Knowledge Object Theory (KOT). KOT is explained in full detail in Chapter 8, which discusses knowledge as an intangible asset. It is not important that you understand KOT here but rather that you recognize the complementary nature of value that information technology delivers and the fact that such complementarity is a crucial characteristic that differentiates intangible assets from traditional ones.

Following is what is called, in KOT lingo, a Triad:

Input	Process	Output
Customer data	Organize, clean, architect	Customer profile information

A Triad is a structured way of expressing any reality of something. Triads require some entity to be put through a process and become something else after that process is finished. In this example, the "something" is customer data. The customer data are put through the process of organizing, cleaning, and architecting for further use. By virtue of customer information being subjected to this process, the end result is clean, accurate customer profiles, which become the basis for the data-mining software to guide managers in making more informed decisions. Again, KOT is used to illustrate the complementarity of a series of sources of value, which deliver the collective value of the software.

Data organization, cleaning, and warehousing are common and critical IT activities today because information and the subsequent knowledge derived from that information can be looked at as the company's source of nutrition, the very sustenance that powers the value creation we're interested in.

In the second Triad (which follows), customer information becomes the new intangible asset that managers seek to leverage.

Input	Process	Output
Customer information	Data mine—search for meaningful patterns	Knowledge—patterns, meaningful customer segments

Management applies powerful data-mining technology to help it make sense of large quantities of clean yet unmeaningful customer information. Data mining helps Dreyfus discover deeper, more revealing behaviors, attributes of this customer information that become the foundation for the strategy and tactics the company undertakes to realize the financial goal—to stop the flow of money out of the company. Dreyfus managers decide to attack the attrition problem along three customer dimensions: life stage, profitability, and investment behavior. It crafts marketing campaigns as well as some tactical activities for its sales force for direct application to the problem around this new segmentation array. The end result is a nearly 25 percent reduction in the attrition rate over a couple of years. "We no longer have a redemption problem—we have a sales challenge, which is basically what we want," Dhore reports.[6]

Input	Process	Output	Performance Impact
Knowledge	Management decision making—analysis and judgment of knowledge	Tactical: marketing campaigns, sales techniques	Reduction in asset attrition

So, how much of the reduction in asset flows—and therefore stabilization of, if not increase in, investment management fees—should be attributable directly to SAS data-mining technology? Deconstruction of the multilayered set of processes that took the company from raw data to a successful financial goal shows how difficult answering this question with any accuracy and confidence is. Dreyfus could have weighted the relative importance of every intangible asset applied to each iteration in the process in getting from raw data to strategy that works. But how to weight the relative importance of SAS tools versus the experience and judgment of managers who had to decide what data elements required inclusion for analysis in the first place? How much credit should knowledge receive? More than software, less than management, or vice versa? The weighting ambiguity in this scenario arises from the multiplicity of elements that contribute to the total value of all the software. To some extent, the value of all software is subject to the contributions of external elements, such as the quality of information being manipulated by the application and the expertise of the people using the system. The forces of complementarity are exacerbated with a technology like data-mining software, however, because the very value proposition of this application type is better decision making as opposed to operational cost reductions, which is at the root of many other kinds of software. Happily, many types of software investment do not introduce weighting ambiguities. The path to an ROI is clear-cut.

How many intangible assets were put to the wheel here? At least five as the business public has defined them: data, information and knowledge, IT, and people. An implied intangible asset in the Dreyfus scenario was the unique culture and company philosophy that shaped all the activities around execution of this strategy. The company did not set itself up to achieve complete results in the first year. The company took a quick win, hitting singles rather than going after a grand slam approach.

Dhore piloted his assertions about what tactics to take toward customer classes before the company implemented this project fully. Not every organization would have worked this way. Unfocused, undisciplined organizations would have swung for the fences immediately. Dreyfus exploited management experience and expertise as well as the right cultural environment, which had the company take a prudently incremental approach to a serious business problem. How do you quantify the value of management wisdom? The financial services industry is one of the most experienced and sophisticated in its use of IT for both operational and strategic aims. It operates in an environment one can characterize as genteel ruthlessness. Competitive necessity might very well inform company culture as that culture dictates management practices that, in the Dreyfus experience, supported intangible asset allocation and in the end proved to be effective.

So we can return to the weighted ambiguity issue and consider the following. We know that company culture at Dreyfus influenced decision making around the course of action to staunch the flow of assets out of the company. How much recognition expressed in dollar terms should company culture receive in the mix of intangible drivers that created value in the form of stopping asset flight? Five percent? Fifty percent? Business intelligence and data-mining software require the marriage of so many interdependent variables—information, data, people, management philosophy—that some might believe attempting an accurate ROI calculation, fraught with so much peril, is pointless.

This is not the case, however. Companies have shown that weighting ambiguity will unlikely stop them from going ahead with technology investments that exhibit these characteristics (witness the success of SAS) whether a rigorous business case is developed or not. Many companies do not think about the weighting ambiguities when considering capital investment because they don't model the possible financial impacts. Yet for those who do make the effort to forecast investment returns, any complementary influences on those returns will come into focus and therefore elevate awareness of all the prerequisites of success. In the case of data-mining software, we know what those prerequisites are: clean, accurate, relevant data, as well as managers skilled enough to know which revelation the software provides is relevant to a particular business problem and, just as important, what action must be taken in response to what the software reveals. Oftentimes economic value models assume the existence of these contributing sources toward total value, and that can be dangerous. An understanding of weighting ambiguity and what elements contribute to it is the beginning of deeper comprehension of potential economic returns from software investment and how to maximize them.

Managers might believe that the reality of isolation and weighting ambiguity in the depiction of IT economic value conspires against management support for technology projects. But this is not the case. At least one study relating to customer-centric technologies—Web-based self-service, call center applications, and sales force and marketing automation, amongst others—contends that CFOs understand the intangible elements of technology impacts and are comfortable using a mix of hard financial and soft nonfinancial indicators to green-light investment.[7] While isolation and weighting ambiguity complicate disciplined, consistent, and clearly portrayed economic value-depiction exercises, the realities of intangible impacts of IT investment do not sabotage investments in these technologies altogether. Companies have found ways around the challenge.

Meeting the Intangibility Challenge

The first step in grappling with the intangibility factor of IT is to recognize when economic value depiction, defined as a detailed preinvestment modeling of all the anticipated cost and benefit drivers, which allows for the calculation of ROI or discounted cash flows such as net present value or internal rate of return, is useful to managers and when it is not. If we accept the idea that modeling the economic value of a proposed technology investment aids in the decision-making process of whether to make the investment, then the issue evolves into a question of what projects to invest the resources in to actually model the expected returns because the modeling calculations will be accurate and can be relied upon with a high degree of confidence by management.

Managers are best served taking a kind of triage approach to economic value forecasting—invest the time and intellectual rigor in modeling some kinds of technology projects, but forgo the exercise with others. The following framework will tell you neither what specific metrics to measure for any given investment nor how to measure those performance drivers. However, this framework will provide guidance as to what kinds of technologies are best suited for modeling and what technologies are not. You should see that some of the intangibility challenge is completely eliminated because by following this framework, managers spend less time fretting over how to measure some difficult-to-quantify outcome for certain kinds of projects and more time looking deeply into the cost savings and revenue possibilities of other projects. Eliminating the obsession with ROI toward some kinds of technology projects eliminates the obsession with measuring the intangibility impacts from that same investment.

Measurement Action Pyramid

A triage approach to the investment of resources in modeling and forecasting the economic returns from a proposed technology investment means you build ROI forecasts and economic models when they are best suited to the technology. A measurement action pyramid (MAP) is constructed along three dimensions:

- the degree of risk associated with the project
- the degree of strategic benefits the technology is capable of returning
- the degree of dependency a specific technology has on other specific technologies for value delivery

Figure 4.1 illustrates the MAP approach.

The idea behind MAP is that companies should be less compelled to conduct rigorous ROI forecasts at levels 3 and 4 than at levels 1 and 2.[8] The reasons are supported along the three dimensions. For one, projects at higher levels of the pyramid are inherently riskier. The narrowing of the pyramid symbolizes the reduction in any room for error; therefore, getting it right the first time is crucial. This is so because strategic kinds of technology introduce complexity and novelty, new ways of conducting business that require business process reengineering and organizational adaptability. More than one CRM initiative has failed because companies did not anticipate adequately the organizational change required to maximize the value out of the investment. Lower-level technologies are inherently less risky in terms of both project execution and operation because the impacts on how business is conducted are lower.[9]

Second, and a related issue, is that strategic kinds of technology found in levels 1 and 2 present opportunities (such as revenue and market growth potential) that lower-level technologies do not. High-impact and high-risk kinds of IT require financial modeling with a higher level of rigor simply because the stakes are higher—not just the risks but the financial payoff. One of the greatest values to be gotten out of a fully

Figure 4.1 MAP Approach

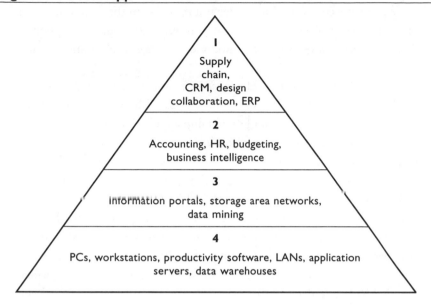

1
Supply
chain,
CRM, design
collaboration, ERP

2
Accounting, HR, budgeting,
business intelligence

3
Information portals, storage area networks,
data mining

4
PCs, workstations, productivity software, LANs, application
servers, data warehouses

thought-out ROI forecast is that if done correctly, it makes visible and foreseeable all the potentialities of the software, as well as all the implications to business processes, job functions, and organizational arrangements. Therefore, the forecast or model does not simply provide some foreseeability into project and operation risk but also some visibility into the true value-creating potential of the technology. The complementary phenomena of high risks and high rewards demand a level of preinvestment assessment and forecasting that isn't required at lower levels.

Third, arguing for a detailed, rigorous financial forecast for investments in PCs, local area networks, and data warehouses is really arguing for an opportunity cost analysis. If the required ROI doesn't materialize after all the calculations have been created, does this mean the company forgoes investment in PC or Office Suite upgrades, new storage, or a data warehouse to support several applications? What is the cost to the company if it decides not to invest in these support kinds of technologies? One answer is that you will never have the opportunity to leverage level 1 or 2 technologies because levels 3 and 4 power them.

This is not to suggest that because infrastructure IT enables strategic IT, all caution about the expenditure should be tossed to the wind. On the contrary, a total cost of ownership approach to a rigorous analysis of the cost implications over the life cycle of the particular technology is crucial. Yet a business case that depicts all the cost implications of the proposed investment, along with some qualitative judgments and assessments that illustrate the investment is a good idea, will suffice for many organizations in place of a decision-making process that devolves into despair when the debate ensues over what dollar value should be assigned to a hard-to-quantify impact revealed in an ROI analysis.

For the reasons of risk, strategic impact, and the enablement reality, detailed ROI calculations are best suited for IT in levels 1 and 2. Insofar as a particular level 1 or 2 technology contains any intangible impacts, managers will agonize more over the challenge with these types of projects because economic value depiction is that much more important for the reasons just argued. Managers are let off the hook with levels 3 and 4 investments for the hair pulling associated with the myriad intangible impacts they present.

Admittedly, the delineation of discrete technology types is slightly arbitrary. A company could make a case that many financial applications do not present any competitive advantage and therefore could be bumped from level 2 to 3 or, alternatively, that data mining has so dramatically changed decision making that it is considered a strategic investment. Generally speaking, however, the logic of the pyramid holds. Not much at level 1 or 2 is going to get done unless investments in levels 3 and 4 are made.

Take the benefits explicated by Oracle for its 9i Application Server:

- Improve business agility by integrating and streamlining business processes.
- Make informed decisions by unlocking information in legacy and packaged applications.

- Collaborate with your business partners using industry standards.
- Gain a unified view of your customers, no matter where their information resides.[10]

In the following order, how does a manager measure improved business agility, measure more informed decision making, measure the value of collaboration, or measure the financial impact of a more unified view of the customer? We'll take Oracle at its word that these impacts are within the grasp of any business that successfully deploys the technology. But are these impacts within the grasp of the manager whose job is to model the costs and benefits in an ROI forecast for presentation to his manager? Not when the benefits are assigned to this technology, one, and not when expressed in these terms, two. (More on this momentarily.)

MAP reveals that application server technology is decidedly a level 3 or 4 investment—not strategic but nevertheless a prerequisite for the technologies that truly will deliver these benefits. In a three-tier client/server environment, an application server in the parlance of techspeak handles the business logic of a software program. The database serves the data, the application server parses the data depending upon what the program is designed to do, and the front end (PC with graphical user interface) presents the data and serves as the point of human interaction with the software. The application server is a hugely important piece of technology, just as an engine is to a car. But it is not the direct source of these stated benefits. It is a contributing source of these impacts, sharing the stage with middleware, the application that sits on top of the application server—CRM, procurement, financials, etc.—and even the hardware that powers all the software.[11]

Just as in the case with SAS business intelligence tools, application server technology creates economic value, but it is interdependent value, created in conjunction with other IT elements because it is not a strategic investment.

Intangibility Challenge Scenarios

While the intangibility conundrum arising from the impacts from IT investment cannot be resolved with some universally applicable formula, there are ways to confront the problem, as illustrated by the three examples that follow.

Scenario 1: Seeking the Tangible in Organizational Agility

The intangibility of impacts from technology investment sometimes resides in how benefits are stated. Articulated impacts, such as employee empowerment, organizational agility, or information quality, while intuitively understood, are actually quite vague and abstract. Annual reports, corporate brochures, and other marketing fluff spout these homilies, while the media will introduce these concepts when supporting contentions that a company has certain strengths and these are it. Most audiences are satisfied with these intangible asset conceptualizations because they can afford to be. When these buzzwords are stuck on the back of a capital investment rationale, however, CFOs might prefer a more nuanced explanation.

Let's return to Oracle's application server example. For the sake of illustration, let's imagine that these exact same benefits have been articulated for supply chain software. (Many ambiguously stated benefits, because of their very lack of precision, are applicable to any kind of technology.) If you look at these statements more closely, you will see that every one of these benefits can be made less ambiguous, if not completely measurable. And the more ambiguity we can eliminate in the statement of benefit, the better we can analyze the nature of the impact, grasp its interdependencies, and isolate its contribution from the contribution of other elements. It's a simple matter of attacking the ambiguity by thinking, from a less abstract level, about what the intangible benefit really means. A useful exercise that managers can deploy consistently when marketing fluff stares them in the face is a simple language deconstruction exercise that can help make more tangible what is believed at first blush to be impossibly intangible: the Tangibility Deduction Grid (see Table 4.1).

In Table 4.1, we attempt to clear away the fog surrounding the benefit "improve business agility by integrating and streamlining business processes." Using this simple process-driven exercise, a manager takes an ill-defined impact from supply chain investment and translates it into phenomena that are observable and potentially quite measurable.

Table 4.1 Tangibility Deduction Grid—Supply Chain Application

Step 1 Intangible Benefit	Step 2 Intangibility Factor	Step 3 Restate for Clarity	Step 4 Descriptor Relevance	Step 5 Observability Factor	Step 6 Measurability
State the hard-to-quantify benefit.	What is it about the benefit that makes it intangible?	Can intangible benefit be recast to clarify its quantifiable impact?	In context of supply chain investment, are speed and flexibility relevant as a benefit? How?	If intangible benefit is relevant, is improvement observable?	If observable, possible metrics
Improved business agility	Difficulty in measuring business agility	Agility is defined as "the power of moving the limbs quickly and easily."* Synonymous descriptors: speed, flexibility	Yes. Speed: gets product to customer quicker. Flexibility: change product mix in response to market demand.	Yes.	Speed: reductions in time to delivery Flexibility: increased market share, increased revenue, inventory reductions, working capital efficiency
	Clarity		Concreteness	Relevance	Quantifiability

*Dictionary.com, The American Heritage Dictionary of the English Language, 4th ed. (Houghton Mifflin, 2000).

Improved business agility might very well mean speed in getting product to market quicker either by cutting down the number of suppliers involved in its creation or by reducing the steps required to procure raw materials. Improved agility is translated into the ability to respond more nimbly to market conditions by redeploying labor and capital into new product development. Any manager will tell you there is nothing intangible about revenue increases or improved working capital efficiency.

Supposing we yoked the same intangible benefit to marketing automation rather than supply chain software? Walking through the same exercise, you might conclude the benefits are observable and therefore measurable, but the impacts will be different because this enterprise software is designed to impact different areas of the business. A speed improvement metric might consist of a reduction in time to launch a marketing campaign once it has been devised. Faster marketing program launch means that revenue from the campaign is captured faster because customers receive this pitch sooner than they would through, say, direct mail. Companies that can ramp up marketing campaigns demonstrably faster using automated techniques and new processes from the software will generate income more quickly and pay for the investment more rapidly.

Flexibility could mean the ability to submit to customers a range of options for them to talk back to the company upon receiving a marketing pitch. They might be given the option to buy, to speak to a customer service person, or to learn more about the offer from the website. In the case of customers who want to learn more, they might take advantage of the detailed product information, which leads to a decision to buy. Assuming that the information is easily accessible and simple to understand, customers might forgo contacting the call center because all their questions have been answered from the self-service environment. In this specific context, flexibility ends up translating into an observable and measurable reduction in product-oriented calls to the call center and cost savings to the organization.

Given the sometimes vague nature of the English language, flexibility as a stated intangible benefit in marketing automation might concern itself more with technical performance of the application. The be-all and end-all of customer relationship management software of any kind, including marketing automation, is the ability to have a unified view of the customer—that is, to develop comprehensive views of customers based upon their complete history with the organization across customer service, billing, marketing, website activity, and product categories. The integration challenges in pulling data from islands of non-integrated software can be vast. At least one vendor pitches the notion that using its software will ease these integration challenges via open standards in defining, modeling, and fusing data in order to present the complete customer picture. Flexibility might turn out to mean the relative ease by which the IT organization can bring together disparate silos of data and translate them into measurable reductions in the time and cost that IT pros must devote to integration activity around the specific investment.

To recap, this simple process is designed to drive precision in articulating and defining intangible benefits of a technology. Here are the steps that can help turn some benefits of IT investment from intangible to tangible:

1. What is the intangible benefit the enterprise expects it will experience by virtue of the investment?
2. Why is the benefit intangible? That is, why is it hard to quantify and measure?
3. Restate the benefit for clarity. Given the fungibility of the English language, for any given intangible benefit, you should find it can be restated several different ways. The simple act of manipulating words and searching for synonyms will bring clarity to what phenomena are driving the impacts from the investment.
4. If the benefit can be restated, how is it relevant? Reduced inventory is the measurable impact from improved agility in supply chain investment. Improved agility might be just as relevant in a customer relationship management deployment, yet the performance indicator or metric that captures the tangibility of the impact is, in many cases such as this, very different. With CRM, flexibility could translate into lower deployment costs or lower call center expenses associated with a particular campaign. Improved agility turns out to be relevant to both supply chain and CRM applications—just in different ways.

5. Once you determine relevance, the next question to ask is whether the restated benefit is observable. Observable in the context of transforming the intangible to tangible means the ability to quantify and measure the specific impacts with some degree of confidence. Observable does not necessarily mean the ability to observe the impact with the naked eye, although plenty of enterprise software brings outcomes that are easy to see. Ask anyone on the short end of an application that automates business-to-business order-entry activities. (Full-time equivalent reductions are one of the most observable impacts from technology.) More often, the observability of the impacts of IT investment—intangible or otherwise—derives from operational data, which capture the improvement. It is difficult to see inventory efficiencies with the naked eye unless one stands in the stockroom every day counting what is on hand. It is obviously easier to pull the data reflecting the improvements from the very software delivering the benefit.

6. If an event is observable, it is measurable. This is a metaphysical certainty. Any positive impact either seen with the naked eye or confirmed in operational data is easily translatable into metrics, expressed as a percentage cost reduction or a percentage revenue enhancement. The impact is one or the other.

Scenario 2: Overcoming the Curse of Small Gains

More than one complaint has been heard from IT executives that a particular expected impact will save a small amount of time—say, two minutes—per event or per day. To these managers, the stated benefit is intangible because it is insignificantly small and defies measurement. Maybe.

Actually, a two-minute productivity improvement in some human activity brought about by automation can be significant. The first question to tackle is whether that two-minute savings is truly observable or did the manager use that as an extreme example to make the point that small improvements—an intangible benefit to him—were difficult to measure? In the context of some repetitive administrative tasks, a two-minute savings per day, even if observable and confirmed, is too small to translate into a measurable impact. A ten-minute savings might be just as insignificant. However, if by installing or reworking some kind of technology an airline cuts ten minutes from the time it takes to load a plane's baggage, such a productivity improvement could translate into a boost in a carrier's on-time efficiency and customer satisfaction, although the causal linkage is ambiguous. Relevance as it relates to intangible impact quantification is highly contextual to both the application under scrutiny and the business the intangible benefit impacts. The measurement may or may not add up to a significant impact.

For instance, one IT manager for a West Coast port authority complained about the intangibility of small gains, having no specific technology in mind. If some software cuts down some repetitive task of a shipping clerk by two minutes a day, then simply translate that into a yearly hourly savings. Say the total is five hundred minutes (or roughly eight hours) a year:

2 minutes × 5 times a week × 50 weeks a year = 500 minutes

If the clerk's hourly labor rate is $30, the organization saves about $240. If the port staff consists of only two clerks, it is true that a two-minute daily savings is not a substantial benefit. That's not the case, of course, if the port employs thirty clerks per shift. As the small gains scale to ever-increasing worker populations, the gains suddenly loom very tangible. Gains of this size, although more rare today because many tasks have been automated, start to translate into head-count reductions.

In both cases, the benefit is realized only if the clerk translates the time saved into another productive activity—taking on more work. Otherwise, there is no savings because labor in this case is a fixed cost. The port is unlikely to cut back the clerk's number of hours worked, and therefore pay, to reflect that $240 saved, especially if the clerk is unionized. One of the biggest pitfalls of IT measurement is for managers to overlook the fact that productivity benefits metrics—in this case, time saved in some administrative task—are predicated upon the sometimes large assumption that the time actually saved is translated into additional, meaningful work taken on by the worker. If half the time saved is consumed in coffee breaks or conversations with coworkers, while these might be permissible activities, they must be subtracted from the total economic impact.

The second problem with this scenario is managers' belief that even if the benefit were possible, it is difficult to observe. Observability does not mean standing over someone with a stopwatch, but it does mean being able to collect relevant operational data out of technology systems. If managers have a proper baseline that provides time-to-task completion within any work flow, presentable data over time will reveal if the savings of two minutes per day is significant enough to document within whatever financial assessment framework was employed—net present value, breakeven, etc.—to determine investment feasibility. Observability also means persistence of the impact; that is, the impact has become structurally embedded in the work flow under analysis and occurs frequently enough that it translates into larger economic benefit. A two-minute savings twice a week or ten times a month may or may not be persistent. It depends on whether its frequency is a measurable enough impact. With two clerks, probably not. With fifty clerks, yes.

The challenge of quantifying the impact of minute, discrete gains did not stop FedEx from announcing that it recently finished a $150 million project arming drivers with new handheld package-tracking devices. The wireless devices will help drivers cut out about ten seconds per pickup per stop and will help the company save at least $20 million each year.[12] Given the scale of the company's operation, it is not difficult to imagine how this ten-second time savings could be rolled up into a significant, quantifiable economic benefit from handheld investment. Assuming one hundred pickups and deliveries a day, this translates into seventeen minutes a day across the thousands of FedEx delivery personnel. Could this savings mean any improvement in on-time delivery efficiency or lower truck fuel consumption? Suddenly the insignificant ten-second gain has a large collective effect on the company's operation. The impact is no longer intangible.

You will notice throughout this discussion that transforming intangible impacts into concrete ones requires validation after the investment has been deployed. Arguably all forecasted impacts from IT investment are intangible until these impacts are validated and confirmed. This may be true for any capital investment but is perhaps more urgent where technology is concerned because of its inherent complexity. For this reason, an increasing number of companies are operationalizing an audit capability post-IT investment, which has the effect of turning the intangible and little-understood impacts into tangible ones.

Scenario 3: Finding the Tangible in the Tactical

Intangibility in IT is a problem when the specific investment under consideration is not tied directly to specific, concrete business goals. Companies make technology investments for lots of reasons: to automate business processes, to comply with regulations, to respond to a vendor going out of business. Rarely is an organization completely blind to the ways in which new technology will improve business operations. Yet by their very nature, some classes of technology more easily model the economic benefits than others. We just saw how intangible can be the impacts from decision support/business intelligence software. Another category of application that poses a quantification challenge is learning.

When you consider the history of training efforts, companies rarely calculated a return on investment for outlays giving employees the opportunity to further their educations with MBAs, technical degrees, or executive workshops. Investments were significant as companies financed tuition, books, and the opportunity costs in days of missed work. Some organizations have invested in multimillion-dollar campuses at company headquarters and have suffered the associated lodging and airfare costs entailed in bringing in employees from field offices. Consultants and university teachers charge substantial fees to run courses. The results of this pedagogical largesse have for the most part, nevertheless, been taken on faith; companies assumed that better trained, more educated workers would deliver operational improvements that translate into success on financial statements. Organizations didn't feel it necessary to determine the ROI of training efforts nor did they know how devilishly difficult it would be to arrive at accurate measures. The goal of having "smarter employees," as noble as that is, presents all sorts of isolation and weighting ambiguity when not linked directly to some immediate tactical business goal. The benefits of financing a master's degree in electrical engineering or business administration can be quite intangible.

Enter e-learning. It was only a matter of time before an industry would emerge to take advantage of advanced information network infrastructures inside most companies today and the desktop computer literacy of most employees. Today, e-learning companies sell millions of dollars' worth of digitized curriculum and software tools for workers to learn a variety of business and technical competencies right from their workstations. (Whether this form of education delivery is more effective than the traditional teacher-student form is a whole other question beyond the scope of this text.) Companies rightly saw that, unlike the traditional form of education and training delivery, e-learning curricula could be deployed rapidly in response to some immediate business need and could reach a far larger target population simultaneously given the broadcast nature of digital delivery. Possessed with these advantages, companies made tactical training investments that lent themselves to ROI quantification. Consider these examples:

- The New York–based cable entertainment company Cablevision hired an e-learning vendor to develop targeted curricula to train two populations of company workers: field technicians troubleshooting technical problems in subscribers' homes and customer service reps handling service issues in the call center. In the case of the technicians, Cablevision sought, by virtue of advanced training, to reduce the number of "truck rolls"—repeat visits to fix problems on the customer's premises, such as TV broadcast glitches or the inability to connect to the Internet. The call center rep's challenge was more daunting: up-sell and cross-sell customers with additional services when they contacted the company. The same e-learning vendor built curricula around the subtle art of salesmanship. Turning inbound call reps into proactive salespeople was a strategic shift for the company.[13]
- The diversified telecom provider Verizon sought the same result as Cablevision—reduction in the number of house calls by field technicians. In this case, the company targeted training at call center personnel who evaluate the customer's problem and decide whether to

initiate a truck roll. The rationale was that having call center personnel who were better educated about the range of technical problems that might arise would result in more informed decision making about the course of action and a reduction in needless field technician visits.[14]

In both cases, the companies made tactical investments whose benefits were, therefore, quite tangible and subject to postinvestment measurement efforts. Cablevision was able to track revenue increases per new service and per rep, as well as more qualitative attributes, such as improvements in a rep's experience rating. The rating is a qualitative measure of customer satisfaction captured through surveys and conducted via phone interviews. Several days after a customer calls in to resolve a problem and, in the process, receives a sales offer, a third-party survey house will follow up by telephone to ask the customer about the experience. In the case of Verizon, the company compared pretraining and posttraining repeat call volume of central office personnel who decided whether field tech visits were warranted and tracked a control group of central office diagnosticians who received no training against a group that did as a way to isolate e-learning's impact.

Neither company was guaranteed any kind of return from investments in new learning technologies. Yet the tactical application of these investments at least allowed the organizations to determine with certainty whether these were wise investments or not. The intangibility factor in the impacts from learning investments was eliminated.

Audits Wring Out Intangibility

A company's assumption that the impacts from a technology investment will meet or exceed economic forecast or an ROI model is reminiscent of this quip, coming from an economist trapped in a burning building: "No problem," he says. "I'll assume a fire hose." While the dismal science lives off assumptions in building theories to better explain economic phenomena, managers are under no such obligation. In fact, the practice might be dangerous.

One of the most pronounced assumptions in IT management practices today is that the cost savings or revenue-enhancing returns forecast in an ROI exercise will materialize on schedule or at all. How else to reconcile the fact that most organizations do not bother to validate the forecast at some point after deployment to determine whether impacts meet plan? However much effort is invested in constructing an economic model as a decision-making tool becomes so much digital dust on someone's hard drive after the fact. The forecast is irrelevant because the project is done—let's move on.

Another motivation than simply assuming certain outcomes is likely lurking behind the absence of postinvestment auditing in most companies—the fear, uncertainty, and doubt about the ramifications should the real-world impacts fall below forecast. No one enjoys evaluations, especially when the outcomes are less than expected, and those who are in a position of accountability—the project champions, those who control the budget—fear reprisal from a project gone bad.

Companies should be encouraged to operationalize a consistent, repeatable postinvestment audit capability to eliminate any intangibility in the expected impacts from an investment. An audit also has larger, more strategic benefits. If you accept the lofty principle that one of the most powerful management practices employees can embrace is the capacity to learn and turn the learning process into improvements in their work, audits are an effective component of IT management. The benefits do not accrete from simply confirming that the returns match the forecast but from improving the technology asset's performance should it turn out that the returns are less than planned. The act of investigating why some element of the deployment is not returning the cost-reducing or revenue-enhancing performance impacts is the act of translating the unknown and disregarded—the intangible—into the concrete. Understanding technology's real-world performance is also the beginning of the remediation process by which maximum value is extracted from the technology when returns are poor. This might be the single strongest argument for devoting the time and money to an auditing process.

For example, a Bay-area hospital decided to enter a new market, the referral lab business. Instead of doing the lab work of hospital patients only, it decided to take referral business from doctors' offices and clinics within a vast geographic area that extended from San Jose all the way to Sacramento. It recognized the revenue potential of leveraging unused lab capacity in the off-hours. This was a big-risk, big-payoff investment in people, processes, and technology—an ideal candidate for a postinvestment forecast validation exercise.

The hospital correctly anticipated that the specialized lab management packaged application it rolled out to support this initiative might introduce some business process incompatibilities that could drag down forecasted ROI. However, it had little visibility into what those exact incompatibilities would look like and how they would impact returns. The hospital's IT team decided to conduct an audit concurrent with technology deployment. It could have waited to audit the returns until some point after deployment, but the risks were high enough that it sought to quickly catch any operating dysfunction.

The audit team soon discovered, when the platform went live, that the procedures for data collection screeners sought from referral lab patients were quite bad. The system was optimized for hospital patients getting lab work in which screeners extracted twenty data elements, everything from next of kin to dietary limitations. These irrelevant questions were being asked of referral patients, when in reality the hospital needed maybe three data points for this customer class: name, age, and insurance carrier. The dysfunction wasn't catastrophic, but it clearly could have compromised the total patient volume and therefore the revenue projections. By investigating how the business logic of the software matched up against the work flow of the referral lab, the IT staff discovered the drag on forecast and made the necessary fixes. Today, this reference lab is a $7 million profit center for the hospital.

In another example, an oil-drilling equipment manufacturer invested in a number of procurement software modules in an outsourcing arrangement to assist it in managing technology acquisition. One module consisted of asset life cycle management software designed to help the company more effectively manage its IT lease arrangements with a number of vendors. It was during a general audit of the economic returns against forecast that managers discovered functionality in the application that could help the organization improve the terms of extended warranties embedded in technology equipment leases. Managers had no idea what the maintenance programs were costing the company in spite of significant expenditures to support more than three thousand workstations in nineteen states.

It was only during the audit that this functionality was discovered and quickly activated. The main question the company will be able to answer is whether it captures any savings by extending warranties on hardware assets or by swapping them out for new ones. A business impact that was truly intangible because of its irrelevance and unknowability is suddenly concrete, tangible, and a driver of true value because the organization bothered to audit the investment's economic impacts.

The purpose of an audit is at once to inject fiscal discipline in information technology capital investment, build the capacity for continuous process improvement, and gain a deeper understanding of all the drivers that collectively deliver value by turning the intangible into the tangible. While beyond the pure scope of this book, here are some high-level considerations in operationalizing an audit function:

- Design the audit around a handful of important metrics rather than get bogged down in hair pulling over impacts that are less significant. In many IT deployments, the bulk of the value is found in a few select benefits. By virtue of conducting an audit, it is possible that other economic drivers will be unearthed. When this occurs, a decision can be made whether to pursue further investigation of that newly discovered performance indicator.

- Build a consistent criteria threshold: decide on a dollar figure above which an audit kicks in as well as the extent of the business impacts that would necessitate such an exercise. Data warehouses can be expensive, but given the infrastructure nature of this technology, a full-blown audit is probably not worth the effort. A software package that drives business change would warrant an audit. Refer to the measurement action pyramid.

- When the results are in, what will be done with the information? Know what you are going to do with the results before embarking on an audit. Is the audit a continuous learning and process improvement vehicle, a means by which IT earns bonus compensation? Both? Will the results become an element in someone's personnel file, whether good or bad? The purpose of an audit is to validate forecast against real-world results, but the existence of measurable results can create a cauldron of political intrigue unless management knows exactly how it is going to act upon the results before the audit is conducted.

• Who owns the audit? This is a potential powder keg. Technology analysts say that the trend is for lines of business to directly receive money for new IT projects, while the IS shop is funded as a service organization, to handle upgrades, code fixes, and routine procurement. This means that although an audit may be an interdisciplinary exercise, LOB is ultimately accountable for both funding the audit and the results up or down.

Conclusions

Quantum theory in physics denies the metaphysical when it argues that nothing exists unless it is observable, a core principle of this science that caused Einstein to ask whether the moon disappeared from the heavens when no one was looking at it. The realm of metaphysics is salient to the study of economic value in technology investment; the expected benefits are unreal to managers unless they are clearly defined, quantifiable, and measurable. Unreal benefits mean they are intangible. The intangibility factor in information technology takes on many dimensions, much to the consternation of managers whose interest in capturing the value in this critical asset is sincere. The fact that technology managers concern themselves with this issue at all is a good thing in the evolution of technology management; there is a sense of urgency in the need to better align IT investment with strategic business goals. This alignment only comes about through a more complete depiction of the economic value of a technology, mostly but not exclusively software. A more comprehensive profile of technology's economic value requires the transformation of intangible phenomena into tangible impacts whenever possible using simple tools and techniques.

It is within these business imperatives that a hard-to-measure impact provokes this consternation. When a technology or operational manager is faced with such an intangible value driver, the most important question to ask is: does the absence of a quantifiable numerical value lessen our confidence in the proposed investment's ability to return business value to such an extent that the investment should not be made? In most cases, the answer is no. Businesses have proved consistently that the intangibility factor in depicting the economic value of a particular investment has not stopped them from making those investments. This is not necessarily a good thing. The reasons are as follows. First, the organization makes no attempt at all to quantify the economic value of a prospective IT investment as a basis for deciding amongst competing projects. If no business case is developed, intangible impacts will not be an issue. Second, quantifiable benefits outweigh the uncertainty around any intangible impacts so that the risks in not quantifying them are minimal. And third, companies make the effort to turn the intangible into the tangible and therefore possess a more complete picture of all the cost and benefit implications of a particular IT investment.

Managers should take solace in the fact that, were companies to halt the level and breadth of IT investment for difficult-to-quantify impacts, we might not have had the intensity of innovation fueled by the revenue of customers that made it possible—innovation in technology that takes the form of intangible assets, such as intellectual property and trade secrets. This happens to be the subject of the next chapter.

Chapter Takeaway

Organizations confronting the hard-to-measure impacts from information technology investment or embarking on a permanent measurement program should consider the following:

• Intangibility in IT investment benefits arises only when organizations bother to rigorously analyze the benefits in the first place. This is so obvious that it almost does not warrant mention. Yet for all the angst the inability to quantify the benefits of IT causes managers, the emergence of the intangibility challenge is a good thing because it means that companies are expending the energy to better understand the economic and organizational impacts of IT investment.

- Some technologies by their very nature possess more intangible impacts than others. Using the measurement action pyramid establishes a kind of triage amongst all the IT opportunities available to an organization. In this way, more time is devoted to economic analysis of strategic, business-improvement projects and less to support kinds of projects. Analysis paralysis can be as dangerous as completely ignoring economic forecasting discipline because energy and time are wasted.

- Management sometimes will—and should—sacrifice the tangible for the intangible if the investment offers more strategic impact potential to the organization. For example, two projects might have equal forecasted ROIs, but one clearly offers the potential for strategic impacts—new market opportunities, new customers, new innovations, etc.—while the other's impacts are found in cost savings only. The impacts from the second project are easy to measure, but that is not necessarily so with the first. Inability to completely forecast results—which means uncertainty in the outcomes—does not necessarily preclude the investment from consideration since big payoffs are usually associated with commensurate risks.

- New to most organizations, even those that have embedded formal economic forecasting into IT investment decision making, audits attack the intangibility of technology impacts. The act of investigating the results after the investment is online can reveal the unexpected and unforeseen in both benefits and costs. Audits essentially provide the ending chapters to a narrative started when someone begins a story about why the company needs a new technology investment. Companies considering establishing an audit capability need to consider the management implications behind it, including project and budget ownership and the actions that will be taken if the audit results fall far below economic forecast.

CHAPTER 5

OPEN-MARKET INNOVATION:

OPENING THE DOORS TO INNOVATION FROM THE MARKETPLACE

As an intangible asset class, intellectual property (IP) suffers from neglect on the balance sheet side of financial statements and, conversely, an embarrassment of attention everywhere else, including textbooks, conferences and seminars, R&D productivity analysis, enterprise software for its effective management, and at least one magazine spawned to carry on a regular dialogue about trends and best practices.[1]

Consulting firms have embedded intellectual asset management practices into their lineups—not to mention legal practices and the armies of lawyers who have chosen to specialize in this area. A few organizations have codified and legitimized IP management as an important job function with formal titles such as vice president of intellectual capital and director of technology commercialization. One software vendor has invented an index like the Dow Jones Industrial Average to serve as a proxy for the market values of intellectual property in patent, copyright, and trademark categories.[2]

Another proxy for the importance of patents as an asset class is found in the sheer volume of patent applications pouring over the transom at the United States Patent and Trademark Office. The wait for patent application review and approval is approaching two years because the USPTO cannot keep up—a potentially huge impediment to the economy's capacity to innovate and generate improvements in productivity.

Inventors might hesitate moving ahead with an idea until the government provides official sanction. The head of the USPTO warned Congress that the total patent filing backlog could exceed a million by 2008. The rate of patenting activity in the semiconductor industry, for instance, doubled between 1985 and 1995.[3] In 2001 alone, IBM was granted 3,411 patents.[4]

While the management of intellectual property is well defined in the literature, a management trend and set of techniques have emerged that could have a profound impact on the extent to which an organization can successfully extract value from these intangible assets. Known as open-market innovation (OMI), this trend describes a set of management processes and organizational conditions that allow companies to in-license intellectual property and intellectual assets (such as trade secrets and other technical know-how) that it does not possess and has little chance of creating internally, while simultaneously providing opportunities for companies that own an extensive IP/IA portfolio to leverage their licensing potential and create revenue streams where none might have ever existed before.

For the purposes of this analysis, it is important to confront yet again a taxonomical issue. Intellectual property includes copyrights, trademarks, and patents. Intellectual assets comprise trade secrets, codified know-how, blueprints and designs, and processes. The difference is how they are treated in the law. IA and IP might prove equally as valuable and financially rewarding, yet IP is a legally sanctioned property right, whereas trade secrets and know-how are not. While this is not a hugely important distinction for the purposes of this chapter, an awareness of the difference is important.

Fully 90 percent of new technology today takes the form of trade secrets as opposed to patents,[5] while 80 percent of licensing and technology transfer activity involves trade secrets as opposed to patents.[6] Another study reports that U.S. manufacturers rely more upon trade secrets and lead-time (first to market) advantages to recoup R&D investment than on patent protections.[7]

Another important point of clarification: while copyrights and trademarks as subclasses of IP are vitally important to many organizations, they are not relevant to this discussion, which is an explication of emerging management trends in the creation of income streams from intellectual assets and, to a lesser extent, intellectual property. Trade secrets, processes, designs, and blueprints as well as patents, unlike copyrights and trademarks, codify the usefulness of technology, which is defined as the commercialization of science. Out of science so applied come the new attributes and features embedded in such things as new dishwashing liquid, automobile engines, and Unix server bus architectures.

Patents, however, should not be considered less important than other kinds of intellectual assets simply because most of today's technological inventions and capabilities are expressed in other forms. Patents are an inherently powerful class of intangible asset because they are know-how embedded in a legally defined property right giving the owner a twenty-year lease, so to speak, to exploit the patent's designs for financial gain. Thieves steal this legally enjoined monopoly at their own peril.

So powerful to the imagination is the concept of know-how having property rights, just like the ownership of land, that our modern belief in this principle is simply a reaffirmation of a mental calculation made five hundred years ago. The first patents were issued in fifteenth-century Venice. It was there that a formal system of granting these monopoly rights was established, containing this preamble: "[if] provisions were made for the works and devices discovered by men of great genius, so that others who may see them could not build them and take the inventor's honor away, more men would apply their genius . . . and build devices of great utility to our commonwealth."[8]

Venetians proved themselves a forward-thinking lot as they took the idea of property rights originally associated with mining activity in its day and applied this construct to the fruits of mental activity. While knowledge management, including all that is freighted in that concept, is a decidedly late-twentieth-century invention, those who participated in the intellectual ferment out of which the Renaissance emerged knew that patents were a critical source of innovation. Innovation was the wellspring of material welfare in a time when rapid increases in living standards were the political issue of the day because they were so low for so many.

Patents: A Negative Property Right

Notice that in this language describing the concept of property rights inherent in invention is the idea of theft prevention. A popular misconception of patents is that they convey an opportunity for exploitation of the ideas encoded within them, when, in fact, patents provide the right to prevent others from exploiting the invention. Patents are a negative right, not an affirmative one.[9]

Understanding the concept of patents as a negative property right brings into focus how fundamentally different and more powerful open-market innovation is than the traditional ways in which companies extract value out of their IP/IA portfolios. OMI fosters an attitude of economic opportunity for both buyer and seller, an alternative to the legal mosh pit that opposing sides fall into during a patent dispute. The traditional approach to licensing is illustrated by way of a simplified example.[10]

Supposing Jane has come up with a great new way of packaging beverages. It's called a can. It is twelve ounces in size and cylindrical in shape, and it has a peel-off tab attached to a ring, which thirsty users can pull off to open the can. Jane patents her invention, and the can is a big hit in the market. Two years go by, and Jim invents an innovation to this can. What if instead of a peel-off top, drinkers could simply pull on a small levered tab, causing part of the top of the can to open downward, exposing a small hole into the contents of the can. Users would no longer need to throw away the pull tab, and this new idea is actually safer. It turns out some users were actually dropping the ringed tab discards into their drinks, causing cuts to the mouth, and, more seriously, a few users swallowed the discards.

Patent law says that Jim cannot realize his invention until he licenses the concept of the can from Jane because she has established an exclusive claim on the invention of a can—which Jim must use in order for his invention to have any value. Jim's invention of a new can-opening mechanism is predicated on earlier ideas already established by Jane, called prior art. Prior art actually has a broader definition. It describes all the publicly available documentation in whatever form (including previous patents) that would invalidate a patent claim because the ideas behind the invention are in the public domain and are, therefore, assumed to be obvious and not novel. (Novelty and uniqueness are critical attributes of patents.) Yet prior art also reflects the fact that many ideas do not emerge from thin air but are cumulative of the established inventions of others. It turns out Jane is equally interested in Jim's invention because it is a measurable innovation in can-opening design. If they can come to financial terms in which Jim shares the wealth with Jane through a licensing agreement without their respective lawyers killing each other, both win. This is a common circumstance under which organizations reap economic rewards for their IP. Jane asserts her negative property right, thereby preventing Jim from realizing the fruits of his invention unless she is compensated. It would be perfectly within her right to choose not to license the new can-opening design, thereby preventing Jim from realizing any economic reward for his invention.

Had Jim forged ahead with his innovation but without licensing the design for a can, Jane could have asserted her patent rights in court, and Jim would have been forced to compensate Jane for her earlier invention. This is another traditional way in which companies extract value out of their IP.

Open-market innovation describes similar outcomes—economic gain to both buyers and sellers of IP and, more broadly, IA. Yet the context under which value extraction occurs is very different from negative property right assertion.

Essence of OMI

Open-market innovation is an arrangement by which one company acquires IP to fulfill its need to innovate, while the seller obliges the buyer through its willingness to sell or license the IP. On each side of this market transaction is an admission of strengths and weaknesses, which each believes it can overcome by partnering with the other. Behind the simplicity of this arrangement, however, lurks a potentially large amount of complexity in pulling off the exchange—complexity that has its roots largely in attitudes and culture that have defined how historically companies have attempted to extract value out of IP. The cultural and attitudinal reengineering that must occur for OMI-based value extraction of intellectual assets to work belies the simplicity of the concept itself.

Some readers might stand back and say, "Wait a minute. Isn't all this just IP licensing? This has gone on for years! IBM earns $2 billion a year from patent royalties."[11] True enough. In fact, companies like Nike are organized around technology acquisition. However, a number of internal and external conditions are being brought to bear on companies, demanding that they recast the sometimes ad hoc nature of patent rental (which is what licensing essentially is) into a process that is operationally more disciplined, focused, and honest about an organization's strengths and weaknesses.

The few companies that consciously operationalize OMI practices to boost financial performance have many senior executives and board members sitting up and asking, "Why aren't we doing this?"[12]

Company-Level Conditions Influencing Open-Market Innovation

A number of conditions exist at the company level that encourage OMI. Let's explore them.

Limited Market

On the seller side, the potentially rich portfolio of IP lies fallow because, for one, there has never been an efficient means by which the owner could announce its availability. While it has been customary for engineers at some firms to make calls on colleagues in the firm's supply chain or at competing firms where the relationship is friendly, in a kind of fishing expedition to gauge interest in its IP, their search was limited to this kind of ad hoc process, bounded by where they had cultivated contacts throughout their careers. By default, the Rolodex was limiting. How many electrical engineers at a semiconductor company know similarly credentialed managers in agribusiness or with consumer goods packagers? Even if executives inside the seller company accepted the daffy idea that maybe the firm could generate some cash flow from its lineup of ideas, where would it go to gauge any interest and work out the details? Points of contact to discuss licensing arrangements have been not only industry concentrated but geographically bound as well. That other engineer's Rolodex likely contained the names of colleagues in the same region.

Where more ambitious outreach was attempted, the results have been mixed. For instance, a Ford Motor Company executive responsible for licensing Ford's patent portfolio used direct mail to generate possible deals. Not surprisingly, the hit rate was low.[13] Perhaps if there existed some global electronic market exchange to lubricate communication flow between Ford and buyers, the company might be able to attract buyers never imagined to have any interest. The imperative is clear: Ford wants to boost licensing revenues sevenfold by 2005 to approximately $20 million.[14] Now it has the means to reach this goal through a much more efficient communications channel, which will be clear later in this chapter.

Blindness to the Possibilities of Patents

A more profound challenge is the owner company's limited ability to envision all the possible applications of its patents outside its own industry. Take, for example, head-mounted displays developed by the military for fighter pilots. In the heat of battle, pilots have little time to gaze at their flight displays to assess critical information about the enemy in their sight. With such data fed directly in front of their eyes, pilots save a few seconds in deciding what course of action to take— precious time that can make the difference between success or failure and life or death.

As it happens, this technology has proven useful to surgeons, who sometimes need to just as quickly make life-and-death decisions in the operating room. A surgeon will wear a head-mounted display into which images of the surgical field are fed from a microscopic camera attached to an endoscope, a kind of long, thin probe inserted into the area of the body undergoing the operation. A neurosurgeon seeking to drain a cyst on the brain, for instance, requires pinpoint accuracy, which the headset provides. The procedure is also less invasive than traditional procedures, requiring a dime-size opening into the brain instead of the removal of a wallet-size piece of skull.

This is exactly the kind of nonintuitive cross-application potential of IP that OMI is supposed to overcome. This example seems obvious with the benefit of hindsight. But how obvious was it to the aerospace engineers who first created head-mounted displays? OMI vastly increases the field of possibilities for future income streams from IP/IA portfolios because it requires the seller to acknowledge that it might be able to conceive of just 5 percent of its total application potential. The seller also acknowledges that the buyer knows better than it what the potential value of a piece of IP/IA is.

The Not-Invented-Here Syndrome

The buyer-side problem is vastly more corrosive. The "not-invented-here" (NIH) syndrome is an insidious attitude in which companies believe that if the patent or technology didn't originate in their own R&D labs, it either isn't any good or doesn't meet their company's business needs. Out of ego, distrust, or misaligned incentives, some companies do not entertain ideas from outsiders even if they don't have a prayer of generating them from within. What's better—building a great new innovative product using the intellectual building blocks from another company in which a share of new profits is foregone in deference to the company who provided the building blocks or assuming the complete dollar value opportunity cost of not pursuing the partnership at all? To some companies, the latter is preferable. OMI argues otherwise.

Take Lucent Technologies. A manufacturer of telecommunications gear, Lucent has historically embraced the attitude of developing its highly sophisticated and IP-driven products in-house. Better to build inside to ensure quality control and technological standards consistency across product lines.[15] That's certainly a legitimate operating philosophy. Yet by Lucent's embracing such a lone-wolf stance, what market opportunity might it have missed in the area of optical networking? Although a market leader in long-haul optical networking equipment, Lucent was swept up in optical technology's move into the local loop, a geographically defined area comprising homes and businesses in a region or metropolitan area. Optical technology represents the next wave in technology-driven innovation and is, therefore, a potentially huge market opportunity, which the company eventually acknowledged with its acquisition of Chromatis Networks.[16]

Had Lucent trudged along, we can speculate its R&D capability would have conquered the need to develop products to serve the metropolitan environment, but at what cost? Given the deployment of resources needed—including time—not only to develop the IP but to shepherd these seeds from patentable ideas to a finished product line, what revenue opportunities might have been lost and what orders of magnitude in greater development costs would have been incurred had it insisted on building the capability completely in-house?[17] In this case, Lucent solved a business problem with an acquisition, which is not OMI as strictly defined. Yet the levers at work that would have given rise to focused OMI practices are the same.

Steering a hidebound culture away from NIH is, not surprisingly, profound. After all, engineers are paid to create ideas, not arrange for the rental of ideas born elsewhere. The move away from this institutional habit of mind can occur only when the company understands the imperative to realign its goals—getting ideas it needs from anywhere—with the reward and incentive structures that tend to encourage a not-invented-here mentality. Should a patent or trade secret emerge from some exotic source, the R&D engineer does not receive credit for the invention, and neither does his or her boss. Moreover, the R&D organization could see budget cuts as a result of management's belief that, because good ideas are originating outside, R&D needs less money for internal idea creation. In the absence of a new incentive and rewards system that supports this new path to innovation as an adjunct to tried-and-true methods, it should hardly surprise anyone that flinty resistance would greet any strategy about reaching out for intellectual property.

And were the organization successful in steering toward this enlightened way of thinking, buyers, just like sellers, would face the same friction-filled communications environment and high search cost challenge. They, too, could use a globally connected electronic marketplace just as desperately.

Time to Market

OMI attempts to fuel a reduction in the time it takes a company to nurture ideas into marketable innovations, even if it has no influence over the ponderousness of government in sanctioning those ideas into property rights.

This type of cycle time reduction is acutely felt when a company such as Pitney Bowes witnesses a rare but profound and sudden shift in market conditions. After the anthrax contamination scare in the mail system following the terrorist attacks in the United States on September 11, 2001, the manufacturer of mail and metering systems believed its business was under threat. How long would it be before customers asked what product innovations it would introduce to help companies detect anthrax or other life-threatening biochemical agents? As it happens, Pitney Bowes was suddenly inundated with calls from companies in search of ways to protect people from this dangerous agent.[18]

A team of engineers solicited a number of ideas that could serve as solutions to the problem. They ranged from machines that created a downdraft and filtered the air around mail as it was opened to the products and services Pitney Bowes actually developed: scanning and imaging capability that sends alerts about suspicious mail as well as guidance to companies in establishing secure mail room procedures.[19] Reaching aggressively outside its walls, Pitney Bowes found the answer to customer problems.

Taken out of context, Pitney Bowes's innovation challenge arising out of an abrupt change in market conditions trivializes both OMI and the R&D capabilities of the company. When this crisis emerged, Pitney Bowes had in place a sophisticated R&D management infrastructure called Advanced Concepts & Technology,[20] which includes a Concept Studio to shepherd IP into innovative products. The Concept Studio works with MIT to identify emerging customer needs, a critical ingredient of innovation.[21] And Pitney Bowes already had in place the organizational habit of mind to look elsewhere when necessary to fulfill its IP-driven business goals.

For instance, the company has researched a concept called Informating Paper, which would embed smart tags in paper. It is exploring the use of Motorola's Radio Frequency ID (RFID) technology in creating this product.[22] The company's response to a profound shift in its operating environment over which it had no control was focused, quick, and effective because it had in place the cultural infrastructure that acknowledged that powerful ideas can originate anywhere. The Pitney Bowes experience argues that OMI is a refinement of—rather than a substitute for—good R&D practices.

Cost of R&D

One urgent condition focusing managers' attention like a toothache, which OMI might ameliorate, is simply the cost of R&D. In 2002, Pharmaceutical Research and Manufacturers of America member companies invested an estimated $32 billion on research to develop new treatments for diseases—an estimated 18.2 percent of domestic sales on R&D—and a higher R&D-to-sales ratio than any other U.S. industry.[23] It now costs on average $800 million to develop a new drug.

As you will recall, R&D is often not capitalized like a physical or financial asset but rather is expensed immediately and is therefore an immediate drag on financial performance. While investors might actually bet on a particular company in near-term rough financial shape because of big R&D investments and the prospect of future innovation and, therefore, profitability, it remains irresistible for executives to manage the earnings game with cuts into R&D efforts, especially if the historic return on investment has been comparatively low. It's costly because the investments are fixed instead of variable, and they are not realized right away (if ever). Furthermore, the labor, or human capital, applied to the undertaking doesn't come cheap. The National Science Foundation estimates that the cost of an R&D scientist has at least doubled in the past twenty-five years to about $190,000 annually.[24] Good scientists deserve the pay, but this value judgment doesn't diminish the financial reality companies face in seeking to turn ideas into revenue.

A number of approaches have emerged to wrestle the R&D cost beast, including alliances and outsourcing arrangements. The semiconductor industry has witnessed a number of R&D partnerships between chip manufacturers in which all participants share the fruits of the IP produced. The medical devices industry is reaping the rewards of outsourcing research efforts.

Companies share many of the same motivations for alliances and outsourcing as they do OMI, including cost reductions. In fact, R&D is perhaps the last internal operation a corporation would consider outsourcing. Every other area of an enterprise has likely felt the sharp edge of the cost-cutting blade wielded by outsourcing: payroll, facilities management, IT, help desk, etc. Open-market innovation is just one more approach to manage the R&D investment equation.

R&D Infused with Fiscal Sobriety

Let's get back to Lucent. Mired in a lackluster telecommunications environment, the company embarked on a $2 billion cost-cutting campaign that has spared no corner of the organization, including Bell Labs. Perhaps the most famous R&D laboratory in the world, Bell Labs can boast some singularly impressive achievements, including several Nobel Prizes and a hand in the invention of the transistor, satellites, fax machines, and the VCR, to name a few.

Lucent summarily cut its budget from a mid-1990s level of $350 million to a third of that during the past few years.[25] Out is the notion of research for the sake of research. In is the abiding principle of applied research (what's R&D done for the company today?). Today, the company seeks far greater alignment between R&D expenditures and success in the marketplace. The president of a leading technical university spoke like a true academic when he called the fate of Bell Labs a national tragedy.[26] Tragedy to everyone except Lucent shareholders, who stand to gain from a far more focused, fiscally disciplined R&D effort.

The need to reduce R&D costs is not a new phenomenon. As far back as the 1970s, when Japan emerged as a global economic power and the globalization of industry basically began, companies became much more conscious of R&D as a kind of capital input (even if R&D is expensed on the books!) that required, like any capital investment, a justification for scarce resources—that is, the ROI of R&D.[27] Suddenly, the free-ranging quality of intellectual inquiry in company-funded R&D labs was fenced with fiscal accountability. Yet while R&D efforts might have become more disciplined and aligned with business goals (a situation not unlike the one IT is currently undergoing), companies did not embrace the logical next step—the acquisition of patents and know-how from outside the organization in those instances when even a retooled R&D capability wasn't delivering what the company's future dictated. The leap from the lean, efficient, go-it-alone R&D lab doing the best it could to a hybrid model in which the company shopped around when R&D's best wasn't good enough has proven to be a jump of decathlon proportions.

Patents Equal Innovation?

It seems so obvious that it wouldn't require specific mention, but it does—"it" being the idea that patents equal innovation. This belief is clearly one of the lead drivers of interest in open-market innovation. A survey taken by Bain & Company of two hundred senior executives revealed that 80 percent asserted "becoming more innovative" as being a top priority for achieving success, while nearly two-thirds admitted they hadn't fully embarked upon OMI practices to bring ideas in-house.[28] The survey reflects unanimity of opinion that innovation equals future profits and that capturing ideas outside the organization, if necessary, is one way of getting there.

Given the arguments underpinning the possibilities in OMI, a crucial question is this: do patents actually translate into innovation? On its face, this would seem like asking whether or not rain helps grass grow. The answer is slightly more complicated. Recent research into this area suggests that patents in and of themselves affect the direction of innovation, not its rate. Other work says that innovation gives the innovator a lead time in the market over imitators, which suggests that copycat products eventually find their way into the marketplace without infringing on the property right of the owner.[29] If the linkage between patents and innovation is not obvious empirically, it is perceptually.

OMI might turn out to be the perfect management trend to prove this, putting to rest any questions about the causal links between patents and innovation. How? The act of seeking out patents from licensing means that the buyer has assessed the know-how in them and at least believes it can build a better mousetrap in renting those capabilities.

Taking a purely rationalist perspective, while some licensing arrangements arising out of OMI will inevitably fail to deliver the desired results, the company that proceeds down this path is interested in renting for precisely the reason to innovate its product line. If OMI becomes standard procedure in many companies, empirical data should demonstrate the causation between OMI licensing arrangements and innovation. Unlike internal R&D, which is sometimes subject to chance discovery, accident, or whim in producing patentable know-how, the existence of already-created patents and technological know-how means the buyer avoids the risks associated with creating the asset in the first place. Visibility into the innovation-creating potential of an idea derived from full comprehension of what the technical merits of a patent or trade secret actually are—which OMI provides—adds significant clarity, even if not certainty, to the issue of whether the company can turn the idea into a profit-producing product. This allows the company to steer its energies to all the remaining steps required to take that idea and deliver an innovative product that proves successful in the marketplace: prototyping, manufacturing, and marketing and sales. OMI does assume the existence of these capabilities as it is no substitute for these crucial elements of the value chain. Yet wouldn't the percentage success rate of patents into innovations increase simply by virtue of the fact that the buyer will only embark on product development in areas known to be needed and from patents known to be relevant and available for rent?

Only time will provide the answer, but it doesn't seem reckless to assert that a company shopping in the OMI arena will know what its market wants, will know what patent might satisfy that want, and will know with some degree of certainty that it is equipped for all the heavy lifting in turning that idea into an innovation that adds revenue—and net income—to the organization. Figure 5.1 illustrates the fit between buyer and seller in the OMI arrangement.

Figure 5.1 Open-Market Innovation Fit—Why It Makes Sense

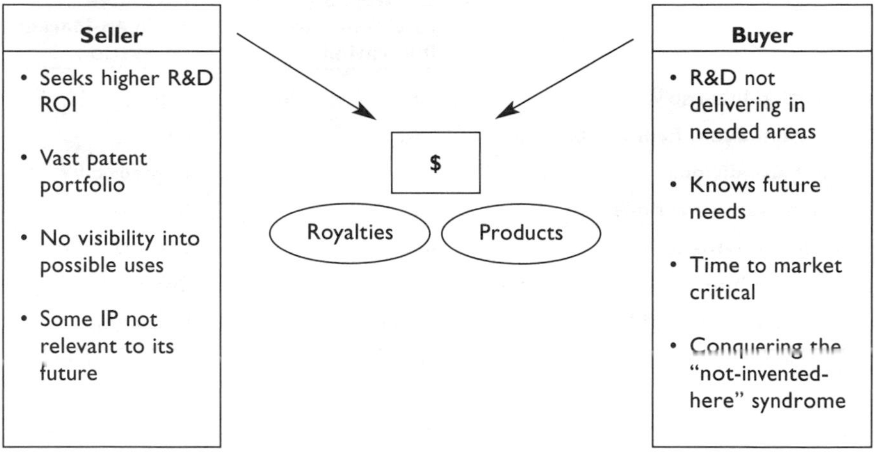

Seller	Buyer
• Seeks higher R&D ROI • Vast patent portfolio • No visibility into possible uses • Some IP not relevant to its future	• R&D not delivering in needed areas • Knows future needs • Time to market critical • Conquering the "not-invented-here" syndrome

$

Royalties   Products

Industry-Level Conditions Influencing Open-Market Innovation

Just as important as the firm-level, or microeconomic, imperatives creating the conditions for increased OMI activity are the industry, or macroeconomic, realities in which OMI will find a warmer reception. Understanding OMI's suitability along several high-level industry environment dimensions is another way to depict this trend's potential value.[30] Table 5.1 summarizes those dimensions.

Innovation Intensity

Consider how often innovations find their ways into products by industry. In software, real innovations might take just months. On the other hand, how often are innovations introduced into vacuum cleaners or dishwashers? Moreover, intensity of innovation speaks not only to how often competitors innovate their products but also to how much they

Table 5.1 Dimensions of OMI

	Unfavorable to Open-Market Innovation	Favorable to Open-Market Innovation
Innovation Intensity	Low	High
Innovation Scale Economies	High	Low
Market Conditions	Predictable	Unpredictable
Cumulative Innovations	Rare	Common
Disruptive Innovations	Rare	Common
Breadth of Innovative Applications	Narrow	Broad
Quantifiable Value of Innovations	Certain	Uncertain

Used with permission from Bain & Company.

rely upon the creation of IP to fuel those innovations. In the security software industry, 14 percent of sales is plowed back into R&D; in pharmaceuticals it is north of 18 percent; and in tires, 3 percent.[31] Unlike the tire industry, software and pharmaceuticals reinvest significant resources into R&D, out of which innovation-generating IP is produced. So we have a situation in which, one, the greater the rate of innovation in an industry, the greater the likelihood that innovations will obsolesce (after all, if new and improved products are coming out all the time—think Intel—previous generations of these products lose their useful life much more quickly). And two, the more an industry relies upon R&D efforts to achieve innovations, the greater the capacity to generate winning ideas. The existence of both conditions argues for OMI activity.

Innovation Scale Economies

OMI is best suited to an environment where economies of scale are not a barrier to the creation of new ideas. While the economies of scale in every facet of aerospace—including R&D—are so enormous that certain markets within aerospace are a near natural monopoly (commer-

cial passenger aircraft, for example), there is no such barrier in starting, say, a software company.

In garages across the country, twenty-year-old kids with authoring
software might be creating the next great game title. The toy innovation industry, also with a low barrier to entry, is populated by lone
inventors tinkering late into the night on ideas that might revolution-
ize the market. In industries where lots of ideas are created by lots of
inventors unencumbered by capital investment required to create those
ideas, entrenched competitors would do well to embrace the principles
of OMI by which they could at minimum conduct IP reconnaissance to
stay abreast of what is happening in the industry.

Therefore, for the patent seller or licensor, barriers to entry in innovation creation are low, yet the product development, marketing, and
sales barriers are almost insurmountable. The IP creator faces low innovation creation economies of scale and high economies of scale for all
other elements to bring the product to market: design, prototyping,
manufacturing, marketing and sales, and promotion. The acquirer has
the existing infrastructure of all these operational functions to take
innovation to market. The fit is perfect.

Market Conditions

Fast-growing industries need to respond to quickly changing market
conditions with innovations, and the only realistic way competitors
might accomplish this is with OMI practices. Volatile market conditions
mean that time-to-market considerations are critical. There simply isn't
enough time to redirect R&D efforts in an attempt to generate an innovation that will co-opt what the competition has already introduced.

A most dramatic example of time-to-market demands that is *not* OMI
is Microsoft's creation of the Internet Explorer browser when it fully
comprehended the implications of the popularity of Netscape's software. The company turned on a dime to deliver within months its own
browser product. Observers thought that this nimble redirection of
resources to execute on a new innovation might have been one of the
most dramatic in the history of corporate capitalism. Whether true or

not, it reinforced the idea that lesser companies would simply fail at undertakings of this magnitude, and if the ideas were available for license, clearly this would prove to be the path of least resistance in meeting the challenge of a competitor.

Cumulative Innovations

Rarely does an innovation in information technology spring to life autonomously from patents or ideas that preceded it. The law speaks to this phenomenon with the concept of prior art, the need for inventors filing patents to include previous patents that inspired the filing, as discussed earlier in this chapter. Because innovations here are largely based upon previous ideas, OMI flourishes in an environment where a company needs small IP building blocks to carry its knowledge forward into something innovative, as opposed to needing that one grand idea. Innovation in some industries is part of a larger ecology of ideas that cross-pollinate.

Disruptive Innovations

Often, large companies will dismiss a new technology as not having relevance to their industry when, in fact, the idea's introduction into the marketplace can turn an industry upside down—dismissal of the PC by mainframe companies is a good example. Famously, a leader at Digital Equipment Corporation (DEC) once said, before the popularity of the PC emerged, that a corporation would have little need for more than just a handful of computers.

When disruptive ideas threaten an entrenched player, it is almost compelled to bring in ideas from outside, lacking the "internal fortitude," as Bain's Darrell Rigby describes it, to create its own innovation in response. This is because the entrenched player finds it extraordinarily difficult to challenge his or her own people, to cannibalize and creatively destruct with Schumpeterian zeal what they know, what they believe, and what they have sweated over in maintaining leadership in their industry segment. Acquiring ideas from the outside might be the only way to save the company. Although DEC morphed from being a manufacturer of minicomputers into an original equipment manufacturer (OEM) of PCs, this foray didn't last long, and the company was eventually acquired by Compaq.

Breadth of Innovative Applications

This dimension speaks to how many different ways an innovation can be stripped for commercial application. If you are a glue manufacturer, your product might have applicability in such areas as aerospace, home repairs, and disposable baby diapers. As an idea seller, you will not have complete visibility into the entire range of industries and their uses. As an idea buyer, you might need to take stock of all the available ideas outside the organization because a particular need might originate from an unlikely source.

OMI drives that understanding. Software innovations are usually applicable across industries and product types. The tire industry, on the other hand, produces innovations that are rarely useful to anyone aside from other tire manufacturers.

Quantifiable Value of Innovations

There are some innovations where the rules of finance and cost accounting are quite applicable. That is, the inputs of financial capital to the process of creating innovations are forecastable, measurable, and fairly predictable. In other words, the company can actually quantify an R&D return on investment. Alternatively, some innovations are considered blue-sky and radical. Nobody knows the potential market size or the revenue opportunity, and dissension grows amongst managers proportionally to the level of uncertainty around their newly created brainchild. In this case, the idea needs exposure to a wider audience of experts who can provide insights into its market potential for the simple reason that the market is much better than the finance department at pricing the value of an innovation.

Biotech is an industry where in some instances the uncertainty and risk surrounding an innovation would require a much higher degree of expert input because its full financial potential is not known.

The ability to gain deeper insight into an innovation's financial potential becomes critically important when scientists and engineers are halfway down the R&D path and the finance department begins hollering that there is no payback or ROI and moves to stop work in its tracks. More than one start-up war story begins with someone who believed in an idea but the company originally funding the R&D didn't. Then the inventor left and started a new company to bring the innovation to life (think Robert Noyce, Gordon Moore, and Andrew Grove, who all left Fairchild Semiconductor to start Intel). OMI tactics through which a company dangles into the marketplace partially completed R&D for future licensing and uses the response as a gauge of whether or not to continue funding is a useful approach when attempts to link R&D ROI with specific innovations are difficult.

The Missing Ingredient No More

While OMI can flourish only in an environment of openness—sellers are open to sharing ideas, and buyers are open to acquiring ideas from outside—the critical ingredient that gives this stew flavor is the existence of intermediaries who smooth communication flows between companies eager to buy and those eager to sell.

Just as Ford realized in its foray into direct mail in order to gin up interest in its IP portfolio, the search costs that companies undertake to find the right partner are not insignificant. Sellers and buyers attempting to find each other are like two freighters passing near each other in the thick veil of fog, never knowing the other is there unless one blows its horn—or they run into each other. The proposition is literally hit or miss.

This challenge is faced when supply and demand for any good or service attempt to find each other. Because markets are fundamentally about information, mechanisms to smooth flows of pertinent information concerning the supply of ideas and the demand for those ideas are required if the OMI vision is ever to be fulfilled.

The Web Makes OMI Possible

As tongue-in-cheek as may have been the earlier observations about the need for efficient market arrangements to propel OMI, it should not have been lost on anyone that the infrastructure for this marketplace already exists—the Internet. A number of businesses have emerged that believe value can be added and money made in drawing the buyers and sellers of intellectual property into a market exchange taking the form mostly of licensing agreements.

While OMI is more about attitudinal and operational shifts in the way companies fulfill their aspirations for innovation, it cannot but accelerate with the emergence of intermediaries who bundle the necessary information off of which informed decisions are made about acquiring or selling the ingredients of that innovation. The success of online intermediaries should not only accelerate the pace of OMI where it already is standard operating procedure but actually legitimize the very idea of turning to the outside world to boost R&D ROI or acquire that patent crucial to product development needs. The electronicization of market information is not a necessary condition for OMI to work, but it is certainly validated and expedited by intermediaries who have built business models around the strategy.

Online businesses pushing the concept of OMI take several forms. One, for example, is the Big Idea Group. It acts as a gatekeeper between inventors and companies in search of new ideas for products in such industries as toys, home and garden, office supplies and storage, and power tools. The inventor submits his or her patent or know-how for analysis by experts. Big Idea Group will determine if it will represent the inventor to subscribing companies looking outside for innovations. This intermediary conducts road shows, not unlike those undertaken by investment banks to generate interest in a stock offering, where inventors make their pitch in front of a panel of experts. Big Idea Group will then expose those ideas that have received the experts' blessing to potential licensing partners. The Big Idea Group business model emphasizes that OMI doesn't discriminate in the size of the organization creating patents with potential value.[32] As we have already seen, great ideas can spring from the lone inventor's garage office as much as they might originate in a $100 million R&D operation. The software industry is perhaps the greatest reminder of this truth.

Now that you have gotten a flavor of the principles behind open-market innovation, the next chapter will demonstrate this intellectual property management trend in action. One entrepreneurial company acts as a kind of electronic marriage broker in bringing together buyers and sellers of intellectual property.

Chapter Takeaway

- Open-market innovation is IP/IA "licensing plus." It is a far more efficient, disciplined way for an organization to extract value out of its IP/IA portfolio than the ad hoc approach of the past. OMI also symbolizes an attitudinal shift away from patents' roots as a negative property right into a mutually advantageous arrangement between buyers and sellers of IP/IA.

- A number of business conditions make OMI a good fit for buyers and sellers, including time-to-market considerations, the existence of the Internet to enhance communication between buyers and sellers, and the need for R&D expenditures to show better returns.

- Bain & Company has found that a number of macroeconomic conditions have emerged that indicate what kinds of industries could benefit from OMI, including high innovation intensity, low innovation economies of scale, and high uncertainty around the ultimate value of innovations into which significant capital was sunk. Bain's analysis suggests these dimensions can be used as a template that businesses can leverage to determine their suitability for OMI.

- The emergence of the Internet can be seen as the octane additive boosting the performance of the OMI engine: OMI could exist without the Internet, but it would not be as effective, as the next chapter will demonstrate.

CHAPTER 6

THE HONEST BROKER— AN IMPORTANT OMI INGREDIENT

Yet2.com is a Boston-based online clearinghouse for the establishment of economic arrangements around the licensing of intellectual assets and, to a lesser extent, intellectual property. It is owned by QED, an intellectual property management consultancy. The goal of the yet2.com marketplace is to provide far greater visibility into the ideas available for licensing and the needs of companies in search of that big idea to support business goals. Yet2.com operates the only pure IP marketplace and exchange left standing from the dot-com collapse, when, by yet2.com's estimates, more than twenty other start-ups sought to establish profitable businesses in this way.

Today, visitors to the yet2.com website (which include a quarter of the Fortune 1000 companies) conduct 100,000 intellectual property searches per quarter. Approximately eighteen companies have concluded licensing deals, and another two thousand are in some phase of the deal pipeline. And while yet2.com does not seek to turn companies into innovation-driven organizations (nor is it capable of doing so), once senior leadership has articulated innovation as an operational imperative, yet2.com is poised to greatly accelerate the journey to that destination. It aspires to be the open market in open-market innovation.

Seller-Side Opportunity

While some users of yet2.com's exchange have institutionalized the OMI philosophy and have operationalized the management tactics required to fulfill the OMI potential, they are rare. More often, they are organizations that approach yet2.com with at least a gut instinct as to the value of greatly ramping up out-licensing but need a tactical road map. Yet2.com's expertise in guiding the company in search of out-licensing income streams provides a high-level glimpse of intellectual asset management techniques that are well grounded in the business management literature and curriculum today but with a decidedly OMI orientation.

The first step in managing these intangibles to identify cash opportunities is to prioritize the portfolio along these dimensions. The following covers the strategic and tactical management considerations on the sell side. (They are applicable as well for the acquirers of IP/IA.)

Step 1: Screen, Segment, and Organize

It is not uncommon for a large organization to have a portfolio of patents numbering in the hundreds if not thousands. Given resource constraints, it is unlikely the company can expose every patent or trade secret to an OMI marketplace even if all had marketability because the organization would, at the extreme, turn into an IP-selling machine with little time to actually sell what they make. So companies must look for those patents that have the highest likelihood of generating an income stream that balances the needs of boosting R&D ROI with the day-to-day needs of doing everything else to succeed in their industry. But as a necessary first step to prioritizing the portfolio, companies must organize and segment the portfolio into meaningful groups using a relevant taxonomy or grouping.

Some companies will organize by groups of patent codes; others will organize by the business unit responsible for the technology. DuPont, for example, segments its portfolio by chemical reaction type, which crosses the boundaries of business units—quite useful, given how chemical oriented is its patent portfolio.

When organized into some meaningful structure, the organization can begin a deeper analysis of the portfolio along several key dimensions that will help it identify those patents with the greatest income potential. Those dimensions include the following.

Trends in Competitors' Patenting Activity

Where are competitors putting effort into building IP because they think that is where the market is headed with technology? For example, QED worked with a manufacturer of oil refinery equipment. Several key questions arose out of intelligence gathering on this company. Should the company spend more time on drilling or on refining technology? If all competitors are investing in generating IP around refining, why is this the case? And is it in the company's interest to follow along, or should it develop an alternative strategy?

Patenting activity of competitors has for some time become one useful navigational aid for future strategic direction of an organization. Although the answers are completely dependent upon industry dynamics, an analysis of competitor patent creation behavior is quite revealing.

In the broad context of the aforementioned strategic questions, the company can begin to assess its OMI aspirations, given that analyzing competitor's patenting activity informs a company as to what technology-based IP it might offer for licensing or sale. The oil drilling and refining equipment manufacturer that has come up with new technology for drilling might decide to license it to as many competitors as possible as a means of accelerating its adoption from as many buyers of the equipment as possible—oil companies. Instead of attempting to sell its products containing the innovation against those of its competitors that do not contain the new technology, the company decides it can make more money from licensing revenue in which all industry players win business using the one manufacturer's IP. This assumes, of course, that competitors will be willing to in-license one player's patents.

As it happens in the oil drilling industry, the oil companies want standardized technology in their equipment acquisitions so if a refinery equipment manufacturer can create significantly new IP ardently desired by Shell and Exxon, competitors might not have much choice (for all the reasons OMI outlines) and might have to buy or rent the innovation. By virtue of out-licensing the innovation, the IP owner might drive the near future of the entire competitive landscape, which it controls until another innovation comes along to disrupt the industry anew.

Citation Analysis

Many new patents contain other patents as building blocks upon which the new innovation is created. For example, QED itself filed a patent around innovative ways its search technology helps visitors find information at its site. QED cited several earlier patents around search technologies that had been filed by such corporations as British Telecom and Procter & Gamble, who for many years have been attempting to improve search capabilities of knowledge bases.

Citation analysis is a proxy for the potential market interest in the IP a company is considering licensing. If few companies have cited the seller's patent in their own patent claims, the inference is that there might be little market interest should the owner decide to expose it to OMI mechanisms.

Purely numeric analysis of patent citations is controversial because of the lack of comparability between citation activity in different technology sectors and because recent patents and patent applications are unlikely to be cited. However, a qualitative review of citations by an industry expert is an important component of a full seller-side portfolio analysis. In this type of a review, the seller can identify both new industry sectors and individual companies that are making use of similar technology.

Market Interest

The existence of a Web-based marketplace in which buyers forage for potential ideas is a baseline against which a seller's complete portfolio can be assessed and benchmarked. Approximately sixty thousand unique users visit the yet2.com website monthly. Suddenly, yet2.com has captured at least a portion of the universal interest from across the globe in particular technologies at a very granular level. Buyer-side market signals of this kind obviously are of great value to sellers who, historically, might have had to rely on the impressions of engineers from conversations with colleagues to gauge the market potential of a patent or technology.

As an example of the power of accurate market signals, one of the hottest areas of interest at the yet2.com site over the past few years has been in electromagnetic actuator technology used in motion control of heavy equipment, including cranes and bulldozers, and which is an improvement on hydraulic systems. A small company called Advanced Motion Technologies (AMT) discovered this interest from yet2.com's search statistics and posted the patent on yet2.com's site. Both Caterpillar and Curtiss-Wright Flight Systems licensed AMT's innovation and are evaluating its use for heavy equipment and military applications, respectively.

Additionally, yet2.com can take a seller's complete patent portfolio and run a simulation of it against buyer interest as captured in site activity over any time frame since it began in 1999. This is useful for companies not ready for true OMI and those that have not yet exposed their portfolios to this kind of public scrutiny but that nevertheless want visibility into the market potential of their portfolios. The simulation calculates market interest as if the seller's entire portfolio was available to the public. The results are far from scientific, but yet2.com believes the results are a useful proxy for the marketability or interest potential of a seller's portfolio.

Once an organization has conducted a high-level analysis providing some direction and clarity into what ideas it has on hand that might lend themselves to OMI, it can move to step 2.

Step 2: Assess Value-Extraction Potential

Once the patent portfolio has been screened along patenting trends, citation analysis, and market condition dimensions and a basket of potential OMI candidates has emerged unscathed from the process, the portfolio must be subjected to a more rigorous analysis in which the specific claims in each patent are scrutinized by someone with licensing knowledge as well as domain expertise in the specific technology. Trend activity might have revealed the high interest in technological know-how around fuel cells or nanotechnology. But what at first blush appeared a promising candidate for OMI is revealed as a bust because the specific claims are minor or antiquated. The expert concludes market interest would be quite minimal.

Forcing the portfolio through the claims analysis gauntlet validates that the specific patent or know-how actually delivers potential innovation to that initial market interest. Patent claims have profound influence on the OMI opportunity, as the company in the next example rudely discovered.

A European-based food-processing company owns technological know-how around the processing of poultry into food products. Historically, the company wrote its patents so that the property right addressed the know-how to chickens only, leaving out any other kind of fowl (such as turkeys) that might end up on someone's dinner table. The specificity of the patent claims limited the opportunities for OMI from the seller side because the patent addressed only chickens instead of a broader category of poultry, where the know-how could have been applied additionally to turkeys or other fowl. Because of the narrowness of the patent claim, the owner of the know-how could license the capability as a trade secret if someone in the business of processing turkeys needed it, but the size of the fees and the duration of payment to the know-how owner would be substantially less than had the licensing revolved instead around a patent as opposed to just a trade secret.

QED showed this company the error of its ways. Had the company written a slightly broader claim, it could have licensed the capability to a far broader population of food processors. The text construction of a patent claim can be as much art as science. In the context of OMI, QED and the yet2.com marketplace are showing clients how true this is.[1]

Once the breadth and scope of a patent or trade secret has been firmly established, the participants in this OMI opportunity analysis—QED experts in consultation with company experts—will be equipped to define the market environment in which each patent or technological know-how that has survived the winnowing process could be placed. Important questions include the following: What is the size of the market? What are the number of total markets into which this idea might find interest? Is the market growing? Is the market in industries conducive to licensing ideas?

The analysis at this stage is much more qualitative than quantitative because definite answers to those questions will emerge only when the technology is put into the marketplace and interest from a specific party is revealed. The business context around which a buyer will leverage someone else's idea—market size, product idea, competitive landscape—sets the terms of financial negotiations. Nevertheless, having yoked the results of step 1 with those of step 2, a company should have a reasonable sense of both the strength of its claims versus competitors and visibility into market potential.

One additional tactic QED will employ in step 2 is a kind of "brain dump," in which the engineers who created the IP along with other senior executives are invited to a roundtable discussion about the future value of that IP. QED finds in some instances that not everyone has a complete grasp of what is so powerful about the IP or IA being claimed. Once roundtable participants fully understand the property right, all sorts of compelling ideas for its use inside the organization suddenly emerge. An engineer who has shopped some know-how in his network with poor response but who believes it could generate an income stream with a larger, friction-free marketplace suddenly has his invention yanked off the OMI pipeline because another executive, suddenly comprehending the know-how's value, wants to develop it internally. Thus, we conclude that communication can be a great thing.

Step 3: Technology Evaluation

So the organization has, say, twenty-five technologies in the form of trade secrets or patents that are the cream of the portfolio. It has learned, unfortunately, that some in this basket are not great OMI candidates for the reasons stated earlier. However, instead of putting them back into the vault, QED assists in helping the portfolio owner determine if there is any other value-extraction opportunity. There are, in fact, several paths beyond just licensing for the seller to explore. They include the following.

Use in Products

This is the situation alluded to earlier in which a final candidate for OMI is pulled because the prioritization process provides deeper visibility to the core know-how. The company discovers the OMI candidate is suddenly a product opportunity to the company.

In a twist on this scenario that occurred after the idea was posted on yet2.com's site, a manufacturer of flame retardant technology analyzed the market potential for products embedded with this expertise and found it dry. The company decided that the IP was powerful enough that somebody might want it, so the technology was put on the OMI block. The licensor received forty responses requesting not the IP but the product the IP would have been embedded in. It pulled the idea and embarked on creating a product in response to these preliminary market signals.

Although not the functional purpose of yet2.com, its marketplace served as a proof of concept for a product idea the company had abandoned. It's quite ironic that the company was ready to license the know-how to someone else when it believed the product that would have been the result of that know-how didn't seem promising.

Sell

Companies sell patents (not ideas) when they don't have any more in-house know-how and have decided that they are not core to company plans. The buyers of patents will seek purchase outright, either because they are already practicing the art and want to have the patent rights or because they want to use it for future defensive purposes.

For example, a client of QED that has a growing business in a specific electronics field is purchasing patents because the client has very few of its own. The client's bet is that sometime in the future it will be sued by others who wish to charge royalties for infringing their patent rights. In order to defend against that possibility, the company is building a "picket fence" of patents that it can use as trading chips in those potential future negotiations.

Donate

There are tax advantages to donating a patent or technology to a university or a research nonprofit when a dollar value can be assigned to it.

This approach is, however, not without controversy, and tax laws continue to change in response to some very public IP donations.

Hold

A company may decide to hold a patent or technology when it is not in the organization's best interest to exploit the idea, but the company also may not want to employ an OMI strategy in which a potential competitor could develop it.

For instance, an LCD screen manufacturer whose product is based on thin film technology discovers a plasma-based innovation through its own R&D. The company does not want to completely retool its manufacturing capability to accommodate production for a competing technology even if it is highly innovative, nor is the company interested in licensing this to a competitor and potentially relinquishing market share for the same product albeit based on a different technology platform. The LCD screen manufacturer locks the idea away, at least in the short term, because there is no internal potential, and the external potential, though large, might prove hazardous to the company's health.

Abandon

This is an option when the patent's twenty-year life span is near expiration and the market has signaled little interest. Other options aren't viable. Just keeping the IP in the portfolio isn't an option either, even though as an intangible asset it requires no maintenance like a piece of capital equipment would. However, administrative maintenance fees to keep the IP official and registered with the authorities can cost thousands of dollars. In fact, the administrative costs for the life of a patent run approximately $200,000.[2] It's the dead-end decision after all other options have been thoroughly explored. QED says that several of its clients have been able to justify the consulting fees around portfolio evaluation in how much is saved in reducing IP maintenance costs. Because clients estimate that only 10 to 20 percent of their patent portfolios support existing products, there is a large opportunity for patent pruning that can save some companies substantial money.

The company that embarks upon this kind of intellectual property prioritization exercise will only do so if OMI is a strategy worth undertaking in the first place. The whole idea of the effort is to prep the IP portfolio for public sale. Although many of these elements are part of the intellectual property management literature, they are quite exotic to those organizations that have recently embraced the notion that their IP portfolio is worth managing more closely to satisfy the desire for more profits.

At this stage, a company is ready to place its gems in the public display case for shoppers to view. Now we turn our attention to companies that are indeed shopping for the next great innovation.

Buyer-Side Opportunity

The potential licensee has determined internally that for a variety of reasons, future innovation imperatives will not be resolved inside the organization, so it is willing to hunt elsewhere. The not-invented-here syndrome has been conquered—or at least wrestled into a cage. The cultural shift moves the company, albeit slowly, to a set of management principles that embrace ideas from the outside.

Yet2.com is not in a position to convince a company that sees little value in OMI of the error of its ways. Yet it is prepared to support the evangelists in the company who need to convince the Luddites of the power of the concept. Yet2.com rarely enters a large organization in the CEO's lair, where OMI can be pronounced an operational imperative with fist-pounding finality. Rather, yet2.com usually enters at layers below, where an executive sees the hints of future value from adoption of OMI but faces the prospect of convincing colleagues of this. Simply by virtue of needing an effective sales strategy to close business, yet2.com is keenly aware that OMI succeeds most effectively when its champions can capture a couple of quick wins and build the necessary momentum and attitude shift that sets the conditions for operationalizing OMI practices—this is actually true for both buyers and sellers. Given the entrenchment and rigidity of NIH, however, the cultural change is arguably more pronounced on the buyer side of the exchange.

When a buyer chooses yet2.com, it will embark on the same early steps as a seller—prioritizing the existing IP portfolio. The buyer's agenda, however, is to gain visibility into its potential sources of future value creation while understanding where the gaps in its path to innovation lie.

The gaps will emerge only when the company attempts to align its business strategy goals against the ideas that are likely to deliver on that strategy. If the goal is to deliver a certain percentage of yearly revenue from products that are no older than two years, the company should be capable of determining whether its portfolio as well as projects in the R&D pipeline will get it there. The alignment imperative will drive the prioritization process in such a way that the organization will have a focused understanding of what innovation needs will require fulfillment outside the organization.

This is the necessary first step to OMI. Yet2.com finds that companies that expose some of their portfolio to the public marketplace occupy all spaces along a maturity continuum, from companies that consist of excellent intellectual asset management practices (in which the prioritization of innovation need is understood across the organization) to novice organizations just emerging from the not-invented-here bog with little expertise in how to vet available ideas or how to structure licensing deals. While yet2.com can guide the company that has just come out of the closet, so to speak, in these tactical considerations, its biggest impact on the buyer side of the OMI equation is providing a wider swath of licensing opportunities than it might have ever imagined possible.

Just as a marketplace provides deeper visibility into the possible uses of its IP, expanding the income-generation horizon for sellers, so, too, have the buyer's options increased incrementally if not hugely in having revealed to it all the ideas available for licensing, ideas that might solve exactly the company's problem in ways it had never thought imaginable.

What a Selection!

Historically, it has not been difficult for a technology scout doing reconnaissance for his or her company to understand what R&D activity—when available—competitors were undertaking. Though patents are often written with great obfuscation in order to obscure the true nature of the IP because filings are public and increasingly accessible by any-one, engineers and researchers, who are subject-matter experts (SMEs) in their chosen fields, will comprehend the property right asserted, the innovativeness of the IP, and the direction of the effort and its poten-tial implications on the marketplace should the competitor turn the IP into something people like. This doesn't mean the idea is even available for licensing from its creator. The point, however, is that the Rolodex approach to hunting for ideas might consign the searcher to the indus-try in which he or she toils. Maybe the buyer gets lucky and finds exactly what the organization needs, and the IP owner is willing to license on reasonable terms. More likely, none of these conditions is true.

The reaction from that same engineer when introduced to an ever-expanding market exchange is not unlike walking into a department store and marveling at the selection. Ten varieties of everything you could possibly want. In the context of IP, ten varieties is high, but the reaction is illustrative. OMI shows its spurs when the buyer discovers the breadth of opportunities in a timely fashion to fulfill strategic goals.[3]

Yet2.com worked with a small manufacturer (with less than $1 mil-lion in sales) of a direct injection-forced ventilation, two-stroke engine. It sought a fuel system to be used with three-cylinder, two-stroke diesel engines in the belief that a fuel system innovation could be leveraged in its engine design in order to open up new markets beyond just heavy machinery, such as passenger ships and freighters. The manufacturer invested time reaching out to automobile companies and railroad engine makers to see if a design existed. No luck. The company had already decided internally it was not in a position to build this capability in-house through the R&D process. The company posted a TechNeed at yet2.com and received responses almost immediately. The know-how the buyer wanted emerged in about four months from a company that worked with NASA and that had expertise in rocket launch systems for satellites. Both companies made engines, but it hadn't crossed the mind of the buyer to reach out to this unlikely source of innovation.

Seeing the need posted on the yet2.com site, the rocket launch com-pany replied that it had know-how around fuel delivery systems and was perhaps what the buyer was looking for. After the idea seeker spent a month analyzing and vetting exactly the nature of the know-how, the two companies embarked on licensing negotiations. Yet2.com might have entered directly into the discussion during the initial dialogue had the relationship building stalled. As it turned out, however, both companies got along well, and yet2.com acted as honest broker, offering advice on how the specifics of the arrangement might be structured, as neither company was experienced in this kind of deal making.

On the buyer side, OMI reveals its promise when a small, resource-constrained manufacturer finds the answer to its technical needs in a company unlikely to have been on its short list of potential sources for the idea. Licensing the blueprints to an engine design innovation is allowing the manufacturer to embark on future product plans, and it doesn't get any more strategic than that.

Cultural Change

One may step back from this exegesis concerning open-market innovation and perhaps wonder what the big deal is. The concepts behind this intangible asset management strategy seem almost childishly common-sensical. Yet many companies have not operationalized OMI. Why?

The cultural environment in which a company operates will influence profoundly whether OMI can succeed, and the challenges in reorienting corporate culture to embrace OMI practices are formidable. The seller is asked to shift away from the attitude that patents are something secret, sacred, and not to be shared, even if they do nothing else but collect dust. The buyer is asked to admit the company's existing IP portfolio is missing the necessary ingredients for revenue growth and profitability, which is why it must rent the idea from someone else.

These concepts may appear at first repugnant to some organizations, particularly the companies that concede the need to acquire IP but are shackled at the ankles by the weight of NIH. Yet as OMI proves its mettle in more and more organizations, companies that have resisted its strategic and tactical appeal for improving intangible asset management should discover its value in helping them reach their goals.

The challenge to reengineering company culture is most clearly revealed in the need to realign employee performance measures with the objectives embedded in OMI tactics. One client company of yet2 .com introduced a line item on every business unit leader's P&L for royalty revenue. The existence of this performance measure is an implicit endorsement for the ideals of OMI because the desire for royalty revenue means managers are required to be on the lookout for any IP in the portfolio that is a candidate for marketplace exposure. A company that can successfully establish reasonable employee performance measures linked to outcomes that OMI facilitates is on its way to true cultural reinvention; if the company rewards OMI behavior, employees are sure to take this imperative seriously.

This fact was demonstrated most emphatically to yet2.com when it launched a series of workshops inside a chemicals industry client company whose CFO declared one day after extensive benchmarking that the R&D organization was spending far too much money relative to the revenues generated from products embedded with R&D efforts.[4] The company sought internal R&D to concentrate its efforts only on projects that would deliver competitive differentiation. Any other ideas R&D seeks should be purchased from outside. Yet2.com helped a senior manager get buy-in from affected employees about the virtues of OMI. The blowback from this evangelization exercise reflected a not unreasonable apprehension that a disconnect existed between the idea that R&D needs to operationalize OMI—buy over build when the product goal is not strategic—and the performance indicators management used to judge R&D worker performance. The worker thinks, "I'm supposed to buy instead of build nonstrategic but nevertheless value-creating ideas for our future products, yet my compensation for the past twenty years has been tied directly to my inventiveness. I am rewarded for coming up with ideas popular in products."

Yet2.com tells every organization seeking the sale of OMI to employees that the effort results in a lot of pretty rhetoric and little more unless management exercises leadership in not just selling the idea of OMI but reengineering incentives to reflect the new way in which the company seeks to leverage its IP. Common sense? The virtues of OMI suggest so.

Why Bother with OMI at All?

Deliberately saved until the end of these two chapters focused on open-market innovation is a brief exploration of another wrinkle in the IP management story. As you may remember from the last chapter, the underlying rationale for patents is that they confer a negative property right to the owner. That Mrs. Smith holds the patent to some invention means that Mrs. Jones is precluded from making money off the same invention. *The same invention* is the operative phrase here. What if Mrs. Jones can tweak her design in such a way as to keep intact the underlying value of Mrs. Smith's idea but offer something different enough in its final form to avoid stepping into any legal crosshairs?

This question must be posed a hundred times a day in the offices of senior management at some companies. The approach, as old as patents themselves, is called a design-around, a slick way to avoid the heavy lifting of R&D. Design-arounds can also be viewed as tacit acknowledgment of the failure of R&D from organizations that insist they must get to market a product that matches the innovations of competitors. There is nothing explicitly illegal in figuring out some hook or twist that can be added to a patent so that it does not infringe on a predecessor. It is quite common in industries with enormous markets that new entrants want to join—for example, auto parts and semiconductors—as well as in mature industries in which the rate of innovation is slow and small changes to a product can mean competitive advantage.[5] But choosing this route increases the likelihood of increased litigation, and litigation appears to be a calculated risk some companies are willing to take, given the fact that some IP lawyers believe this IP management tactic—if it can be called that—is growing in popularity.[6] (There is no clearinghouse that captures design-around activity.)

In one example, a cattle rancher received a patent for a remote-controlled flashlight that rotated 360 degrees, allowing him to inspect his range cattle at night from inside his truck. Wal-Mart wanted to sell this flashlight through its Sam's Club stores, but the rancher turned it down, worrying that this would damage distribution relationships he had already established.[7] Not long afterward, Sam's Club was selling its own version of the light with one small modification—a plastic part was added to limit the light's rotation to a range just less than 360 degrees. The rancher decided to sue even after Sam's Club stopped selling its version of the product once supplies had run out. A federal court in Denver awarded the inventor nearly $500,000 in damages as well as court costs. How might yet2.com and open-market innovation have altered the course of events here?

We will assume that the inventor would decline posting his invention at yet2.com's site because he wasn't interested in licensing to anyone else. Wal-Mart, on the other hand, had an immediate desire to put this type of invention into the marketplace. Were an innovation available in the form of a patent at yet2.com's site, Wal-Mart could have licensed it and avoided patent infringement. The rancher might have sued anyway; OMI doesn't necessarily mean avoiding infringement lawsuits. However, the existence of a patent at yet2.com's marketplace means there exists a lawful alternative to Wal-Mart's illegal design-around ploy, and the retailer would have prevailed in court.

The value of OMI and an IP/IA exchange like yet2.com's is their potential to serve as an alternative solution to design-around attempts when organizations need a quick way to introduce a competing innovation into the marketplace. The challenge for yet2.com—one faced by any exchange, including eBay—is to scale the supply side with enough choices so that any appetite for innovation can be satisfied. Assuming that an available patent at yet2.com's site satisfies the specific needs of a company (admittedly a big assumption), we have to conjecture that choosing the design-around path anyway means the company doesn't want to pay royalties for the fruits of someone else's labor and/or it feels the process of negotiating a deal for the idea is undermining its go-to-market timetable. Either motivation is flawed; attempting to profit from someone else's legally sanctioned ideas is un-American, and any organization that needs an innovation bad enough can close a deal quickly. It's not as if sellers are inclined to protract negotiations since making known publicly at yet2.com's site the availability of their ideas means they want to deal—and one of yet2.com's jobs is not just to lead the horses to water but to then make them drink.

Conclusions

The importance of innovation should not be underestimated—as hard as that might be, seeing as the word seems to spout from the mouths of CEOs and consultants at least on an hourly basis. Innovation is not a new idea. Johannes Gutenberg, Guglielmo Marconi, Alexander Graham Bell, and Thomas Alva Edison were all innovators. What has changed is the urgency around the need to innovate. The capacity to innovate has evolved from an important goal to a fundamental ingredient of market survival.[8]

Evidence of this intense interest in innovation is all around us, even in the area of public policy. Michael Porter from the Harvard Business School and Scott Stern of MIT have constructed the Innovation Index, a method for scoring the quality of a country's innovation potential, for the Council on Competitiveness.[9] Built on advanced mathematical techniques, the Innovation Index comprises several key metrics, or performance indicators, that these professors have determined drive innovation in a nation or in some political subset, such as region or state. These indicators include:

- total R&D personnel
- total R&D investment
- the percentage of R&D funded by private industry
- the percentage of R&D performed by the university sector
- spending on higher education
- the strength of intellectual property protection
- openness to international competition
- a nation's per capita GDP[10]

The Innovation Index is a benchmarking tool and navigational aid for government personnel and policy makers who are in a position to nurture private sector innovation. And as both Porter and Stern like to point out, "History teaches us that the private sector is the engine for innovation."[11]

Corporations now routinely set goals around innovation. Consider percent sales targeted from products less than four years old or percent sales targeted from products in the market for just one year. These metrics have been the concrete sales goals of 3M.[12] The importance of the ability to innovate as the critical competency in the organization is undisputed. Why innovation is so important is the interesting question and helps to explain why intangible assets have supplanted physical ones as the source of value creation.

Industrial-era companies were heavy with physical, tangible assets: equipment, machines, and real estate. In this paradigm, organizations discovered that economy of scale in production was the secret to competitive advantage in the marketplace. Through sheer size and scope, companies that were the low-cost producer in an industry held an edge. Yet these companies were also quite large and organizationally unwieldy. They were often vertically integrated; that is, one company controlled or manufactured every component that went into the finished product. For instance, it was said that Henry Ford owned herds of sheep out of which cloth was made for seats in his cars.

Economists have shown, however, that economies of scale have limits. Although they offered a competitive advantage, scale economies reached limits far below the ability of any single company to dominate a market.[13] Several firms in oligopoly fashion ended up controlling a market because economies of scale exhausted themselves way before one organization could control the entire market. Companies simply became too fat to manage effectively.

So where was competitive advantage going to come from if not from the economic laws of production? From innovation.

Companies discovered that developing the capacity to deliver new and improved products to the marketplace, each better than the last and perhaps better than the competition's, was the new source of competitive advantage. Yet when everyone builds this capability, innovation ceases being a strategic capability and becomes the price of admission: "innovate and kill the competition" morphs into "innovate or die."

The change in strategic focus from physical asset ownership as the means of capturing economies of scale and thus gaining a competitive advantage to building the capacity to innovate was the invitation for intangible assets to invade the organization and occupy a place of such prominence as they do now. It is easy to see why they did.[14]

Suddenly, the drivers of value creation shifted. Machines were out, and the complementary elements needed to innovate were in. So many interdependent elements became crucial, and they all happened to be intangible: people, knowledge, IT, R&D capabilities, unique organizational structures, and collaborative alliances. Manufacturing and the physical assets that supported that activity became commodities, something that could and should be outsourced.

These economic forces highlight the importance of IP/IA as the source of business-sustaining innovation and open-market innovation as the vehicle for the acquisition and exploitation of those intangible assets. The next chapter will demonstrate problems of and solutions to managing what can be conceived as the raw material that is shaped and manipulated into IP/IA—knowledge.

Chapter Takeaway

Companies pondering a jump into the open-market innovation deep end should consider the following:

- The initial step must be a complete and accurate organization and assessment of the existing IP and IA portfolio, such as QED's methodology, explained in these pages. No OMI strategy can possibly work without this understanding. What do the IP and IA look like, and, as the engine of innovation, can they serve management's vision for the direction of the company? The literature and consulting expertise available on the subject are extensive.
- Complete visibility into the IP/IA portfolio will help the organization answer the following fundamental question: given perpetual budget and time constraints, is the path to innovation achievable in-house? The cell phone manufacturing industry is asking this very question. Traditionally, handset makers—Nokia, Motorola, etc.—have created in-house the software that powers the phone. The emergence of Symbian and Microsoft as creators of software innovation in this market space is causing the industry to rethink vertical integration and instead adopt a personal computer hardware–OEM/Microsoft licensing part-

nership model. And while this circumstance is not pure OMI, the questions this trend is causing cell phone makers to pose are exactly those that OMI would require a company to ask: What is the advantage of continuing to build cell phone operating systems in-house? Do we own any IP/IA that can satisfy the anticipated future needs of consumers? What do we surrender versus gain in licensing the software to run our products?

- Company culture is as amorphous an intangible asset as they come. Yet culture weighs heavily on an organization's ability to profit from OMI. At the highest level of generalization, think of innovative companies having either an engineering culture (such as defense contractors like Boeing) or a management culture (such as General Electric or Procter & Gamble). Companies that will succeed in OMI will need to act more like the latter and less the former. Because there is no magic template for changing a company culture, companies may be best served employing a start-small approach by launching one or two OMI projects—regardless of which side of the market exchange they might find themselves.

- The good news for engineers is that for OMI to succeed, engineers will serve the critical responsibility of translation bridge between the technical merits of available IP/IA and business strategy that joins the battle in turning this know-how into successful products. The engineer equipped with deep technical expertise who can articulate how available IP/IA can meet strategic goals will win the rapt attention of workers in product development, operations, and marketing and anybody else who makes up the ecumenical team deciding OMI policy.

CHAPTER 7

A LITTLE KNOWLEDGE MANAGEMENT IS A DANGEROUS THING

What is knowledge? The dictionary defines it as the state of knowing; understanding gained through experience; and specific information about something. As the economy has evolved and companies have come to realize that the know-how, the experience-based expertise, and the information in the possession of employees are truly assets that need managing for their value in some way, the answer to the question "What is knowledge?" has descended rapidly from its epistemological perch onto the desktops of managers.

As managers conceptualize knowledge as an asset, they seek codified techniques and principles that could be applied to its manipulation and exploitation. Enter knowledge management, the inevitable attempt to provide a consistent approach, not to mention lend managerial respectability, to this particular intangible asset value-extraction imperative.

Definitional Challenge

What can we say today about knowledge management as a set of precepts for managing this intangible asset called knowledge? By some lights, plenty. No fewer than 844 book titles emerged at Amazon.com when that term was applied to a search.[1] This compared with thirty-one titles on the subject of open-heart surgery. Yet this reminds one of what a British official said about the bumbling Ribbentrop, Hitler's foreign secretary during World War II. To paraphrase the official, "He said so little in more words than anyone I have ever met."[2]

Consider that despite—or because of—the profusion of titles, there seem to be as many definitions of what knowledge management is as there are attempts to explain it between book covers. The more words that have been spilled, the more confusion that has been created over exactly what KM is. Following is a representative sampling of definitions—the choice is yours:

> *Knowledge management caters to the critical issues of organizational adaption, survival and competence in the face of increasingly discontinuous environmental change. . . . Essentially, it embodies organizational processes that seek synergistic combination of data and information processing capacity of information technologies, and the creative and innovative capacity of human beings.*[3]

> *KM is the process through which organizations generate value from their intellectual and knowledge-based assets.*[4]

> *Knowledge management is the collection of processes that govern the creation, dissemination, and utilization of knowledge.*[5]

> *Knowledge management involves the identification and analysis of available and required knowledge assets and knowledge asset related processes, and the subsequent planning and control of actions to develop both the assets and the processes so as to fulfil organisational objectives.*[6]

> *Our working definition is that knowledge management refers to strategies and structures for maximizing the return on intellectual and information resources. Because intellectual capital resides both in tacit form (human education, experience and expertise) and explicit form (documents and data), KM depends on both cultural and technological processes of creation, collection, sharing, recombination and reuse. The goal is to create new value by improving the efficiency and effective-*

ness of individual and collaborative knowledge work while increasing innovation and sharpening decision-making.[7]

Likewise, conduct a search for "knowledge management products," and results will include content management software, data visualization tools, secure collaboration platforms, bioinformatics applications, data-mining utilities, and R&D administration management applications.[8] No such confusion will result if the search had been for "cardiac surgery products." But we know that software vendors are notorious for slapping a label on their products that seeks to reposition them to a particular class of software application even if the product in question is only faintly similar in functionality to more well-known products in the class. The point is that anything having to do with information is KM.

Practitioners will freely admit that there is no common definition of KM, so this isn't breaking news. The existence of a chorus line of definitions, however, is worth noting for managers contemplating an initiative directed at leveraging value out of this intangible asset because a multiplicity of perspectives suggests the absence of consistent, well-grounded, and universally accepted techniques, which give any management discipline its legitimacy. And the absence of a structured, universally understood body of knowledge around any management discipline, including KM, is potentially dangerous. Open-heart surgery is conducted to solve a number of problems, and KM can be deployed to solve a number of problems, too.

The profound difference is, of course, that the act of conducting open-heart surgery to solve those lifesaving medical problems—for example, artery blockage, tumor, and valve replacement—comprises a strict set of techniques and empirically proven methodologies universally understood by any cardiac surgeon. Not so with KM because the approaches to reach those business goals—the metaphorical equivalent of artery blockage, tumor, and valve replacement—are as myriad as the problems to be solved. Going in, organizations should understand that there is no structured body of knowledge around knowledge management; KM strategy could wind up being defined by whomever is discussing the subject at any given time. This is a recipe for chaos and paralysis.

It is not that KM doesn't work. There are proven success stories within some definitional domains of what KM is. However, organizations will often get bogged down in the definition of knowledge management as a discipline, which might help it better exploit knowledge as an intangible asset. Managers have no such challenge when implementing Six Sigma or the Balanced Scorecard because these tools have been well defined. The proposition that managers are first faced with is determining which definition in the earlier list to hitch the organization's future to. That prospect is both a crucial step and a potentially time-intensive distraction, a momentum killer—and the first point of vulnerability to succeeding with a KM strategy. Choice of definition will dictate strategy, tactics, and execution.

In the estimation of Nathaniel Palmer, KM initiatives often fall between the two extremes of approaching the project from a very theoretical, pedantic perspective, which gets lost in the definitions, and an overly tactical return on investment approach, which limits KM's strategic effectiveness. Palmer, a principal at Delphi Group, is a management consultant who has rolled up his sleeves to help companies create and execute a KM strategy while also helping some organizations salvage what became KM failures. Following are two scenarios by way of example.

Machine-Age Metaphor

The pedantic, academic approach is obsessed with defining knowledge. The stakeholders aware of the need to deploy strategies to manage this intangible asset find themselves drawn into a debate about what KM is rather than what it can do. This debate is an understandable and natural response to the varied definitions of KM that populate the literature today, and it manifests itself in attempts to conceptualize knowledge as something distinct and more important than information. Consider the rendering shown in Table 7.1.

In this academic stylization, knowledge is viewed as the value-added result of transforming data and information. Data about some operational reality inside the enterprise are manipulated and treated in transforming into something better than data, something more useful on its

Table 7.1   An Attempt to Conceptualize the Creation of Knowledge

Data	Information	Knowledge
Raw list of customers and products they purchased from a website in the past 30 days	Structured table of purchasing information with key fields for customer name, monthly and yearly purchases by product category and total revenue by customer, and variable costs per customer	Structured list of customers grouped by contribution margin
→	→	↑

way down the assembly line toward the final product, knowledge. The second step is the crucial phase in the production process, as we turn important information, useful in itself, into something upon which strategic and tactical decisions can be made.

Because the information in the last step is "actionable" in corporate-speak,[9] this information is no longer information but knowledge. In this instance, information about customer profitability is knowledge upon which a whole host of decisions concerning marketing, customer service, and call center operations (to name three operational domains) can be made. Notice that according to the logic of this exercise, information can be knowledge but knowledge is not just information—it is something more.

This way of thinking has an almost mechanistic, machine-age quality to it as thinkers attempt to superimpose a manufacturing, factor-of-production template on top of the discussion. It is not an inaccurate way of thinking about knowledge assets and is, arguably, a reflection of the very conceptualization effort managers invest in intangible assets in order to get their arms around what the nature of the assets are and how they can be managed. Yet Nathaniel Palmer's experience says that this template should be viewed as no more than a thought experiment because it is not very useful as a way to inform KM strategy. Why is this approach problematic?

For one, creating distinctions between information and knowledge is arbitrary and counterproductive. Defining information as something one step removed from knowledge and therefore not a "knowledge" asset that won't be part of a KM initiative diminishes the importance of information as something that is arguably knowledge in itself. That entity called information in the context of this example might have just as easily been transformed into a piece of knowledge constructed along not a contribution margin dimension but a product popularity dimension.

Table 7.2 shows data transformed into the same information entity as in Table 7.1, yet the value-added step that turns information into knowledge takes a different turn here. The piece of knowledge, now constructed in terms of product popularity, might affect a range of internal resource allocation decisions in design, production, supply chain, and marketing and sales. The manager would be presented with a whole new set of decisions to be acted upon.

If information is not knowledge, does this mean that the structured table of customer and product information is not part of the knowledge base that becomes the inevitable physical space into which knowledge is archived and stockpiled? If information is not knowledge, does this mean this specific piece of information is no longer available for the creation of a new piece of knowledge? We have already seen how one table reflecting site activity was turned into two discrete pieces of knowledge—first, a table of customers grouped by contribution margin, and

Table 7.2 A Further Attempt to Conceptualize the Creation of Knowledge

Data	Information	Knowledge
Raw list of customers and products they purchased from a website in the past 30 days	Structured table of purchasing information with key fields for customer name, monthly and yearly purchases by product category and total revenue by customer, and variable costs per customer	Structured list of most popular product categories
→	→	↑

second, a table of most popular product categories. There might be five more.

This fungibility of information and knowledge brings us to the second problem with a machine-age metaphor. Because knowledge can proceed in many different directions since it possesses many different iterations arising out of many different contexts, managers could find themselves dragged down by attempting to direct the information into knowledge that might not be useful. For example, workers at a steel mill know that low-grade ore is a factor-of-production input meant for one output—steel. However, data and information as a production input have as many outcomes as the users of the data and information can find uses for them. How can a manager know in advance all the potential uses of a piece of information that is turned into knowledge in advance of the knowledge use? Adopting a command-and-control approach to knowledge management in which someone directs information into a preconceived idea of what knowledge is, is in fundamental conflict with effective knowledge management practices in which the transformation happens bottom-up from the point of use.

The factor-of-production approach also loses sight of the fact that turning data into knowledge is not the end of the company's value transformation, while the transformation from low-grade iron ore into steel is. Turning raw data into knowledge is the first step of a much longer journey in which knowledge is leveraged by people to produce some product or service twenty steps down the line. Anyone adopting the production metaphor and following the factor-of-production logic must concede that knowledge is actually an early factor of production, not the end.

Another related problem to the machine-age construct of KM is managers' belief that because knowledge is this precious asset targeted for value extraction, it must occupy its own dedicated physical space, separate and unsoiled from all other data and information that reside on hard drives across the organization. In this way, knowledge is approached as if it were inventory—discrete, individually boxed, and requiring its own directory and subdirectory scheme for proper access—when, in fact, where the knowledge is located is far less important than the content of the knowledge, its usefulness to a worker, and its accessibility via good search technology.

In one example, an organization embarked upon an audit, a means by which known knowledge in a recorded state and tacit knowledge (that which is in the minds of employees) were each directed toward a special repository. Each individual was required to add his or her knowledge to the online database through a process coordinated by a team of internal subject matter experts. The SMEs sought to cull every known fact about their subject area into this special online information index.

An even more perverse reaction to a misguided understanding of what knowledge management really is manifests itself in orders from KM project owners for employees to brain-dump what they know. Palmer of Delphi Group witnessed one company that actually had all its employees go through the process of emptying their heads of what they knew in seeking to document this expertise as part of a KM project. The exercise was akin to mom-and-pop retailers conducting a manual, end-of-year stock check in order to reset the books going into the new year. The results were less than optimal. And by necessity in undertaking such an activity, knowledge, however defined, winds up bounded not only by definitional limitations but by physical and spatial limitations as well. Consequently, managers are inclined to exclude information that might be quite useful in a knowledge base.

Perhaps a more effective way to think about archiving knowledge is to tag the information with the proper label and taxonomy so users can access it intuitively. That a piece of knowledge resides on a server at the London office instead of downstairs in the cold room housing the server farm is far less important than that the knowledge attached to it has the appropriate descriptor so that search tools will be able to retrieve it quickly and efficiently. Companies have been working on this problem for years, and the technical challenges to the creation of effective metatags that act as the homing beacons the search tools key in on are not insignificant. (XML has emerged as the meta-definition scheme for Web-based information. HTML describes only how a Web page looks; XML tells us what it is.)

The machine-age mind-set conceptualizes knowledge as a physical store of value, like bars of bullion. Only the gold is allowed in. That customer list reporting product popularity and customer profitability could very well be viewed as silver. It has some value but isn't a candidate for our Fort Knox.

Show Me the Money

The other extreme is to view KM exclusively as a tactical cost-saving proposition, without considering the contribution to strategic goals KM might deliver as an intangible asset tool. This habit of mind is particularly prevalent when discussions around the need for a KM strategy are rooted in technology when some "knowledge management" packaged application is introduced to managers. When KM is deliberated around technology and not strategy, one can hardly be surprised that cost savings, cost-benefit analysis, payback, and all the other economic value lingo that has insinuated itself into technology investment assessments become the focus.

The tactical approach would proceed something like this: by virtue of our KM initiative, we use 25 percent less paper. Automation, digitization, and electronic access have replaced paper and the means of communication and documentation. Therefore, our organization has saved such and such dollars.

Cost savings are fine as it goes, but such goals miss the strategic impact companies can leverage by managing knowledge better, with more discipline and focus. Is the organization changing meaningfully because it uses less paper? Are products designed more efficiently? Has collaboration in some process around production improved? Is the company responding to opportunities more quickly because it communicates electronically instead of on paper? These are legitimate questions that are precluded when KM is lashed to cost-saving benefits only. A document management company, such as Xerox, positions KM in precisely this way, in its mind, using its scanners to digitize documents it considers at least one element of KM.[10] It's in Xerox's interest to position automation and document management as KM activities, and who is to argue with them given the variety of definitions KM suffers from?

Good KM at Work

In order to demonstrate the full potential of knowledge management through a project possessing a number of tactical and strategic impacts to the organization, it is necessary to return to yet2.com, our OMI friend from Chapter 6. As it happens, yet2.com is selling a KM package to organizations that seek to extract more value out of their intellectual property portfolios. Yet2.com does not position this product within the knowledge management realm explicitly, and given the confusion surrounding the management discipline today, this should serve it well from a sales and marketing standpoint. Call it intellectual asset management or intellectual property asset management—the project would find acceptance amongst practitioners were it called knowledge management. This mini–case study might represent the best knowledge management can aspire to as an approach to managing a key enterprise intangible asset.

Yet2.com anticipated that as much as some companies want to drive open-market innovation practices with external partners, it would also want to capture some of the same operational benefits within its four walls. Yet2.com created a product called the i-4C Knowledge Engine, a packaged application embodying much of the functionality found in its publicly accessible exchange environment. The idea behind this internal application is to improve visibility across business units as to what patents, trade secrets, and technological know-how are part of the company portfolio, as well as who the authors of that expertise are and how they can be contacted. Here's how i-4C worked for one large aerospace company.

Engineer A found that an aircraft design with which he was involved required a new lighting design that at once was more durable and used less energy, a capability that was not readily available to him. Using i-4C, the engineer posted the need across the corporation for technical know-how around interior lighting. Not long afterward, an engineer in a different subsidiary posted a response that his team had just completed a project in this domain and provided documentation around the know-how. Neither of the two engineers knew each other, but in a very short time they set up an appointment to meet.

The buyer (engineer A) confirmed that the innovation would meet the technical specifications of his project and arranged to hire the engineering expert from the subsidiary for a few days of consultation. The domain expert not only provided schematics and blueprints and elaborated on the technical details of the know-how embodied in the new lighting design but also showed the engineer in need how to incorporate the innovation in the design specifications, identified the best parts suppliers to work with, and guided the acquiring engineer on how to ramp up production of this important aircraft component.

What seems a quite simple solution to one employee's problem—ask a coworker—actually reveals some challenging organizational tensions apparent in large organizations, not the least of which is the fact that in a company of many thousands of employees, the search costs the engineer in need might have incurred could have been substantial. What took engineer A only minutes to nail within this system might have taken days or longer had he embarked on a quest to determine whether the expertise and technical know-how resided somewhere else in the organization. Where would he have searched for this capability? How would he find the exact expert the project required? Did he have the time to devote to such a search? In a hierarchical organization such as this one, are there any negative political implications when an employee freelances to help someone in another business unit or affiliated organization? Multiply one engineer's experience across the multiple technical needs that arise in a large organization building complex products, and the productivity drag that could emerge from R&D folks on a constant treasure hunt for answers is clear. Worse, the engineer might not have even bothered, instead resorting to starting the process of developing new lighting technology from scratch. The not-invented-here syndrome rears its ugly head once again with Loch Nessian menace.

This aircraft manufacturer's experience is instructive, revealing how KM lives up to its methodological potential, as follows:

- **KM demonstrates strategic implications:** Not only did the domain expert explicate the technical know-how for the engineer in need, but he also provided valuable insight and expertise into the best way to take the idea and turn it into a necessary part of an aircraft.

The domain expert expedited the engineer's learning curve around critical product development issues, including third-party sourcing and production. Any sanctioned collaboration that improves the process of innovation is the strategic playing field on which KM can shine.

- **KM emphasizes experiential knowledge:** Delphi Group's Palmer believes the most powerful knowledge leveraged by an organization is not documented in files but is, rather, the expertise and hard-to-quantify wisdom of colleagues, vividly at work in this example. This kind of "wisdom," as Delphi Group likes to call it, is often not captured in document form. An in-house exchange platform encouraging communication sets the stage for this experiential knowledge transfer from owner to acquirer in a consultative and collaborative environment. The domain expert could have documented the knowledge conveyed to the engineer in need, but it is unlikely he or she would know in advance that a colleague at an affiliated organization would have a compelling need for new aircraft lighting technology— and it would be impractical to spend the time putting all the advice on paper in advance of the need actually emerging. Experiential knowledge is that knowledge hidden in the recesses of an employee's brain matter that doesn't come out until someone else poses the need for it. In fact, most people don't know everything they know until challenged to solve some challenge. Again, demand will drive supply, not vice versa.

- **KM provides rapid access:** Yet2.com's proprietary search technology and content presentation structure in which an IP and technical know-how portfolio is packaged in plain English, with relevant pointers directing acquirers to related materials (including R&D proposals and white papers), allow engineers to quickly zero in on what they need.

- **KM leverages reuse:** A fundamental precept of knowledge is that just like any digitally created entity—Word file, software product, etc.—it can be created once, replicated an infinite number of times at almost no cost, and spun in many directions. A ubiquitous knowledge base of a company's IP and know-how portfolio linked to the appropriate domain expert supports the idea that if the expertise exists, it is important to take advantage of it before reinventing the wheel.

Imagine, however, if this aerospace company had reversed its strategy. Instead of establishing a needs-based KM platform, in which the "buyer" of the IP initiates engagement and sets off the chain of events—communication, consultation and collaboration, knowledge transfer, and acquisition—which collectively constitute a KM strategy, suppose the aerospace company had all the engineers document what they know, just in case someone wanted it down the road. What a colossal waste of time. Good KM means supply responds to demand, not vice versa.

Goals Drive KM Strategy and Tactics

Just as we witnessed in Chapter 4 (which addressed intangibility factors in IT), where impacts to an e-learning initiative become quite tangible when linked to concrete strategies and tactics, so too is an aerospace company capturing value in KM out of the practical solutions it provides for the problems large organizations face by their sheer girth. Palmer asserts that looking at the endgame of the KM project—what will it deliver strategically to the company?—is the most potent way to approach KM as a management discipline. It is a philosophy shared by others.[11]

In this one small example, an aerospace company boosts worker productivity in cutting the search costs around finding an answer to a technical problem; it enjoys the cost avoidance of not having to re-create the intellectual property wheel (an expensive wheel at that); and it drives improvements in the process of innovation when one expert shares his experiential knowledge with a colleague. The impact from one incident, such as the story of the engineers, might be too small to measure on its own, but if similar scenarios are replicated across all companies, the benefits are sure to be quite tangible.

It's Nice to Share

While confusion surrounding what knowledge management is as a set of management principles causes companies to go off in ill-considered directions, another element of effective knowledge management is often completely overlooked—how do managers encourage employees to actively contribute what they know to a larger store of knowledge accessible to anyone? When the organization implements a knowledge management strategy, a rather large assumption sitting underneath the effort is that employees will freely contribute their expertise. This assumption not only is large enough to drive a mainframe through but is potentially dangerous.

There are several reasons why knowledge sharing is undermined, including the absence of a technology platform to make knowledge sharing easy, siloed organizations that discourage communications with anyone outside a worker's immediate domain, and just plain inertia. But the biggest reason might be the perceived value of knowledge itself as a lever for personal gain.

The hard-won expertise and know-how that employees have developed over time become a key element of the reputational capital they are building for themselves in the company. Knowledge or know-how that others do not have is an employee's legitimate skill differentiator, a lever they perceive can be used to their advantage. Knowledge really is power, and getting employees to part with it requires that organizations figure out how the contributor will be recognized for the value delivered. Attitudes about doing what's good for the company have definite limits, particularly in dysfunctional, top-down organizations, where ideas from the grass roots traditionally have not been welcome or other accomplishments have not been consciously and appropriately recognized.

How do you reconcile the need for constant feeding of the knowledge base that effective knowledge management insists upon with the proper motivational drivers that encourage the very contributions KM needs? Let's look at some possible approaches to overcoming the sharing challenge.

Counting Beans

In the late 1990s, Hill & Knowlton, a global public relations firm, built a company portal that would contain a variety of information, including employee bios with areas of expertise, client case studies, and speeches and articles written by consultants.[12] Chief Knowledge Officer Ted Graham, who works out of the Toronto office, felt the company needed a way to accelerate contributions when it built the portal. While H&K kicked around some ideas on how to accomplish this, a client emerged with a clever approach to the problem.

Beenz.com was one of these highly innovative, if unsuccessful, Internet start-ups that attempted to do in a digital economy what S&H Green Stamps succeeded in doing back in the 1960s. It acted as a proxy of value and alternative payment mechanism. People were rewarded beenz for participating in any number of Internet activities, such as answering a questionnaire, filling out an identification profile, or buying that second product from some online merchant. When they had accumulated enough beenz, people could turn them in for merchandise from merchants participating in the program. One of the problems with the business model was that the company behind the beenz could not get many blue-chip retailers to participate, thus limiting its appeal. High adoption from brand-name e-commerce efforts was critical for the company to gain traction with consumers, and this never materialized. On paper, however, the idea made great sense.

Beenz.com was a client of Hill & Knowlton. A colleague of Graham's suggested the launch of a program in which beenz would be rewarded for knowledge contributions to the company's new intranet portal. Clark Aldrich, a former analyst at Gartner, the IT research firm, termed the arrangement a "mini-economy" and viewed this as a significant event in the evolution of KM. The more Graham thought about it, the more sense it made. Beenz just might be the way to kick-start the effort. He and colleagues structured a reward system using beenz for both knowledge contributions and knowledge consumption, which they believed would accelerate the accumulation of useful and relevant information at the company portal. Hill & Knowlton bought beenz for cash and then put them in a virtual bank account for distribution to employees. Table 7.3 depicts the beenz reward program at Hill & Knowlton for the consumption side of knowledge management.

Graham figured that offering small inducements to use the various elements making up its knowledge repositories would get employees comfortable with the navigation schemes in front of it while instilling the habits that would ensure its constant use to drive operational efficiencies and work performance improvements. Benefits would only accrue, however, if there was information worth consuming, so Graham and colleagues also constructed a reward program for knowledge contributions. Table 7.4 outlines this.

On both the consumption and contribution side, the absolute value of beenz rewarded for particular knowledge-related tasks was less important than the relative values each activity was assigned versus another. On the contribution side, more than twice the number of

Table 7.3 Hill & Knowlton's "Mini-Economy" Incentive System

Knowledge Consumption Activity	Number of Beenz Rewarded	Reason for Reward
Browsing general content	10 (one time) intranet home page	H&K wanted to promote "search first" to save time before sending an e-mail to someone asking for the answer. This sought to encourage self-service.
Browsing featured content	25	This ensured that people were reading targeted info. For example, H&K changed its branding, and the company wanted employees to read about the change.
Advanced searching	30	Advanced searches could get employees to previously created work-related content that could be used in their current engagements. Content reuse when applicable avoids re-creating the wheel and boosts productivity.
Subscribing to updates or search agents	40	This created loyal consumers of knowledge who saw updated content—alerts sent when new content was added to intranet or someone did a search under a specific word.

Table 7.4 Hill & Knowlton's "Mini-Economy" Incentive System No. 2

Activity	Number of Beenz Rewarded	Reason for Reward
Contributing a biography	50	Required activity of all consultants. However, some were archiving them on local servers instead of global intranet. This would help get them over that hurdle.
Filling out a profile	75	Asked more detailed questions about work history, client projects, other skills. Colleagues would be able to quickly assess other employees' appropriateness to offer advice and guidance concerning a work-related issue.
Contributing a case study	100	Takes more time than any other activity; expectation that some research is required to discover impact; must be deemed presentable to clients before points are granted.
Adding a speech or an article	125	Goes beyond job responsibility; asking someone to share their personal insights.

beenz was awarded to employees for posting a speech presented to some industry or professional group than for simply posting their professional biographies. Because writing and presenting a speech or getting an article published in a professional journal was outside the bounds of employees' jobs, required serious effort, and offered potentially high added value for a specific consumer of the information, Graham established the relative rewards accordingly.

While employees liked the program, an unforeseen twist emerged in the story. Graham thought employees would start cashing in beenz for the various merchandise that honored this virtual store of value. Yet upon review of the company account, Graham discovered that not all beenz were tendered. While some employees cashed in beenz for magazine subscriptions and CDs, others were hoarding their personal stashes of beenz for their symbolic bragging rights. In the eyes of some employees, beenz became a proxy for their relative worth in the organization: "How many beenz you got?" went some of the conversations between employees.

Alas, Hill & Knowlton abandoned the beenz project for the simple fact that beenz.com went out of business. The company could have sustained the effort using some other proxy for value, like a points program with a credit card, but the attraction of the beenz model was its novelty as a new payment mechanism as well as the ease of use in managing rewards. The rewards were embedded in the intranet upon which employees either consumed or contributed knowledge. Assignment of beenz to specific employees and total program tracking were engineered in Beenz.com's back office IT infrastructure. Graham ultimately questioned whether a more cumbersome reward system could be managed with as little effort as the beenz program. Management of a rewards-based knowledge-sharing program can't exceed the resources needed to run the global KM effort because sharing is only one component, albeit an important one.

Four years after the program was launched, Graham is still asked about his mini-economy idea at industry functions and in conversations with practitioners. The moral of the Hill & Knowlton story is that rewarding knowledge contributions in perpetuity might be counterproductive, as employees could come to view rewards for contributing knowledge as an entitlement, a prerequisite for contributing. This is a truly dangerous outcome. Employees should discover that ideally, over time, they will get as good as they give, and if their work lives are made easier or more productive through the availability of knowledge repositories, then sharing in an implicitly understood barter/quid pro quo arrangement makes sense. Yet an inventive effort like Hill & Knowlton's beenz program has its place as a vehicle to kick off KM initiatives or build buy-in—no pun intended.

Making Markets

Another approach that encourages knowledge sharing and holds great promise is not even considered knowledge sharing per se.

Economists have long argued that markets do an excellent job of forecasting events and trends, and they are not expensive to organize.

Why couldn't companies organize markets internally that predict the likelihood of future events actually happening as a way to drive better decision making? HP tried exactly this.

Employees bought and sold shares in an artificial internal market established to forecast future sales month by month. While the markets involved only a couple dozen employees over a three-year period, the market results outperformed official sales forecasts 75 percent of the time.[13]

Perhaps the most well-known futures market outside of industry is the Iowa Electronic Markets, founded in 1988 at the University of Iowa's business school. Open to anyone, it is organized to allow participants to buy and sell shares of futures contracts based on the outcome of political elections. The market uses real money, from $5 to $500. This technique was seen as a way for academics to study market behavior and to teach students the power of markets in decision making. The accuracy of this marketplace has been impressive. In the 1988, 1992, 1996, and 2000 presidential elections, the IEM's market price on the day some six hundred different polls were conducted across those elections was closer to the actual results than the polls 75 percent of the time.[14]

How would a market inside a company work? The company would set the reward, say, 100 units (real money, Monopoly money, points— it doesn't matter), for payout around some business event. Any future event the company is interested in forecasting could be a candidate for such a market: sales forecasts, earnings, end-of-quarter market share growth, inventory turns, etc. We'll say the company is interested in forecasting market share growth of a new product for the quarter. Therefore, employees would buy and sell contracts for the right to win 100 units, or points, if market share growth at the end of the quarter is 5 percent or better. Both the reward and the terms of the contract have been set. When the market begins, employees would "buy" futures contracts depending upon their belief that market share will indeed exceed 5 percent. Someone who "pays" 50 points to get the 100-unit reward at the end of the contract is betting even odds that market share will indeed meet or exceed the forecast—betting 50 to get 50 more.

What does any of this have to do with knowledge management? Plenty. The price of the futures contract at any given time is a synthesis of the collective judgments of the people participating in the market. A participant's personal knowledge is embedded in the investment decision he or she makes, and the market investment price is the collective wisdom amongst all participants. Employees are, in an organic way, sharing their expertise, and we can have high confidence that that expertise is the best employees can give because each participant has a stake in the outcome of the market exercise (particularly when it's real jack, as in the case of IEM). The act of sharing is merely organized and manifested differently than the beenz.com exercise with Hill & Knowlton.

Economists call the capture of collective wisdom around markets decision markets, or opinion aggregation. KM practitioners could call it knowledge sharing even though contributing expertise is not an end in itself but rather a means to an end—winning the payout from the market.

Can markets work as a decision-making tool inside companies? Can the collective judgment of a market trump the analysis of statisticians and business analysts who are otherwise the sources of forecasting that management relies upon? Some markets' accuracy in forecasting cannot be denied. And the inherent features of markets are compelling. For one, the wisdom of the group is better than the wisdom of the smartest individual in the group. Two, markets are democratic. Unique and unorthodox perspectives are not shut out in the name of conformity or in the name of not making waves while the company is inoculated from the virus called groupthink that characterizes much decision making in industry today. These elements are also perhaps the reason why markets have not caught on in organizations, because that would require senior management to acknowledge it doesn't have a monopoly on wisdom.

A market most emblematic of the notion that useful knowledge can conceivably originate anywhere and not just in the boardroom is the Hollywood Stock Exchange (hsx.com). Players can register at no charge to predict box office forecasts of films ready for launch. Players trade securities whose prices are tied to box office forecasts for new films in their first four weeks of release. The market represents the collective judgments of about a million people who have registered so far.[15]

Because a futures market for new movies is still a novel idea, studio executives have yet to replace market research, focus groups, or gut instinct as the primary decision drivers behind green-lighting investment in a movie. But they are watching it very closely. A Harvard marketing professor studying the market says the last trading price of a film just before its release is a more accurate metric of future box office than any other metric used by studios in decision making. The market's variance runs about 16 percent under or over actual receipts.[16]

Far from perfect in its predictive value, futures markets nevertheless give you an idea of how poorly traditional research and other information sources perform that movie companies rely upon. If this market proves its mettle over time, studios could easily fold these forecasts into their risk-adjusted ROI models for movie capital investment.

What other techniques for leveraging the critical value of knowledge might join up with the use of market tactics to improve the state of knowledge management? As it happens, a new and radical approach has been in development for the past several years, which makes up for in cleverness what it lacks in a track record inside the enterprise. It just might help knowledge management solve some of its woes and is the subject of the next chapter.

Chapter Takeaway

- Knowledge management suffers from too many definitions; if something is everything, then it is nothing. Some have argued this is natural with an immature management technique, and over time a set of proven techniques will emerge to lend structure to knowledge management. But for now, managers should choose the definition that best suits the needs of their particular situation and what problems they hope to solve deploying it.
- Effective knowledge management means adhering to some broad principles. Consider the strategic implications of a KM strategy: focus on experiential knowledge (what's in the head of workers), provide rapid access to information employees need, and understand the reuse possibilities of existing knowledge.

- Knowledge is power and a kind of leverage employees use to assert their standing in the organization. Assuming employees will share their hard-earned expertise, particularly in situations where a lot of time and effort are expended by the knowledge holder that takes him or her away from formal job duties, can be treacherous.
- Market arrangements might be a lasting methodological contribution to knowledge management. They can be a fun and effective way to encourage knowledge sharing and the leveraging of experiential knowledge for some tactical or strategic goal.
- Because sharing is fundamental to KM, how can it be engendered? The market approach is quite new to knowledge management, but it has large potential to encourage sharing if designed correctly. Markets are inherently about sharing information. Using market mechanisms in the context of knowledge management means aggregating the wisdom of many employees. Companies intrigued by the market approach should set test cases for its use. Try it in the sales organization (as HP has) or in the IT organization, or run contests to forecast the ROI for several technology projects. Look at the variance in results from the market versus actual. A university keen on the subject might be willing to provide expertise in market design and validate results in exchange for inside data to enhance research efforts. If it turns out that market forecasts fall near actual results many times over, the organization can then rely upon market mechanisms as a basis for decision making.

CHAPTER 8

A RADICAL NEW APPROACH TO MANAGING KNOWLEDGE

A new methodology has just emerged that could prove to be a fundamentally new and powerful set of tools managers could deploy in the practice of knowledge management. Invented by the Future Knowledge Group, a San Jose–based consultancy, the methodology is called Knowledge Object Theory (KOT). Its roots are found in such disciplines as predicate logic, graphical network diagrams, and graphical knowledge modeling. Although KOT does not redefine what KM is from the conceptual level—managers are still required to articulate what the business impacts from KM will be—KOT does show its tactical usefulness in a couple of ways.[1]

Knowledge Object Theory Overview

KOT is fundamentally about one insight: all realities in the world can be expressed consistently in a structured and formal way. That structure looks like the one shown in Figure 8.1.[2]

Consider real-world applications of this simple construct (see Figure 8.2).

Figure 8.1

Figure 8.2 Illustrating Input-Process-Output

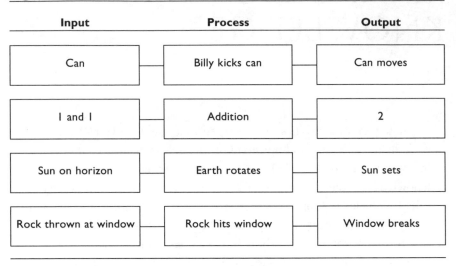

Figure 8.3

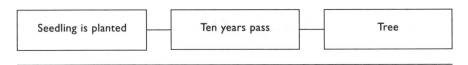

What is the pattern that emerges in Figure 8.2? Any entity, be it a can, the numeral 1, the sun, or a rock being thrown, undergoes a process of some type, after which an output or outcome takes place.

The I-P-O process, called a Triad (introduced in Chapter 4, which dealt with intangible impacts of information technology), is the first step in understanding Knowledge Object Theory. A Triad is a consistent, formal, and structured way to explain *any* reality in the world. It is consistent and structured because knowledge is expressed in terms of an input, a process, and an output. It is formal because it contains rules. As these examples show, the input is any reality or knowledge about the universe. The process is any phenomenon that will cause change to the input, including the passage of time. A time-dependent Triad expression might look like the one shown in Figure 8.3.

The output of the I-P-O expression in Figure 8.3 is new knowledge produced by the act of the process impacting the input. Another important element of Triads is that it should be easy to see that they contain causation. (The idea of causation and its implications will be explained in more detail later in the chapter.) The process of time causes some reality about the world (in Figure 8.3, the planting of a seedling) to change through the process of time passing, giving us the output in the form of new knowledge (here, a tree).

Intent Is Key

The next step in understanding Knowledge Object Theory is to show the critical importance of the intent of the knowledge—that is, its purpose in being expressed. Knowledge Object Theory includes what is called an Intent Indicator, expressed as *ii* or *eye*. Figure 8.4 demonstrates this. An Intent Indicator joined to the Triad for any expression of knowledge is called a Knowledge Object Machine (KOM).

Figure 8.4 A Knowledge Object Machine

Intent Indicator (ii) = Describe seedling transformation into tree

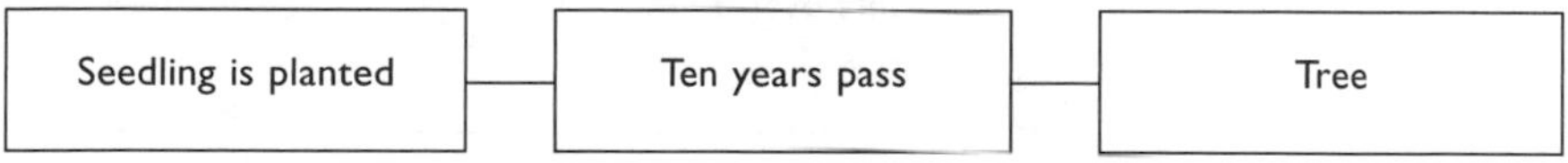

Seedling is planted	—	Ten years pass	—	Tree

This KOM example is very broad. Consequently, the Intent Indicator is very broad as well. The creator of this KOM has decided to explain how a seedling will turn into a tree over time. We know this is the agenda of its creator because he provided the Triad (seedling is planted → time passes → seedling grows into a tree) with an Intent Indicator (an explicit expression of what this Triad is about). This KOM doesn't really tell us all that much other than the fact that if a number of years go by, a seedling will eventually turn into a tree of an unspecified height. The Knowledge Objects technique allows the creator of the knowledge expression to depict it as broadly or as specifically as wished.

Theory in Action: R&D Scientist Scenario

Supposing we worked for a lawn care or forest products company and wanted to know the effect of a new strain of fertilizer on the growth of red maples. This lawn care company has been working on an innovative new fertilizer that causes plants and trees to grow faster with greater resistance to disease than any other product in its line. An R&D team has been slaving away on the project for many months. The KOM broadly describing the application of this new fertilizer is depicted in Figure 8.5.

The intent of the knowledge in Figure 8.5 is to demonstrate the effects of a new strain of fertilizer on the rate of growth of red maple seedlings. The intent of this captured knowledge is fundamentally

Figure 8.5

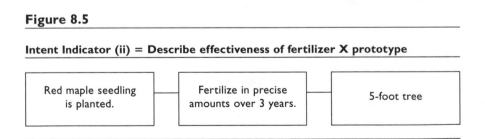

Intent Indicator (ii) = Describe effectiveness of fertilizer X prototype

| Red maple seedling is planted. | Fertilize in precise amounts over 3 years. | 5-foot tree |

important because, as was demonstrated earlier, knowledge is fungible and flexible, and it is a candidate for many purposes or contexts. Let's look at an example of intent outside the red maple scenario first to understand completely the importance and context of the Intent Indicators. We'll use the kicking can scenario to illustrate the point. Consider Figure 8.6.

What is the intent of this Triad?

- ii = Example of Newtonian physics
- ii = Advertising concept for new shoe launch
- ii = Describe children's game
- ii = Example of Billy's bad behavior

Any one of these is a plausible intent of the Triad depiction of Billy kicking the can because the Triad does not tell us any more than the fact that the can was kicked and therefore moved. Again, the intent of the Triad is the same thing as the purpose for which it is being created, and the intent depends upon who is creating it and for what context. What is the reason someone would create a specific Triad within the discipline of knowledge management? Let's return to the red maple seedling example.

Figure 8.5 depicts the application of the fertilizer innovation to a red maple seedling, but again, it doesn't provide much specificity about the impacts of the solution, other than the fact that it was indeed applied over a three-year period. An R&D scientist would be very interested in documenting the effectiveness (or lack thereof) of the new technology in order to determine how much faster a maple would grow than if

Figure 8.6

Intent Indicator (ii) = What is the intent of this Triad?

| Can | Billy kicks can. | Can moves. |

it had been treated with no fertilizer or with a previous version of the company's product. So what the scientist might do is test different amounts of solution applied at different intervals and observe the rate of growth of a red maple seedling. As a world-class arborist, the scientist will establish three studies to test varying quantities of solution and study the impact. Figures 8.7a, 8.7b, and 8.7c illustrate the results.

Figure 8.7a

Intent Indicator = Describe fertilizer X prototype effectiveness—case study 1

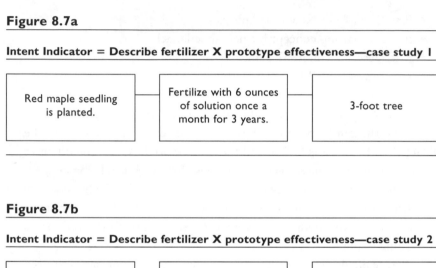

| Red maple seedling is planted. | Fertilize with 6 ounces of solution once a month for 3 years. | 3-foot tree |

Figure 8.7b

Intent Indicator = Describe fertilizer X prototype effectiveness—case study 2

| Red maple seedling is planted. | Fertilize with 10 ounces of solution twice a month for 3 years. | 4-foot tree |

Figure 8.7c

Intent Indicator = Describe fertilizer X prototype effectiveness—case study 3

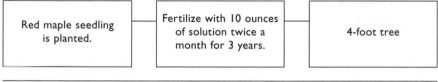

| Red maple seedling is planted. | Fertilize with 12 ounces of solution twice a month for 3 years. | 5-foot tree |

Each case study involves the application of a different quantity of solution at varying intervals to red maple seedlings to measure the technology's effectiveness. For illustration purposes, this example has intentionally been kept simple and excludes such factors as weather, soil composition, and other variables scientists engaged in this R&D exercise might be interested in measuring. All three KOMs are expressions of what happens to red maple seedlings (all of the same height to start, of course) when different amounts of solution are applied with varying frequency, and each contains its own Intent Indicator to reflect the specifics of the respective Triad. These KOMs become elements in a global knowledge base the scientist will use in testing a product prototype. He discovers that increasing the amount and frequency of the solution provides the best results.

Just to add complexity to the scenario, let's say that the scientist used three different variations of the solution—A, B, and C—comprising different levels of chemicals. The scientist is interested in capturing the performance of the different solutions and those solutions' relationship to the results of faster-growing, more disease-resistant red maples. Adding this wrinkle to the example demonstrates further functionality of KOMs and the KOT methodology. To keep the example simple, solution A is associated with case study 1, B is associated with 2, and C with 3. The new KOMs are shown in Figures 8.8a, 8.8b, and 8.8c.

The KOMs in Figures 8.8a, 8.8b, and 8.8c express with more detail the outcomes of the case studies, this time when red maple seedlings are fed equal quantities of different solutions over a specified time period. Should the scientist apply eight ounces of each solution in an attempt to determine whether increased quantities have any appreciable effect on red maple seedling growth, he would create KOMs expressing those results.

An R&D effort testing a new technology for introduction into a product line would be interested in capturing knowledge with much finer detail. So in building a database of results expressed in the causal structure of Knowledge Object Machines, the scientist decides to create another set of KOMs, which expresses the fact that three chemical agents interact in some way to arrive at solutions A, B, and C. We'll confine the illustration to solution A only (see Figure 8.9), although the

Figure 8.8a

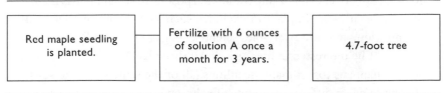

Intent Indicator = Describe fertilizer X prototype effectiveness—case study 1

| Red maple seedling is planted. | Fertilize with 6 ounces of solution A once a month for 3 years. | 4.7-foot tree |

Figure 8.8b

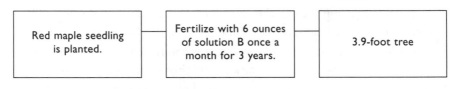

Intent Indicator = Describe fertilizer X prototype effectiveness—case study 2

| Red maple seedling is planted. | Fertilize with 6 ounces of solution B once a month for 3 years. | 3.9-foot tree |

Figure 8.8c

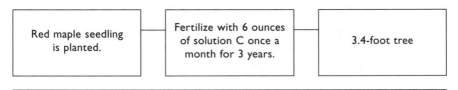

Intent Indicator = Describe fertilizer X prototype effectiveness—case study 3

| Red maple seedling is planted. | Fertilize with 6 ounces of solution C once a month for 3 years. | 3.4-foot tree |

KOM process could be repeated for as many solutions as are being tested.

The scientist has documented the fact that chemical agents 1, 2, and 3 are used in solution A. Using the KOM methodology to capture information about the progress of these solutions, our scientist would

Figure 8.9

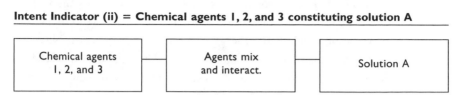

Intent Indicator (ii) = Chemical agents 1, 2, and 3 constituting solution A

| Chemical agents 1, 2, and 3 | Agents mix and interact. | Solution A |

Figure 8.10

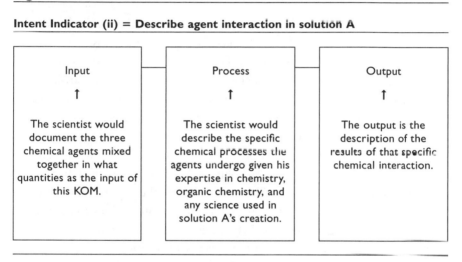

Intent Indicator (ii) = Describe agent interaction in solution A

Input	Process	Output
↑	↑	↑
The scientist would document the three chemical agents mixed together in what quantities as the input of this KOM.	The scientist would describe the specific chemical processes the agents undergo given his expertise in chemistry, organic chemistry, and any science used in solution A's creation.	The output is the description of the results of that specific chemical interaction.

certainly be interested in documenting the nature of the specific chemical reaction these agents undergo in the creation of solution A. This is illustrated in Figure 8.10.

This is really only the beginning of knowledge base construction around the development of solution A as a viable technology that could be leveraged in a commercial product. To get the full value of Knowledge Object Theory as a way to build a knowledge base, the scientist would create many more KOMs relationally linked to case study 1, which concerns itself with the effectiveness of solution A. He would build as many KOMs for solutions B and C as well. As you can see, the scientist starts with a very broadly stated KOM that expresses the fact that a solution he is working on will be applied to red maple seedlings—and a tree of some height will emerge sometime in the future. Next, the scientist creates KOMs that explain in more detail the nature of the solution applied to the red maple seedlings. Then he digs in even deeper to express the chemical reactions the agents constituting the solution undergo to cause the seedlings to grow. The process of continuously breaking down various components of the issues at play in the creation of a new fertilizer is the act of decomposition, a process that forces the knowledge creator to get at the fundamental forces at work on the subject under analysis—in this case, the various forces that at the highest level give us a fertilizer that helps seedlings grow into trees.

Supposing soil composition is a factor affecting the potency of the solution. The scientist might also be interested in expression knowledge about soil composition as a variable in the rate of growth of seedlings. Assuming experimental growth beds contain many different soil types (type 1, type 2, etc.), the scientist would create KOMs providing a formal expression of their impact on seedling growth. See Figure 8.11.

The scientist might be testing solution A's effectiveness in a number of soils of varying pH values. Should he want to, the scientist could create a KOM that expresses the specific chemical interactions that occur between the solution agents and the acids, alkalines, or other nutrients in the soil, just as he described the specific properties that caused the agents in solution A to interact. The scientist could create as many KOMs expressing as much knowledge about this new fertilizer as he wished. For each KOM, the scientist will provide an Intent Indicator, a description of the purpose of the specific KOM. Successive KOMs are created capturing knowledge about this R&D activity, all of which can be hyperlinked to each other so that users can see interrelationships between each KOM put into the repository.

Theory in Action: Marketing Scenario

Now let us suppose that the R&D team's hard work is done and solution A works significantly better than any other product of its type in

Figure 8.11

Intent Indicator (ii) = Describe effects of type I soil with solution A

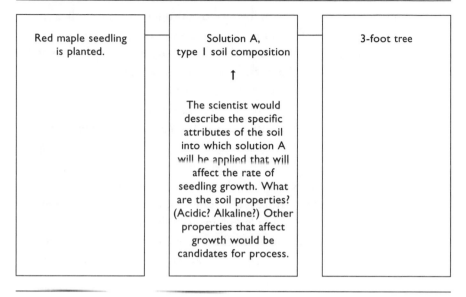

Red maple seedling is planted.	Solution A, type I soil composition ↑ The scientist would describe the specific attributes of the soil into which solution A will be applied that will affect the rate of seedling growth. What are the soil properties? (Acidic? Alkaline?) Other properties that affect growth would be candidates for process.	3-foot tree

Figure 8.12

Intent Indicator (ii) = Describe new product in final form

Solution A	Add new packaging.	BestGrow

the marketplace. The company is ready to take the product, which we will call BestGrow, to market. What kind of KOMs would a marketing executive create?

She could start with a broad KOM (see Figure 8.12) expressing that the new product, BestGrow, derives from the innovation solution A.

The broadest statement is simply the fact that solution A will be placed in a container and labeled. The result is BestGrow. Let us imagine the company decides to save money and keep its brand consistent by choosing the standard bottle it uses for its entire product line. The labeling will be new, however, reflecting the marketing executive's desire to communicate clearly how innovative this product is against all competing brands. The KOM in Figure 8.13 doesn't reveal much in itself, but it is a starting point to think about how to position the product. This KOM will serve as the starting point for decomposition of important elements in constructing a marketing plan.

Figure 8.13 expresses how the marketing team will take the visual and text elements planned for the label and add a unique selling proposition extolling the virtues of BestGrow. The result is the new packaging for this new product. This KOM shows that the team needs a unique selling proposition for the features of BestGrow, a fact they obviously would know even had the KOM not been expressed. However, documenting marketing plan elements using KOMs adds structure to the process while provoking the strategy leaders to think clearly about how to address the marketplace in such a way as to maximize the

Figure 8.13

Intent Indicator (ii) = Describe packaging in final form

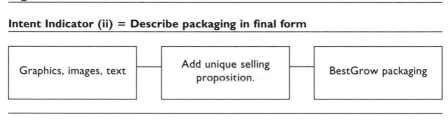

Figure 8.14

Intent Indicator (ii) = Describe unique selling proposition

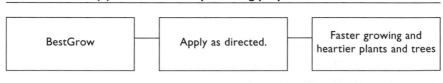

sales possibilities around the new product. Figure 8.14 shows a KOM that begins to delve into the details of a positioning strategy.

The marketing executive will now want to break down the unique selling proposition into its component parts in order to answer these questions: What is it exactly about BestGrow that makes it the best plant fertilizer product on the market? What would we want to communicate about it? The process of decomposition using KOMs (shown in Figures 8.15, 8.16, and 8.17) is one way to analyze the unique selling proposition issue.

Figure 8.15

Intent Indicator (ii) = Describe product differentiator 1

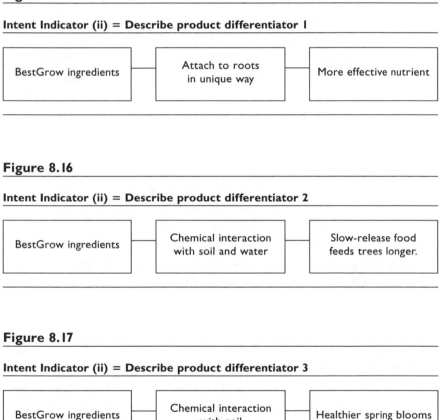

Figure 8.16

Intent Indicator (ii) = Describe product differentiator 2

Figure 8.17

Intent Indicator (ii) = Describe product differentiator 3

In these three KOMs, the marketing executive is asked to articulate the benefits of this new fertilizer solution using a consistent, formal technique to any level of detail desired as a marketing campaign for BestGrow is prepared. Depending upon what the marketing team wants to communicate, she could have created an additional KOM off the third product differentiator (in Figure 8.17) to explain in even more detail why BestGrow is uniquely qualified to deliver more vivid spring flowers on a red maple. Decomposing the KOM that is shown in Figure 8.17 demonstrates this additional detail (see Figure 8.18).

In acidic soil prevalent in parts of the United States, red maples accumulate foliar manganese, which, at toxic levels, inhibits the ability of red maples to photosynthesize.[3] The KOM in Figure 8.18 explicates the fact that BestGrow contains ingredients that neutralize the effects, certainly a product feature that marketing would like to highlight. As the marketing chief constructs a comprehensive marketing campaign, the analysis might have had her build other KOMs in such areas as the competition's products, the BestGrow pricing strategy, or the promotional efforts the company might launch concurrent with BestGrow's market introduction.

Knowledge Object Theory doesn't argue that in the absence of this exercise the marketing executive would fail to create a marketing strategy needed to maximize the revenue potential from this fertilizer innovation. Rather, KOT is designed to force the marketing manager to think with more clarity about the business issues surrounding a marketing campaign: What is the innovation? Why is it better? Why should people run right out and buy a bottle of BestGrow? The act of thinking about a business issue in the form of causality—take an entity, put

Figure 8.18

Intent Indicator (ii) = Describe reasons for more colorful blooms

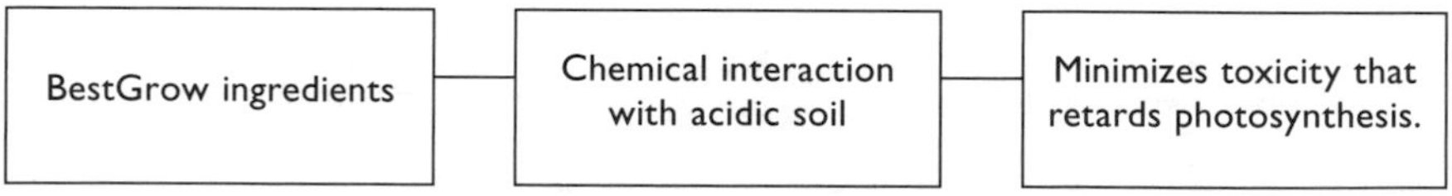

| BestGrow ingredients | Chemical interaction with acidic soil | Minimizes toxicity that retards photosynthesis. |

it through a process, and conceive of the outcome—enables the knowledge creator to think more deeply and with greater insight into the problem at hand because the methodology requires the creator to cast the knowledge in the form of causal forces at work on any phenomenon under analysis. This approach to knowledge creation and analysis is consistent, formal, and structured.

Toward a Universal Language

The Intent Indicator feature of KOMs can drive reuse and global comprehension between creator and consumer. In a global data repository consisting of KOMs, the marketing executive could easily access the R&D scientist's work for her own uses. Although the marketing executive would not understand the specific science behind the creation of BestGrow, the Intent Indicator would give her guidance as to what the purpose of the KOM is: What is the scientist attempting to show? What is it about these KOMs the marketing executive is interested in learning to leverage for the BestGrow marketing campaign?

An Intent Indicator provides the consumer guidance about the knowledge so a quick decision can be made as to its relevance for any particular problem for which the knowledge base is accessed in the first place. If a technical-oriented KOM poses a particular challenge to the marketing executive, she can barter for some time with the research scientist. Why would she be interested in a scientist's specific KOM that explains the chemistry behind this fertilizer innovation? She might want to write a white paper or include a detailed instructional guide with the product for the hard-core gardening warriors in the United States—and there are lots of them—or the professional lawn care community, who would be interested in the technical details of the innovation.

The contextual nature of the Intent Indicator is a critical element in the KOT methodology because accessibility and comprehension of created knowledge by others has such a singular importance that, in its absence, any KM effort is bound to fail. In the case of BestGrow, who else other than the marketing chief might be interested in the scientist's work expressed in KOMs? The CEO has a board meeting and wants to update members on the status of research in this new product line, the CFO has budgeted $5 million for R&D and wants some visibility into the scientist's progress, and the marketing chief has already begun to sketch out approaches to a marketing strategy. The team needs to understand her thinking.

Knowledge Object Theory in general and Knowledge Object Machines in particular do not lose sight of the fact that accessibility of knowledge is critical in any knowledge management strategy, and a critical element of accessibility is the expression of the purpose of the knowledge—the Intent Indicator. Through the Intent Indicator, the expresser clearly states the purpose of the KOM, and the consumer quickly grasps whether or not a particular KOM is relevant to his or her needs.

Other Features and Considerations

The previous pages were meant to serve as a primer on Knowledge Object Theory, a new approach to knowledge expression and analysis. The two brief imaginary scenarios involving a lawn products company scientist and marketing executive point to a number of issues and realities about Knowledge Object Theory broadly and Knowledge Object Machines specifically, requiring explication so that readers' understanding is complete.

Discover What You Don't Know

You will notice that Figures 8.10 and 8.11 did not actually identify the specific phenomena in the process module of the Triad, nor did Figure 8.9 describe which chemical agents undergo what kind of chemical interaction to give us solution A. There is a good reason for this. I don't know a great deal about either R&D or product features in the lawn care industry, nor am I an expert in soils or the chemistry that describes a chemical interaction. Complete accuracy of the scenario isn't the purpose of the exercise. Acquainting readers with the dynamics of Knowledge Object Theory is. Nevertheless, it is important to qualify the scenario for two reasons. One, I do not want to misrepresent the R&D

process in the lawn care industry, even though the purpose of this chapter is to educate readers in the basics of KOT as a tool set that can be leveraged in a knowledge management strategy, not to explain how companies make fertilizers. The example was used for its illustrative power.

Two, the implication of this example is that anyone attempting to build a repository of KOMs will quickly reach the limits of his or her ability to create them if he or she is not a subject matter expert in the domain put to the wheel of this methodology. Start digging into the phenomena around that fertilizer, around that growth, and the need for deep expertise in the subject becomes immediately apparent if KOT is to offer any value at all. This is so because KOT, as stated earlier, is primarily a tool created for use in strategic planning and risk analysis with applications in a number of contexts, including warfare and fighting terrorism. The way in which KOT works forces domain experts to think carefully and deeply about a situation in need of expression in more detail. The causal impacts expressed in KOMs are useful as an analytical and knowledge expression methodology to the extent that subject matter experts are building them.

What users of KOT as a tool set in knowledge management will discover are the limits of their expertise and understanding as they decompose and break down some issue under scrutiny. This is a powerful feature of the methodology—helping people realize what they do not know. Scary but very useful and very healthy. Out of the acknowledgment of ignorance begins enlightenment and understanding because the capacity to learn is a prerequisite for success in modern society.

In our BestGrow example, it took me only two layers of decomposition to realize I was out of my league. In a less dramatic but more nuanced and subtle way, the scientist and the marketing executive might very well hit a wall at some point in the decomposition exercise within their respective domains even though they are experts. This is natural. In decomposing the causal elements of a complex set of chemical actions, the scientist might discover he does not completely understand why one agent binds with the others in a specific way. The marketing executive might discover she does not completely understand a competitor's market share position. If KOMs are used correctly, the causality embedded in a Triad will point out to the expert ever so diplomatically the holes in his or her analysis.

Validating the Knowledge

Discovering unknowns using Knowledge Object Theory is tightly related to another problem. Without exception, the various approaches to knowledge management today assume that the information or knowledge under management and control is correct. That is, the knowledge is unimpeachable and is an accurate portrayal of some reality. This is true in most cases—but not all. Knowledge management broadly defined does not include implicitly any quality control of the assets under new management unless someone in the organization is expressly responsible for ensuring the knowledge is of the highest quality. Knowledge can become dated, losing much of its revelatory or analytical value, or it can be flat-out wrong. KOT and KOMs take aim directly at this problem.

KOT states that KOMs come in three varieties: invalid, valid, and sound. The following figures illustrate this. Because most readers are, like myself, not experts in lawn care products, I won't use the BestGrow scenario to drive home this point but instead will return to the rock-through-the-window scenario, which is universally understandable by anyone.

Figure 8.19 shows a valid KOM. Why is it valid? Because it is *possible* that the Triad is true. A rock is thrown at a window, and the window breaks. However, it might turn out that the rock is thrown so lightly that it barely makes contact with the window and the window

Figure 8.19 A Valid Knowledge Object Machine

Intent Indicator (ii) = Describe how a window can be broken with a rock

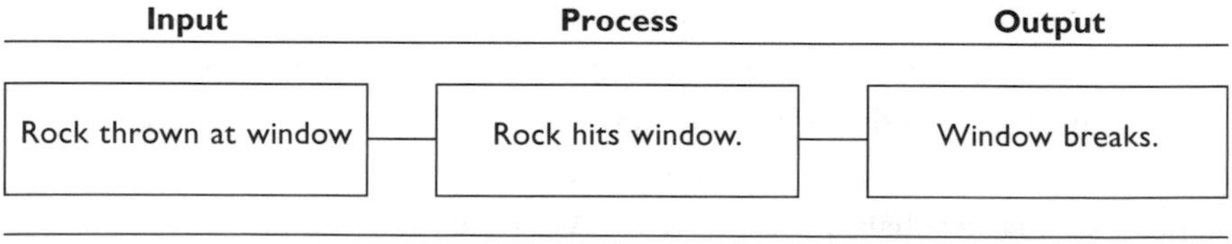

Input	Process	Output
Rock thrown at window	Rock hits window.	Window breaks.

does not break. Or it might be true that the window is made of material that prevents it from being broken. The creator of this KOM must decompose it to determine the truth of this expression of knowledge.

The knowledge creator digs a little deeper and determines that the KOM in Figure 8.19 is not a valid KOM after all. It is invalid because it is not true. Figure 8.20 shows us why.

Figure 8.20 depicts an analysis of what exactly constitutes the window that is an actor in the KOM of Figure 8.19. The knowledge creator discovers the window is made of impenetrable Plexiglas. A missile might breach it but not a rock. Nothing says that the creator can't deliberately introduce a false or invalid KOM into a knowledge base. There are no independent KOM police officers ready to arrest the perpetrator of an invalid expression of knowledge.

However, the act of analyzing the elements of causation that serve as the architecture for all KOM-based knowledge expressions demands accuracy from the KOM's creator if the undertaking is going to work. A lack of confidence in the veracity or accuracy of a KOM requires its creator to undertake some independent research—such as consulting a colleague, buying a report, reading a trade magazine article, or observing the phenomenon himself or herself—to ensure its validity. Had we learned that the window in question was made of ordinary glass and the

Figure 8.20 An Invalid Knowledge Object Machine

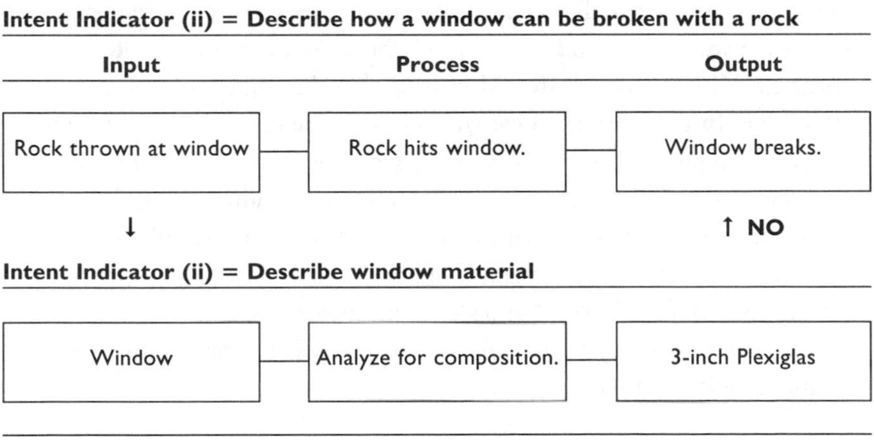

Intent Indicator (ii) = Describe how a window can be broken with a rock

Input	Process	Output
Rock thrown at window	Rock hits window.	Window breaks.

↓   ↑ **NO**

Intent Indicator (ii) = Describe window material

Window	Analyze for composition.	3-inch Plexiglas

rock weighed a pound, the KOM in Figure 8.19 would return to a state of soundness—it might or might not be true. We will imagine an eyewitness told the knowledge creator she witnessed the window's destruction. Therefore, the KOM is definitely valid.[4] Knowledge management quality control is an implicit feature of Knowledge Object Theory because of the analytical rigor demanded of the creator.[5]

Knowledge Object Machines Complement Other Knowledge Types

Neither is it the purpose of KOT nor is it practical to argue that the entire company's store of knowledge should be transformed into KOMs. Not only would companies face an extraordinary cost, but such an endeavor would cheapen the value of knowledge captured in traditional forms, such as PowerPoint presentations, spreadsheets, memos, e-mails, or notes. Gratefully, KOT does not obsess over what knowledge is, which is a truly losing proposition for anyone jumping into the deep end of knowledge management.

Any information upon which analytical value can be added is a candidate for the methodology. Yet companies might be best served using KOMs as pointers to the vast trove of non-KOM–based information scattered across the network. The scientist who constructed a dozen KOMs to explain the innovations in BestGrow might have ten documents of various types associated with this innovation. It would not pose a great challenge for the company to architect a knowledge repository in such a way as to build hooks and hyperlinks to create relationships between KOMs and non-KOM information that supported their construction. In this case, the challenge is to ensure the links remain valid from an infrastructure point of view (the document hasn't moved to another drive) and from a relational level (the document is still pertinent in supporting intellectually and informationally a particular KOM). Therefore, there is no getting around the expense of a gatekeeper necessary to keep KOM-based knowledge assets fresh. Companies find the refreshment imperative is equally true for non-KOM–based knowledge management initiatives.

KOMs Provide New Search Capabilities

Imagine doing a search on the company intranet for any specific topic, but instead of conducting the search around a phrase or a keyword, you build your search around inputs, processes, outputs, or Intent Indicators. A KOM-based knowledge store makes this not only possible but inevitable. The scientist might decide to run a query in which the primary dimension is all processes that various combinations of ingredients undergo in creating the various solutions out of which the big breakthrough is achieved. Or the primary dimension is all outputs from a particular soil type. He might query all Intent Indicators around root absorption of solution C—whatever the scientist needs to know.

There is nothing revolutionary about KOM-based searches; nevertheless, the formal structure of KOMs will allow searches along these attributes. For that reason, consumers of an enterprise knowledge base will get unique looks into the repository not possible with more conventional keyword searches, which tap into unstructured collections of information. Searching against Intent Indicators might significantly reduce search costs because an unambiguous definition of the purpose of the knowledge will allow the consumer to more quickly decide if the knowledge is relevant for a particular need. In fact, Intent Indicators themselves could be part of the data definition format when architecting the database infrastructure supporting the knowledge base.

Knowledge Object Theory's Potential in the Enterprise

Is Knowledge Object Theory a radical innovation in the practice of knowledge management? Because this methodology is just being turned loose on the world, it is too early to say definitively. Real-world, empirically sound results validate the worth of any management methodology. Yet the R&D that went into KOT's creation was significant, comprising about five years of formulation and testing. Certainly, the potential exists for KOT's addition into the tool set companies deploy in managing knowledge as an enterprise intangible asset. The potential value of KOT can be summed up by revisiting the dimensions along which knowledge management offers value, as argued in Chapter 7 through the experience of Delphi Group's Nathaniel Palmer and the yet2.com internal marketplace scenario:

- **KOT demonstrates strategic implications:** The analytical capabilities inherent in KOT mean the methodology is not just another scheme to organize information but a technique to help managers get at the root of any business problem in the organization. If decision making and resource allocation are improved by virtue of analytical rigor inside Triads and I-P-O, forcing employees to think carefully about how knowledge is to be expressed for themselves or others, the linkages to enterprise performance can materialize.
- **KOT emphasizes experiential knowledge:** KOT makes no distinction between explicit knowledge taking the form of a technical memo versus the more experiential knowledge or wisdom of employees that does not lend itself to explicit documentation—such as the example of the aerospace engineer who helped a colleague plan the evolution of an aircraft lighting, from design to finished product. No documents existed that showcased the engineer's highly valuable production knowledge that a colleague needed. While asking employees to undergo a brain dump as a means to capture (in Word or PowerPoint) everything they know can be a distraction, the act of expressing knowledge in the structured form of KOT means that this kind of tacit know-how of employees is likely to leak out for the good of others. Had the aerospace engineer with the necessary expertise to get a new aircraft lighting design produced constructed a KOM-based knowledge store around production strategy and planning, some of that tacit, hidden experiential knowledge unexpressed in any other form would find expression in KOMs. A detailed knowledge base consisting of KOMs analyzing the aerospace company's production capabilities would have certainly revealed preferred manufacturing suppliers. The engineer in need might have obtained the necessary expertise in this way. Of course, this conjecture assumes such a knowledge base would be built in the first place.

- **KOT provides rapid access:** The purpose for expressing some knowledge declared unambiguously in the Intent Indicator sets the context for the knowledge consumer. Is this relevant for what the consumer needs to learn? Searching by Intent Indicator also speeds the process of burrowing into exactly what information the consumer is attempting to lay his or her hands on.
- **KOT leverages reuse:** Intent Indicators advertise the potential suitability of a piece of knowledge to the consumer. Hyperlinks and pointers within KOMs that provide directions to non-KOM–based information ease accessibility of all kinds of knowledge as well as increase the likelihood that consumers can "steal" what they need from an existing document rather than having to re-create the wheel. The realities of information economics—work effort is front-loaded and reproduction costs are near zero—cry out for knowledge management efforts to exploit these realities in order to drive operating efficiencies in the organization.

Conclusions

Knowledge management's identity crisis means that a body of universally proven practices and principles is more difficult to come by, managers run the risk of spending too much time debating what KM is rather than what it can do, and vendors will most likely take advantage of the situation (as all software vendors do) to stake a claim of legitimacy for their product versus competitors'. This state of affairs does not mean a KM initiative won't succeed, but it does mean that managers must focus on what benefits the organization hopes to gain from leveraging this intangible asset rather than allowing one of the myriad definitions of KM and the software following it to dictate the direction of the effort. (More on this point is covered in the takeaway items at the end of the chapter.)

Knowledge Object Theory is a potentially important innovation in KM for the ways in which it helps solve some of its current weaknesses. One, because KOT forces the expression of knowledge in terms of causation, it is more structured than expressing pieces of knowledge—proposals in Word, strategy road maps in PowerPoint, etc.—in open-ended expository English. Two, linkages between Knowledge Object Machines reinforce the cross-functionality of knowledge—KOMs started in operations and marketing might be just as useful to someone in finance or product development. Cross-functional use is an important feature of KM. And three, the rigor built into a KOM forces its creator to verify knowledge accuracy, reducing the chance of inaccurate information populating the knowledge base.

The one weakness KOT shares with any KM methodology is the unstated assumption that employees will indeed share their hard-earned wisdom so that others might follow the light shone. The context in which this methodology is used will be key. If workers find KOT a highly useful analytical tool that improves their productivity and effectiveness in everyday work, then they might freely post their KOMs to some global repository for others to access. If, on the other hand, employees are somehow bullied into learning the complexities of the methodology to create KOMs in the name of some grand knowledge management initiative, not only might the results fall short of expectations, but employees might hold back the full fruits of their labor unless the proper incentives are established that acknowledge the heavy lifting involved. KOT is a radically different way to approach understanding of business issues. Its potential effectiveness will not be understood or appreciated by everyone. Therefore, the knowledge creation (KOMs) and sharing impact will occur residually from those who discover how useful the methodology is as an analytical tool. If KOT becomes an indispensable business tool, knowledge will follow.

Chapter Takeaway

Organizations contemplating a knowledge management initiative should consider the following:

- Think of KM as a system to encourage information flow across the entire organization, keeping these broad principles in mind:

1. **Accessibility:** Is the information or knowledge available to anyone in the organization on demand? This speaks less to its physical location and more to its availability through the deployment of robust, easy-to-use search capabilities.
2. **Reuse:** The inherent value of knowledge is its applicability to many different contextual situations. Once created, knowledge can be leveraged elsewhere (for example, pieces of a strategy memo might be useful in a sales proposal). Although knowledge is difficult to measure with precision, workers can over time offer anecdotal information about productivity improvements (how their work is made easier) by having the ability to take advantage of trails blazed before them instead of having to re-create the wheel with completely new documents.
3. **Relevance:** A top-down gatekeeper approach in deciding what information or knowledge may or may not be useful is counterproductive and should be avoided. A ten-year-old sales performance sheet might be just what a manager is looking for in providing historical context for a new product or service idea. Employees are the best judge of what information or knowledge is relevant at any given time.
4. **Interaction:** Because important knowledge will not appear in some repository but will remain locked in the gray matter of its owner, collegial interaction amongst employees fostering the exchange of ideas should be an operational objective of any KM project. Some businesses are culturally attuned to this way of working (for example, the professional service consulting firms, whose stock in trade is ideas). At least one information technology research firm wants its analysts to document the time they spend speaking to the media because press relations is an important tactic to the company. Organizations similarly committed to idea exchange amongst employees as part of knowledge management efforts will encourage them to document the face or phone time spent with colleagues in these consultative events.

CHAPTER 9

CUSTOMERS AT ANY COST?

C ustomers are not intangible assets in the strict sense of the definition. They are not intangible like knowledge or intellectual property, which go unseen by those who attempt to manage them. Customers are quite tangible, making themselves seen and heard when they initiate a big purchase or make a shrill call center complaint. Neither are customers under the control and ownership of the organization, a fact made all too real every time they walk across the street to the competitor.

Customers fail the definition of what an intangible asset is. Yet no business today would argue that, from a rhetorical and perceptual perspective, customers are not indeed assets worth managing for value. Certainly some equity investors assess who a company is doing business with as well as the strength of those customer relationships—independent of revenue or profit margin—as an important asset in the collection of other intangible assets, providing indications of the company's future growth potential. The valuation jocks will price customer lists in mergers and acquisitions, too. In acknowledgment of the idea that customers are assets, they are sometimes referred to as "relational capital."

Taking some license to include techniques in the management of customers as one category of intangible asset is not too radical if you think about it; performance of this asset is an affirmation of sound manage-

ment of all other intangibles in the enterprise portfolio. How the customer behaves in the marketplace is the cold verdict rendered about the
business competing for his or her business. Has knowledge management
as practiced in our organization given us the distribution of expertise
across the organization that allows us to manage customer relationships
consistently and with greater insight? Have the impacts from information technology delivered any additional capacity for us to better identify, win, and serve customers? Have our intellectual property and
innovation management strategies delivered products with real innovations faster than the competition?

While the income statement and balance sheet are the final voice in
deciding these questions, the customer, as any manager knows, has a
great say in how financial statements look at any given time. Therefore,
customers are an intangible asset, and advances in techniques to better
manage them have emerged, which deserve explication.

Including customers as a category of intangible assets is also warranted because a couple of attributes of their value that influence financial performance are only beginning to come into focus for many
companies. In all the literature that has been written about the customer, in all the advanced marketing techniques that have been prose-
lytized in how to sell to the customer, in all the empirical evidence that
has been amassed about customer behavior beginning with the Sears,
Roebuck and Co. catalog in the late 1800s to serve rural customers via
mail order and which gave rise to modern merchandising, we possess a
phenomenal amount of information. Customers are profiled by race,
ethnicity, hobby, religion, zip code, gender, age, job title, education, and
income. But what are businesses doing with this information? Are they
maximizing their customer management efforts with what the information is telling them? And does this information really tell businesses
all they need to know to maximize those efforts?

Two management approaches have emerged that are worth exploring for their viability in a comprehensive customer strategy.

One approach is measuring customer profitability, or lifetime value.
The concept is not new, but both its measurement and application in
customer strategy are new. The second technique is tied directly to
clearer thinking about human capital's influence on customer behav-

ior—the quantifiable link between employee and workforce strategies—and how it impacts the amount of business customers will conduct. While conceptually this is not new, many companies struggle with how to align human capital into effective customer strategy.

Customer profitability revolves around the fairly understood if not regularly tracked concepts of lifetime value and customer contribution margin. Some companies, particularly in a business-to-business context, know not only how much a customer has spent with it in the past but also the customer's net contribution to the bottom line after all variable costs to serve that customer are accounted for. Possession of this data influences decision making in three categories of customer management. They are:

1. **Support:** Companies that understand the profitability segments into which customers fall can differentiate levels of service in alignment with those segments. High-profit customers receive relatively more support and service investment than less-profitable customers.
2. **Retention and loyalty:** Companies that understand profitability segments can make more informed decisions as to which customers it is a priority for the organization to retain, lest they go elsewhere. As dandy as it would be to attempt to retain all customers, resource scarcity in competitive markets suggests a more surgical approach.
3. **Growth:** In the mix of highly profitable and negligibly profitable categories is a population of customers who, under the right incentives, might move into a more profitable category. They are found somewhere in the middle of the spectrum from worst to best, and knowing who they are is the first step to their migration into a higher value category.

The relentless pressure on company profit margins in the face of much faster communication flows, new supply chain arrangements, and the ability of consumers to price compare as never before, coupled with the result that corporations have limited pricing power over their products and services, argues for a far deeper understanding of customer contribution to profitability. Figure 9.1 depicts the value proposition of this approach.

So what is intangible about customers that new management trends and technologies can make more tangible? Many businesses manage customers as if they all present the same universal profitability impact when this is clearly not the case. Also, the causal linkages between human capital strategy and customer behavior have been informed mostly by guesswork, hunches, and some qualitative analysis—until now.

New methodologies have emerged that provide businesses analytically rigorous ways to understand how a company's employees and the policies and procedures that guide them have a direct bearing on a customer's propensity to do business with it. A deeper understanding of these dimensions and the commitment to refining business practices in response to the customer realities they reveal wrings out the mystery and intangibility associated with ignoring them. If you can't manage what you can't measure, certainly you can't measure what is ignored or overlooked.

Drawing customers into this kind of management focus might also have implications for investors. As mentioned, customer acquisition activity is an important trend investors will include in investment decision making. It is a barometer of management effectiveness. Yet Geoffrey Moore, noted consultant and author of *Crossing the Chasm*, asserts in a foreword to the book *One to One, B2B*, by Don Peppers and Martha

Figure 9.1

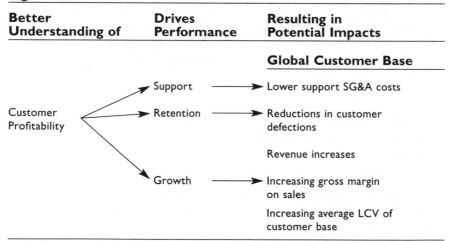

Better Understanding of	Drives Performance	Resulting in Potential Impacts
		Global Customer Base
	Support	Lower support SG&A costs
Customer Profitability	Retention	Reductions in customer defections
		Revenue increases
	Growth	Increasing gross margin on sales
		Increasing average LCV of customer base

Rogers, that investor behavior in response to company customer management practices swings wildly from overexuberance to irrational pessimism. Assuming that a company has successfully retained customers, investors will overvalue the actual value of the customer base by investing too heavily. This causes the business to go on an acquisition binge because, no matter the cost to acquire each new customer, the act of reeling them in as if albacore in a fishing net bids the stock price up even further. This is what investors want!

Then when companies cannot sustain the relationship with customers after they have been acquired, the zeitgeist turns overly pessimistic, investors sell off their positions, and companies respond with the sudden desire to retain existing customers because they are escaping from the nets and diving back into the deep blue sea. The company feels compelled to halt investor defections by halting customer defections. And so the situation oscillates from one extreme to the other—companies chasing customers, investors chasing customer growth, companies chasing fleeing customers, investors following fleeing customers.

Could a more insightful and even-handed approach to customer management leaven this market neurosis? Perhaps an approach that acknowledges that for many companies—with the possible exception of start-ups—customer acquisition simply for the sake of acquisition and market share is not a winning strategy.

Hey, Customer—What Have You Done for Me Today?

This is a question companies will rarely articulate publicly, but behind the curtain this attitude is finding increasing acceptability as it runs right over the received and unquestioned wisdom of a generation of executives who believe the customer is always right and we should win customers at almost any cost. Market share is losing much of its currency in companies that recognize the need for a more nuanced approach to boosting revenues and profits. It's as important to increase the amount of business done with existing profitable customers as it is to steal them from competitors.

Before we get into the core of this chapter, note that in the sidebar is a review of how to calculate contribution margin and lifetime customer value (LCV). These are easy but important concepts to understand in the context of measuring customer profitability.

UNDERSTANDING CUSTOMER PROFITABILITY[1]

Lifetime customer value (LCV) is a performance measure at the root of a strategy to allocate internal resources more efficiently.

Let's consider an apparel retailer whose customers Joe and Sally buy the same dollar value of merchandise during one year. Even though sales are equal, upon further exploration the company finds their lifetime values to be quite different. Why?

First, figure out the gross profit for each customer's purchases. Then divide gross profit by sales to arrive at the gross profit margin percentage. Gross profit margin percentage is a good indicator that can help you determine which customers will be the most profitable. Gross profit margin percentage may change over time, but for our purposes it remains constant.

The company reviews transaction data and learns that in four quarters, its gross profit on Joe's apparel purchases is as follows: $60 on $200 in sales; $15 on $50 in sales; $45 on $150 in sales; and $30 on $100 in sales. Obviously, different apparel products carry different margins. In this case, gross profit is $150 on total sales of $500. This represents a profit margin of 30 percent.

Sally's transactions look like this: $80 on $200; $20 on $50; $60 on $150; and $40 on $100. Sally has also bought $500 from the retailer, but her LCV is based on a profit margin of 40 percent.

To calculate LCV, we need to determine Joe's and Sally's contribution margin (CM), defined here as gross profit on sales minus variable costs. The variable costs are all those incurred in having Joe and Sally buy from this retailer. We'll assume $10 variable costs per quarter for both Joe and Sally. Sally's CM for the year is: $80 - 10 = 70$; $20 - 10 = 10$; $60 - 10 = 50$; and $40 - 10 = 30$. Joe's CM is equally simple.

LCV is then calculated by determining the net present value (NPV) of the CM for each economic quarter and adding those values. We use the NPV calculation—which Excel does on the fly—to take into account the cost of capital as well as inflation. NPV is simply the CM × NPV factor. Using a standard search engine like Google, you can find several websites that feature a table for calculating the NPV factor. The table will provide the proper NPV factor depending upon the time period and the discount rate, which in our example is 4 percent over four quarters.

In period 1, Sally's NPV is 70. There is no discount in the first time period. In period 2, the NPV is 10 × 0.925 (the NPV factor for period 2 at a discount rate of 4 percent). In period 3, it is 50 × 0.890. In period 4, it is 30 × 0.855. We arrive at an LCV of $149.40 when we add up the four NPV calculations. If the retailer's relationship with Sally is ten years, the managers could calculate an LCV over forty quarters to get a better look at the long-term value of Sally's business.

Using the same process, it is easy to calculate Joe's LCV.

Consider these issues when calculating LCV:

• Measuring LCV from top-line revenues offers little value. A big mistake companies made during the dot-com boom was calculating LCV from top-line sales figures. For LCV to offer insight into the most profitable customers, managers must first calculate the contribution margin. In its purest definition, the contribution margin equals sales minus variable costs. This phenomenon was especially prevalent during the height of the Internet craze, when top-line growth drove companies' stock prices. But contribution margin is what really drives profits, and profits are really what drives market value.

• Calculating LCV from top-line sales may skew the data. Someone who buys $1,000 of goods in a year might have a lower LCV than someone who buys half of that if there's a lower-margin product mix purchased by the higher-revenue customer.

• A higher gross profit margin percentage is a good early
indicator of which customers are most profitable, but it's not
definitive. You might have a situation in which the customer with
the lower-margin percentage has the higher LCV because some
of the variable costs—acquisition, retention, and customer
service—surrounding the purchases may be lower than those of
the customer with the higher-margin percentage.
• LCV starts with rich data. Accurate lifetime value calculations
demand detailed data sets that identify the costs associated with
a customer. As rigorous as they are to track, capturing
acquisition costs as well as ongoing retention, marketing, support,
and customer-care costs is a prerequisite to accurate
measurement.
• Understanding the discount rate reinforces the power of LCV.
When used in conjunction with a net present value table—which
calculates today's value of future cash flows—the discount rate is
the cost of capital or the opportunity cost of investing in one
project versus another. The rate is less important than the idea
that LCV represents a new way of investing in customers as an
asset. A company that scores its customers might devote more
time and spend more marketing money on those with a higher
LCV. Managers make more productive use of labor and capital by
investing in customers who represent higher profit potential.

There is an old joke in the computer industry reflecting this attitudinal shift that goes like this. The Acme Computer Company sells a PC
to a customer, and suddenly the company is inundated with calls from
the customer ranging from trivial but time-consuming tech support
questions to complaints that he paid more for his machine than his bud-
dies paid for theirs. Furthermore, he doesn't like the color. Analyzing
call center logs and doing some rough activity-based costing calculations, Acme realizes that the cost to service this customer is far above
average, and the profit margin on this sale is low and moving in the negative direction because each additional customer service call costs the

CUSTOMERS AT ANY COST?   *197*

organization between \$10 and \$15. At a loss to do anything to satisfy this nag, one customer strategy executive says, "Let's buy him a Dell."

While the details of this story might be slightly apocryphal, the ideas behind it are not. Some customers are worth having and devoting the internal resources to, and others aren't. While most customers are not so noxious or unprofitable that they should be consciously gotten rid of, companies are increasingly aware of the need to know who its most profitable as well as its most "growable" customers are in the belief that future profitability is achieved from a "share of customer metric," which tracks how much that person buys over time with the goal being that customer's continuous patronage. In this extreme example, a PC company pays to rid itself of the long-term unprofitability of a particular customer, surmising that the up-front cost is small relative to the future costs it is likely to incur over time keeping this individual as a customer.

Profitability Scoring Can Reduce Customer Support Costs

Hints of heightened sensitivity to the need to align internal resources with customer classes began to emerge in call center operations several years ago. Once again, the financial services industry proves itself to be the know-it-all kid who sits in front of the class, hand constantly raised because he has all the answers.

In possession of very granular customer profile information, financial services companies match up customers by score with classes of reps working in the call center. Caller ID technology at the call center plant would tell the company who was contacting the organization. Rules engines would route the call to particular employees depending on the customer value score assigned by the company. Helen Hotshot, one of the most experienced and polished reps on the staff, would handle calls from Flush Frank, who had \$2.5 million in assets with the company and a propensity over five years to increase the dollar volume of assets held by the company. Novice Ned would field calls from Johnny Gypo, who had \$10,000 in a money market fund and hadn't invested a dime in two years.

The idea is obvious. Give your best customers the best resources you have. The customer's profitability score justifies this alignment.

This kind of scenario has grown quite common in the financial services industry, and scoring profiles will affect everything from whether an overdraft charge is waived to the interest received on a credit card. One bank sends to branch managers every morning a report depicting which customers bounced checks the previous night and the penalty assessed. Historically, the branch manager relied upon tribal knowledge about customers—nice person, next-door neighbor, etc.—to decide whether to enforce the penalty. Now the bank scores customers along a profitability profile, and the results of that scoring appear in the overdraft report. The decision to enforce the penalty has not been automated—it is still the manager's judgment call and not a rules engine that determines the decision. But the guidance now is to waive overdraft penalties from higher-scoring customers and enforce them with lower-scoring customers. Enforcing overdraft penalties accomplishes two goals. It demonstrates to good customers an appreciation for their banking business in a vivid manner far beyond rhetoric like the occasional thank-you. With lower-scoring customers, the policy has the added effect of actually raising their profitability score, however slightly. Bank overdraft charges are stiff and a high-margin business in light of the actual cost the bank incurs to cover the bounced check.

Frequent-flier miles have been a kind of proxy for this thinking; better customers—those who fly a lot with an airline—get perks while others don't. Yet even this way of thinking has taken on new shades. Delta Air Lines announced a change to its frequent-flier miles program in which customers paying the full fare get more miles than someone who bought a ticket on Expedia for 25 percent the cost flying to the same destination.[2] Again, we see better alignment between what value the customer has demonstrated to the organization with the internal resources supporting the service given to the customer. Delta's policy change makes so much sense, we have to wonder why it took so long to be implemented. And where are the other carriers?

Companies terrified of a war of attrition with unprofitable customers—the idea of losing any customer is unthinkable!—should talk to Weyerhaeuser's door manufacturing unit in Wisconsin. Before the

Internet, it had no idea which product distributors were contributing to the company's bottom line. Customer-ranking software took care of that. It wasn't long after implementation that the company jettisoned half its customers. Blasphemous on the face of things. However, in one year it doubled its total sales of doors to 800,000.[3] This is the precise value proposition that proponents of customer scoring argue is possible—the elimination of customers contributing little or nothing to company profitability and the addition of redirected and focused energy toward customers with relatively higher profitability and high potential future value.

Some industries have engaged in customer profitability profiling but haven't thought of their efforts in these terms. Consider the health insurer who uses actuarial science to determine the risks of insuring a company. It's a fairly low-risk occupation for exposure to injuries, yet actuarial science says people will inevitably incur diseases, some fatal, as well as injuries. The carrier actually has two customers: the employer who foots most of the premium bill and the employees who collectively make up the company. It will analyze the risky business in which employees are involved—for example, smoking, alcohol use, a sedentary lifestyle—and implement tactics to confront these controllable medical exposures head-on.

To the carrier, this is simply risk reduction and good insurance operations practice. What the carrier is really saying is that it has a class of unprofitable customers it is interested in moving into a more profitable segment. Education and wellness programs might be the path to get them there. The insurer's task is complicated by the fact that law prevents it from cherry-picking only the more desirable employees at a company to insure, yet the levers at work are unmistakable.

As a last example, let's do a thought experiment that was inspired by a stay at a Seattle-area Holiday Inn in the early fall of 2003.

Apparently, Holiday Inn is losing substantial money from guests stealing the towels emblazoned with the company logo. Sitting innocuously on the bathroom counter in my room was a plastic placard with an artfully constructed message from management that simultaneously attempted to avoid confrontation and convey a tone of friendliness yet without compromising the seriousness of an issue it needed to face head-on. The gist of the note was that guests loved the towels, and if I loved them so much that I considered tucking one in my luggage upon departure, Holiday Inn would say, "Go right ahead. You are welcome to them." However, my total room charge would reflect the additional cost of the towels. The towels are not free. Now, I do not know for sure if Holiday Inn is bluffing or if it would follow through on its warning. I must assume the company is serious. How might it contend with a real cost problem in the context of profitability profiling?

The hotel industry has pretty rich data about who its customers are and how frequently they stay at its establishments. It would not pose a significant challenge to Holiday Inn were it to build customer profitability scores that took into account such dimensions as a customer's overall revenue, frequency of paying retail or corporate rates as opposed to using Priceline, and amount of incidental income generated (does the customer ransack the outrageously priced minibar, or does he hit the 7-Eleven before check-in to stock up on snacks?).

Highest LCV customers might get a complete pass in the Case of the Purloined Terry Cloth. The company could reason that the cost of towel replacement is minimal compared to the margins the customer is generating in the course of a year. The second highest class might get a pass for the first or second incident, but if it turns out the guest is a terry cloth kleptomaniac, a carefully worded letter might be in order. Holiday Inn would have to judge exactly how many classes of customer profitability make sense. But once the customer tranches are built, it could begin differentiated, nuanced problem management informed by where a customer falls in the spectrum from best to worst. Alas, I would certainly find myself subjected to room charges had I surreptitiously snuck one of the towels into my luggage, given that I have absolutely no brand loyalty to any hotel chain and simply seek two-and-a-half star or better quality when routinely using Priceline to make lodging arrangements. Holiday Inn has probably never heard of me. I certainly cannot remember the last time I stayed in one until that trip.

The large assumption undergirding a more sophisticated approach to customer management for Holiday Inn is the argument that a scorched-earth approach to its defensible policy of charging guests for boosting its towels might cause more problems than it solves. Customers loyal to the Holiday Inn name might take great offense at the policy, with the company facing the risk of losing them even though it is within its rights to reduce this substantial operating cost. (No guest would rationalize his right to lift a TV set out of a property.) Yet a differentiated approach to dealing with this problem can succeed only in possession of clean data that drill down into contribution margin and lifetime customer value attributes of suspected thieves.

Out of this exercise emerges a well-defined portrait of customer profitability performance from which the appropriate policy is built. Managers who reject the idea of a differentiated response to customers based upon their profitability classification must then believe that the only thing subject to customization are the products and services they offer, as is the case in many industries today, but not the internal resources allocated to the very customers being offered these customized products and services.

Profitability Scoring and the Interplay with Retention and Loyalty

The Holiday Inn thought exercise was presented in the context for the company to establish a set of differentiated responses to a customer support problem—towel theft. It was pointed out that there are elements of loyalty and retention built into the issue as well. How will customers respond to the deftly crafted accusations of theft? Customer profitability assessment argues that Holiday Inn should be concerned with the answer for only a percentage of its customer population. For guests (such as myself) who exhibit a very low or nonexistent profitability score, the company would charge their credit card had they taken any towels. For highly profitable, long-standing customers, an entirely different response is warranted because the company should care deeply whether those customers decide to end the relationship over Holiday Inn's risky yet justifiable decision to seek compensation for the theft of towels—retention.

Customer profitability assessment is not just about service and support cost savings through differentiated treatment brought about by a better understanding of what customers contribute to the bottom line. It also informs how an organization retains its best customers. In the case of Holiday Inn, retention is sought through a conscious decision not to require compensation for the theft of towels. It just might not be worth it.

This idea of loyalty and retention is as old as the village shopkeeper giving the customer merchandise on account because he knows the buyer will make good on the purchase and he wants to keep the customer happy. Or as old as a friendly bartender buying the customer an occasional beer because she knows that the customer has patronized her establishment for years. In both cases, the owner is making resource allocation decisions based on knowledge about customer contribution margin, as unscientific as that calculation is. Using tribal knowledge as the basis to make tactical decisions about customer management is fine in these small market situations but does not scale well when the shop is Safeway and the restaurant is the Olive Garden or the Cheesecake Factory. A more consistent, disciplined approach is necessary.

Frederick Reichheld's 1996 book *The Loyalty Effect* was a groundbreaking work because it recast loyalty from a foggy intangible element in the customer profile to a hard, economic driver of enterprise financial performance. He removed the intangibility surrounding loyalty by demonstrating convincingly that the most loyal customers deliver the largest percentage of profitability to an organization. This insight contributed to a profound shift in our understanding of what elements of the customer relationship drive financial performance and argued that companies were required to think about customer management functions with a much higher degree of sophistication than had been previously directed toward the subject.

Reichheld's bottom line is that loyal consumers tend to make larger transactions, buy products at higher price points, and buy more often. As their familiarity and satisfaction with a particular company grow, they refer more new customers, respond more readily to cross-selling offers, and cost less to support. Retaining customers clearly has a significant impact on a company's revenue and cost structures, and so loyalty amongst its customer population when possible emerges as a key strategic marketing goal of the organization and is not seen as just some residual benefit of a customer's satisfaction with products and services. Figure 9.2 reflects this.

Implementing tactics to drive loyalty and retention upon the foundation of customer profitability and LCV carries risk because the approach succeeds only when incremental loyalty is greater than defections from the new policy. Consider the following thought experiment.

What if a supermarket chain surveyed its customers and learned that long waits in line were the number one problem? The supermarket could load every lane with cashiers to relieve congestion, but even then the waits would still be quite long on weekends, when Mom and Dad are doing the family shopping, complete with screaming savages in tow. What if the survey also revealed that customer loyalty was at risk if the chain could not alleviate long waits at checkout?

Figure 9.2

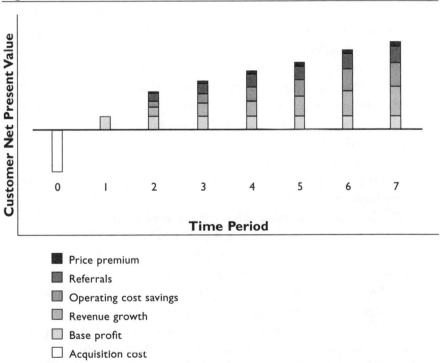

I always thought grocery stores organized customer service in a completely counterintuitive way. Speedy checkout is rewarded to customers with the fewest goods for purchase. The express lanes are devoted to customers holding fifteen or ten items or fewer. Now some of these customers might have high lifetime value because they are regular shoppers, but others are not. They could be just visiting relatives or vacationing, or perhaps they are patrons of another store but necessity required them to visit this particular supermarket.

The chain decides to test a new way to organize internal resources in order to drive loyalty. The supermarket will now devote a majority of its checkout lane capacity at busy times to customers having the highest lifetime value to the chain, regardless of the number of items being purchased. All others will be directed toward the remaining lanes, which most likely will require a longer wait. The first issue that needs to be confronted is how supermarkets can know who their most valuable customers are.

It turns out that a pure contribution margin calculation might be impossible because the supermarket has no reliable way to roll up the variable costs associated with each customer.[4] Even if it did, the variable costs to service its entire customer base might not differ greatly. However, the chain can capture a rough proxy of contribution margin by measuring aggregate revenue per customer. This is easily accomplished with customers who are members of certain card-based discount or loyalty programs that some chains have instituted. Customer profitability assessment must begin by linking what products are bought by what customer, and this is now accomplished with a card-based system. The chain knows both.

So the chain implements this program in which customers wielding a loyalty card are directed to a dedicated checkout lane. What happens when best customer #1, buying only a box of laundry detergent, is stuck in the premier lane behind best customer #2, the Waltons, buying for John Boy, Jim Bob, and the rest of clan for the next month?

Technology is the answer. Some restaurant chains have been using portable point-of-sale systems for years. The waiter can run credit cards or make change right at the customer's table using a handheld cash register. Why couldn't a supermarket employ a couple of roving cashiers to handle this anomaly? Cost? Well, the supermarket will have to determine if additional labor and capital are required to satisfy the loyalty imperative made real in its customer survey. Remember, this thought experiment assumes that wait time in the checkout line is a big deal to customers.

Realigning internal resources with customer profitability profiles might not always mean cost reductions when the goal is retention. In this case, costs will go up. Yet the incremental cost to execute the tactic might be far lower than the benefits captured over time. Is it worth it? The chain will have to decide this as it weighs the incremental cost of measurably better service against the opportunity cost of lost customers if the survey is accurate in suggesting patrons might find another supermarket if the checkout problem is not resolved.

The good news is that if time savings in the checkout line is an important feature for the customer, as important as selection, price, hours of operation, etc., some customers who are not card-carrying "best customers" might be induced to join the loyalty program when they witness how much faster checkout moves as a result of this new store policy. The next question might be, what if everyone joined the loyalty program to avoid long lines? This is not likely to happen, but if it did, the supermarket ought to count its lucky stars because a customer profitability strategy has just migrated a huge population of customers from occasional to loyal. (More on growth strategy in the next section.) Or the customers were loyal but the store had no way of knowing this because the customers did not bother to sign up for the loyalty card. The store should not underestimate the value of turning unknown loyal customers into known loyal customers, one of the most obvious benefits of this customer migration. Possessing this knowledge removes some of the intangibility of customer assets as the chain gains clarity into their behavior and financial performance. As stated before, many companies have no idea who their customers are—and clearly, the beginning of any refined customer strategy requires that they do.

In this example, a supermarket chain reallocates internal resources to improve loyalty amongst its best customers while migrating unknown or marginally loyal customers into a more loyal category. What happens if marginally loyal or infrequent customers defect? Again, only empirical evidence from the results of the policy will tell the supermarket if the benefits outweighed the costs. They might not. The store must assume this risk, however, if it is committed to a strategy that acknowledges the need for better service for the customers who bring home the bulk of its financial performance. Theory is nice, but real-world results are better, and there is no way to validate the approach until it is launched.

Customer Profitability Scoring Drives Growth

Progressive Casualty Insurance Company runs TV ads communicating a competitive quote value proposition. The company's agents will notify customers if competing carriers' rates are lower for comparable types and sizes of coverage. Customers love it, and Progressive successfully executes its profitability strategy, the substance of which says that if the customer is going to buy on price alone, he or she is likely not a "growable" customer and might actually cost more on a lifetime value basis over the long run. This tactic is an effective way of finding out who is part of the growth-potential population.[5]

Purposely and consciously introducing a new risk of actually losing some customers on top of all the other risks companies already face just being in business seems very gutsy and, to some, even loony. But the tactic makes perfect sense when understood in the context of using customer value profiles to determine which customers companies should invest in for future growth and which not to. Over time, the carrier will be able to determine whether higher lifetime value customers equate to a better loss experience for the carrier.

A key element of a customer's lifetime value in the insurance industry is the rate and extent of claims the carrier incurs. Insurance, ironically, might be the only industry in which great customers do not use the company product. Is it possible that higher growth potential or higher-margin customers are a better risk? The law of large numbers says probably not, but if a carrier like Progressive is addressing the marketplace in terms of lifetime value and growth potential, the causality with loss experience will be interesting for it to tabulate.

This growth potential attribute, closely linked to loyalty and retention, is referred to in industry lingo as growability. It's a lousy word, but it has gotten traction as a way to explain how companies attempt to shift a customer cohort from a lower lifetime value to a higher one, so growth essentially is referring to the potential to grow the financial depth of the relationship with the customer. The customer profitability assessment imperative doesn't argue that there are just two cohorts, highly profitable and marginally profitable, but that there exists a vast middle range of customers presenting solid if not spectacular profitability. The challenge is for the organization to figure out effective ways to migrate some of this tranche to one with higher profitability, assuming it can offer real value to the customer poised to become part of the new cohort. Some companies will view loyalty and retention in terms of preventing customer defection. Customer growth, on the other hand, actively pursues additional business from the customer.

Putnam Investments, a Boston-based mutual fund company with $270 billion in assets, responded to explosive growth in the mutual fund industry in 2000 and 2001 with investment in customer relationship management applications in sales for automation and marketing.[6] As a load mutual fund company, Putnam sells its financial products only through financial professionals (advisers, banks, and brokers). It makes no sales directly to investors. To cover its customers, Putnam employs both salespeople in the field as well as dedicated Boston-area phone-based sales and service personnel.

The old model consisted of sales reps personally visiting sales partners, but the company saw that this business development model would collapse under the sheer weight of increases in the number of advisers it started relationships with as well as increases in the sale of its financial products. There was no other way to scale operations unless aspects of sales and marketing were automated. The company desired to allocate internal resources more efficiently through scoring its sales partners by how much business each conducted with the company. The data that sales force automation and marketing automation applications captured allowed Putnam to conduct customer profitability assessments, out of which it could decide the most appropriate channels through which it could communicate and support its sales intermediaries. Channels include visits on-site to a partner's office, a call center, the Web, and snail mail.

Not only could visibility into customer profitability allow Putnam to allocate internal resources more efficiently, but the fund company could begin thinking about ways in which a lower dollar-value sales partner segment might move into a more valuable segment. As it happened, the company launched a college savings mutual fund with an attractive tax deferral feature. The company closely watched sales partner interest in this product because it reasoned that partners who sold large numbers of this financial product to the end user seeking help in financing a son's or daughter's college education might be interested in selling the company's portfolio of equity and bond funds. The success or failure of a new product launch gives the company that bothers to score customer profitability some signals about lower-scoring customers' propensity to migrate to a higher profitability cohort if the organization offers something of real value.

Delta Hotels, a Toronto-based company with thirty-seven properties across Canada, built a master repository consisting of customer purchase and profitability profiles that integrated easily with its central reservation system—the cardiovascular system of the hotel industry.[7] Burrowing into large volumes of transaction data, Delta scored its best customers into several subclasses:

- Green: Those who might want to participate in a Delta loyalty program but are not in one at the time.
- Gold: Those who stay five times in a calendar year.
- Platinum: Those who stay fifteen or more times in a calendar year.

Delta created a direct mail campaign establishing a base population, defined as anyone in the Green class who had stayed with the hotel chain at least twice in one year, surmising that a person who lodged with Delta at least two times a year might be willing to join its loyal customer program. In that campaign, it invited Green customers to stay with them three more times in a five-month period to bump them to Gold. Then Delta invited Gold members to stay three more times to bump them to Platinum. Customers taking advantage of the offer would be bumped to the next level, receiving all the benefits that go with a move into the new class. For each cohort, Delta offered additional benefits as incentives to encourage migration. The result was that Delta upgraded about 9,000 customers into Gold from Green out of 138,000 in that class—a bump of 2,000 more than it had projected.

Could Putnam or Delta Hotels arrive at the same results had neither approached their marketing and sales efforts with the knowledge of their customer profitability scores? Technically, yes. But the whole point of their efforts was to turn good customers into better ones, not to win new ones. Winning new customers could have easily been the theme of the campaigns—particularly in the case of Delta—were both organizations completely blind to the contributions its customer base was making to the bottom line. Whether the campaigns succeeded or failed, using profitability assessments injects clarity and focus into marketing and sales efforts when the organization acknowledges that getting customers to do more business is as important as, if not more so than, acquiring new ones.

B2C Versus B2B

It should be clear from the Delta Hotels example that the customer profitability imperative does not mean that each individual customer will receive a unique internal resource treatment but, rather, that customers will be grouped into cohort classes with each group receiving the resource allocation the business decides is appropriate based upon the profitability of each of those classes. Therefore, a company with 100,000 customers it knows by name and for which it has assigned a contribution margin and lifetime value score can discern profitability patterns that serve as the starting point for the construction of cohort classes.

Software tapping into a data warehouse might show the organization that five thousand customers have a lifetime value of $1,500 and that, over a year, fifty thousand have an LCV of $950 a year, twenty-five thousand have an LCV of $700 a year, and twenty thousand have an LCV of $400 or less. Each customer will be labeled as a member of a cohort. The company might decide to call them Platinum, Gold, Silver, and Bronze cohorts, respectively. Differentiated support, service, and marketing and all the other internal activities that constitute customer management will flow from this cohort blueprint. The point is that a company can use statistical modeling to create customer cohorts when it has lots of customers whose names it knows, whose purchasing history it knows, and whose profitability it knows. It is not necessary to build a unique set of customer management tactics for every single customer.

This is not necessarily the case in the business-to-business arena. B2B markets contain a number of unique challenges the consumer market does not face.[8] While consumer companies contend with thousands if not millions of customers, many B2B players do business with far fewer. In the extreme, think of L.L. Bean or Williams-Sonoma versus Boeing, which has only a handful of airline customers. At first blush you would think that building profitability models for B2B companies would be less complex by virtue of the small population involved. Actually, the reverse is true.

B2B companies face amazingly complex political and organizational environments into which they sell. The nature of the complexity can be unique to each customer. Because customer companies have unique cultures and somewhat unique organizational structures, vendor organizations are faced with a hornet's nest of issues that have individualized answers: Who is authorized to buy? Who is our chief evangelist? Who has influence to stop our ability to build a successful relationship? Who is actively sabotaging our efforts in the customer organization? How does our value proposition fit with a change in strategic direction in the customer organization? How do we build momentum for a sale or an engagement win when a multiplicity of decision makers have a say?

The consumer is an individualized decision-making unit; companies are not.[9] The B2B customer environment does not lend itself to statistical modeling of broad trends in purchasing behavior out of which profitability cohorts can be built. Therefore, the customer profitability assessment exercise is much more customized to the unique circumstances of each customer in the vendor's orbit. For this reason, the customer profitability strategy in B2B environments provides potentially higher knowledge takeaway for those interested in the techniques around this approach to customer management.

A good example of managing customers around a profitability score in the business-to-business environment is introduced at the opening of the next chapter. From there, the concept of loyalty as a phenomenon that bears directly upon the intangible asset value of customers is explored in more detail.

Chapter Takeaway

- Customers fail many of the definitional tests of an intangible asset, yet they are an asset just the same in the eyes of most managers. Customers make or break companies.
- The ideas of lifetime customer value and contribution margin are not new concepts, yet a shift in attitude has drawn into prominence the idea of managing customers around these dimensions.
- Frederick Reichheld's *The Loyalty Effect* advanced our understanding of loyalty, that sustained relationship between business and customer, by demonstrating the economic implications of having a loyal customer base.
- Customer support, retention, and growth patterns can be influenced by a better understanding of the profit profile of each customer or cohort of customers that does business with an organization.

CHAPTER 10

PROFITABLE CUSTOMERS AND THE LOYALTY IMPERATIVE

Convergys is a huge Cincinnati-based billing, receivables management, and customer support outsourcing operation with $2 billion in revenue and forty-four thousand employees across the globe. Its customers include credit card companies, insurance carriers, and retail banks in the area of financial services; hardware and software companies in the technology sector; and wireless and wireline telecommunications carriers. There is a good chance that the call you make to your credit card or cell carrier's support center is fielded by a Convergys employee contracted by the vendor (although your vendor does not want you to know this).

Convergys came to a fundamental conclusion that it needed to reengineer its marketing and sales strategy in response to several realities:[1]

1. The differing lifetime values each Convergys customer represents require that Convergys prioritize its sales and marketing function to better align internal resources with profitability of its customer base.
2. Customer acquisition in and of itself is not necessarily as profitable as a customer growth strategy in which less time is spent on pure

acquisition and more on deepening the customer relationship with additional services it is well positioned to offer.

3. As a result of this strategic shift, the company realized that the operating principle for its sales force going forward would morph from finding customers for its products into finding products for its customers.[2]

This shift in thinking reinforces how valuable customers are in a competitive market because what the approach is saying is that it is easier to acquire new capabilities to sell to customers than it is to find new customers for existing capabilities.

Scoring for Value

In this context, Convergys constructed a kind of customer performance matrix, or a scorecard, which employed financial and nonfinancial measures to capture what the future value of its customers would be. This became the company's sacred text around which sales efforts would revolve. For Convergys, the contribution margin was important, but it was only one of many key performance indicators used to calculate customer value.

For instance, the company knew that calculating lifetime customer value—the net present value of future profits from a customer—should reflect not just the amount of business customers were giving currently and future business the customer was committing to giving but also the dollar value of additional business above and beyond that which was contractually obligated. The LCV of existing and contractually obligated future value it called actual LCV. The incremental dollar value of additional business it termed strategic LCV—that is, business the Convergys marketing and sales organization wins after the relationship is already under way.

Given the breadth of the company's service offerings, the customer might need a second or third service somewhere in the company, and it would be up to the sales organization to identify the opportunity, make a compelling pitch, and close the deal. The LCV matrix Convergys constructed was designed for use as a navigational aid for sales and marketing executives to win just that kind of new business.

Convergys thought of the issue this way: if one client is doing $20 million a year with Convergys, but realistically the most business that client will ever do is $25 million, is that client more or less valuable than a client doing $10 million in business but that Convergys believes could do $100 million? Both clients are important to Convergys, but which one would it want to apply more resources to? Deepening relationships by identifying those customers that presented the highest potential future value and reallocating internal resources to pursue those opportunities became a strategic principle because the company believed that chasing market share (new customers) alone would not guarantee future company profitability. How did Convergys know who presented a higher value? Because of the lifetime customer value matrix, as shown in Table 10.1.

This index analyzes seven important dimensions of the customer profile. A few items are more self-explanatory than others.

Table 10.1 Convergys Lifetime Customer Value Matrix*

Index	Measures	Weight
Average Revenue Score	Current and projected spending	15 percent
Revenue Change Score	Year-to-year actual spending	15 percent
Profitability Score	Customer contribution margin	20 percent
Current Relationship	Signed contract length Total years as a client	10 percent
Technology Entanglement	System integration Reporting	20 percent
Share of Client	Outsourcing potential	10 percent
Partnership	Level of contact Referenceable Future value	10 percent

* This was a second iteration of the original index created when Convergys embarked on this customer profitability strategy in 1998 and 1999. That original index is published in *One to One, B2B: Customer Development Strategies for the Business-to-Business World*, on p. 147 of the draft version of this text. This particular iteration of the index introduced contribution margin as a line item with a 20% weighting. The introduction of CM into the index is less important than the idea that the index is meant to be a living, breathing, flexible guide complementary to business goals and conditions, not a rigid set of rules. These revisions were provided to me by Convergys for a piece I wrote in *eCFO*, the defunct supplement to *CFO Magazine*, titled "Lifetime Customer Value: New Business Is Great, but Generally It's a Lot Cheaper to Hold on to Existing Customers" (September 15, 2001).

- **Average Revenue Score:** This dimension takes the average of a customer's revenue for the current year and projected revenue for the next year.
- **Revenue Change Score:** This dimension gives the difference between what the customer spent with the company last year versus this year. This dimension allows Convergys to see the rate of growth or decline, year to year.
- **Profitability Score:** This is the contribution margin, which is figured as the total present dollar value of the customer after all the variable costs associated with that relationship are accounted for, such as marketing, sales, service, and support costs.
- **Current Relationship:** This dimension measures the current level of commitment the customer has made.
- **Technology Entanglement:** Given the nature of Convergys's business—billing, receivables management, etc.—it is often necessary for the customer organization to integrate at a technology level with Convergys's IT infrastructure so that Convergys can provide seamless and uninterrupted service. The need for programming hooks to be written in between the operational software of Convergys and the customer creates both lock-in and a potentially high switching cost should the customer want to leave Convergys for a competitor. Higher technical integration makes it more difficult for the customer to simply forklift the outsourced service to another company. Technological lock-in and high switching costs constitute one of the most formidable components of IT industry business models. It makes perfect sense that Convergys should want to measure the extent of the lock-in with each customer because it differs by service utilized as well as by the amount and type of service a customer contracts for.
- **Share of Client:** What is the customer's total budget for services Convergys provides, such as contact center support? What percentage of the customer's budget is outsourced? Although Convergys had a difficult time capturing accurate data, understanding that a customer has outsourced only 30 percent of its total contact support needs means there is room to deepen the relationship if the sales force can make a compelling case that it is cost effective to outsource these activities to Convergys.

- **Partnership:** This dimension attempts to determine such phenomena as whether the client buys on price only, how high in the organization the salesperson's contacts are in the customer organization, and whether the customer would be a good reference.

You will notice that the first two dimensions are highlighted. Revenue does not lose its saliency in determining customer value even though it is not as accurate a measure of customer profitability as is contribution margin. Because revenue is quantifiable down to the penny, it comprises a significant weighting in calculating the entire LCV matrix for each customer. Coupled with contribution margin, these three quantifiable metrics represent half the weighting in determining customer LCV. The first iteration of the Convergys LCV did not include contribution margin, but it was added to the index later. The more subjective measures are given less weighting, yet they are nevertheless important because each conveys an attribute about the customer that informs sales and marketing strategy, attributes that were historically intangible and therefore unmanageable simply because the company didn't consider them.

Using this matrix, all customers are run through a scoring exercise and are ranked accordingly. A funny thing happened on the way to the scorer's table. Customers that ranked high based on revenue alone dropped, and customers that scored lower on revenue alone moved up. A technology company customer that ranked ninety-fourth on revenue moved to sixth because of its high change dimension and partnership score. A telecom company that ranked third on revenue alone fell to tenth when these additional attributes were added to the total score.

Drilling down below pure revenue into a number of objective and subjective dimensions redraws the customer value rankings and provides further insight into which customers require additional dedicated resources in an attempt to conduct more business with them. Even though a number of the metrics are subjective and open to interpretation, their very existence means that Convergys thinks about these customer attributes when calibrating its sales tactics and strategy when they hadn't been a part of the company's collective consciousness historically. At least some of the intangibility of customers as a key company asset is removed.

Realigning Resources

The resource realignment required to pull off this strategic shift in how Convergys addressed the marketplace was profound, and it hit the sales organization right where it lived. Some salespeople refused to embrace the new vision and left the company. For those who stayed on, working under a lifetime value-scoring regime would be very different. For one thing, the company lightened the customer load by as much as half for some salespeople in acknowledgment that more time—a hugely valuable internal resource—would be spent cultivating customers that were candidates for more business as opposed to chasing hot leads in the Rolodex. Salespeople also had to bone up to a much greater degree on the complete portfolio of Convergys services. There's no point building business with existing customers by selling them additional services if the sales force doesn't know what they are. Therefore, specialization shifted from knowledge of a couple products or services directed toward as many prospects as possible to deep knowledge of the company's entire portfolio directed at existing customers with whom salespeople were expected to capture more business. The demands on salespeople consisted of two dimensions: breadth of product and service expertise and depth of understanding of the customer's business.

Of course, compensation changed as well when this new strategy was implemented. One quarter of a salesperson's bonus was tied to growth in the customer's lifetime value index. The salesperson's bonus, however, was tied not just to increased sales from existing customers but also to an increase from other qualitative measures that constitute a lifetime customer value index.

Consider also the technology entanglement dimension. If a PC manufacturer has outsourced its tech support for a product line to Convergys, it is likely the manufacturer has exported all its customer profiles to Convergys so that a Convergys call center employee can best respond to the needs of a PC user calling in with questions. If a salesperson can deepen the relationship with the manufacturer so that other information stores are integrated with Convergys's IT infrastructure—say, winning tech support for an additional product line with all the data that go with it—technology entanglement increases, and so does the customer's lifetime value. The salesperson isn't going to spend his or her time simply trying to get the customer to provide more operational data as a way to increase technology entanglement and, therefore, boost the matrix score. Technology entanglement is not a stand-alone objective. There has to be a reason for the entanglement, and winning business in a new product line is it. However, under the new arrangement, although the salesperson is rewarded for the incremental revenue brought into the company, he or she is also rewarded for bumping the customer's score in the technology entanglement category. Incentives were reengineered to reward impacts to each dimension in the matrix, not just new revenue from a sales win.

Suitability

Are there businesses that by virtue of industry and business model are more naturally suited for a customer profitability assessment strategy? It's hard to conceive of the Coca-Cola Company calculating LCV of its customers even if it knew who they were. On the other hand, could knowing the lifetime value of customers that Coca-Cola is aware of (such as restaurants) appreciably change the way it would do business with them?

Geoffrey Moore and his business partner Paul Wiefels argue that companies fall into two broad domains: operations-centric and customer-centric.[3] Operations-centric businesses sell high-volume, low-complexity products and services. Examples include Charles Schwab, McDonald's, Coke, Exxon, tire stores, and local dry cleaners. Customer-centric businesses, on the other hand, sell high-margin, low-volume products and services. Examples of these include EDS, IBM, Boeing, General Electric, and Convergys. Customer-centric businesses predominant in business-to-business environments are characterized by complex products or services and consultative approaches to winning business. Operations-centric organizations focus on design, manufacturing, distribution, and marketing that can scale to the enormous volume of product and services consumed in the marketplace. Operations-centric businesses are essentially simple, standardized, and often sold on price.

Cast this way, it would appear that customer-centric types of industries are more suited to a customer profitability strategy. Yet some industries attempt to straddle both worlds. Airlines sell a low-complexity, high-volume service, yet loyalty programs attempt to boost the amount of business American and Northwest attempt to do with customers. Online businesses of all sorts that would at first glimpse seem operationally oriented (dealing in apparel, books, toys, and music, for example) might have significant opportunities in refining marketing and sales strategy were they to score customer profitability, which they can do given the fact that they automatically know who their customers are the first time they buy.

Does a shift in customer strategy informed by profitability offer any sustainable financial performance improvement to the company that embraces it? Convergys saw a 16 percent bump in operating income in the first quarter of 2001, when the program was fully launched and the company was confident enough to say a substantial portion of that increase could be causally linked directly to the new strategy. Yet revenues for 2002 declined 1 percent from the previous year, and revenue is revenue whether it comes from a new customer or from an existing one.[4] A customer profitability approach is no magic bullet for recession.

Implementing this approach at the expense of new customer acquisition might also run the risk of the company relying on too few customers for the bulk of its business. At the time, Convergys generated nearly 40 percent of its revenue from outsourcing services for three customers: AT&T Wireless, AT&T, and Sprint PCS.[5] Just like any other business, Convergys's financial performance is tied inextricably to the performance of its customers, although it is more pronounced here given the concentration of its customer base. Embracing a customer profitability strategy, however, is not meant to be an absolute trade-off between building upon existing relationships versus winning new customers. After all, there is very little customer growth if you don't have customers in the first place. Neither did Convergys lose sight of the need to bring in brand-new business. The company is very acquisition-minded.[6] It is not inconceivable for an organization to grow through acquisition and then throw its new customer base into the arms of a profitability scoring strategy so the company might obtain visibility into the possible future value of these newly obtained customers.

Customers are the living tissue of any company. If you don't have them, you cease to exist. This statement is fatuous only to the extent that businesses have a solid grasp of the future value of their customer base—and plenty do not. For many companies, their customers remain incorrigibly intangible because they do not or will not make the effort to remove some of the mystery around their value contribution. If there is any intangible asset (loosely defined) that begs for concreteness and tangibility, it is the one asset over which a company has little control and which sometimes controls it—the customer.

Challenges to Implementation

Understanding customer profitability for internal resource allocation does not mean that highly profitable customers receive good customer service and everyone else receives mediocre or worse customer service. Within a company's cost structure, its best customers receive great and exceptional customer service, but all customers must receive good customer service. Otherwise, the company risks alienating customers who are not necessarily the organization's most profitable but who are important to its financial performance nonetheless. What defines good versus great service might mean using industry norms and benchmarks as a guide in establishing that baseline.

A second challenge is acquiring the necessary information from which to continuously measure the profitability of customer cohorts. Table 10.2 outlines the information required.

It should not be surprising that this customer management technique has gained traction as an outgrowth of the almost crushing volumes of customer data available to businesses today coupled with the software to synthesize and analyze what the data mean. Information technology is not the reason why companies are better aligning internal resources with customer scoring exercises, but it docs invite contemplation of such

Table 10.2 Hierarchy of Information Needs for Capturing Customer Profitability*

Sales revenue per customer	Aligning internal resources with profitability profiles means knowing how much customers buy, which means knowing who your customer is.
Direct costs per transaction	What direct variable costs were incurred to win the transaction?
Indirect costs per transaction	What indirect costs were incurred (e.g., brochures, sales literature, samples)?
Lifetime value	Calculate the present dollar value of all profits delivered by a customer, including profits earned on referrals by the customer.
Share of customer	This dimension means knowing the lifetime value plus the potential value of future business a company could win were it in possession of a strategy to get it.

*Adapted from "Analytical CRM—a Worthwhile Investment?" Extraprise white paper (2002), p. 6.

an approach since rich data sets give organizations much deeper visibility into both buying patterns and the financial inputs required to support those customer transactions. Internal resource allocation alignment with customer profitability requires very granular data about specifically what the customer has bought and all the traceable, causally linked costs that went into that sale.

While big-box retailers, such as Target and Wal-Mart, might never reach a place in which they know every customer by name and know all the costs that went into each discrete sale, a growing number of businesses that have data linking specific product purchases with specific customers are scrutinizing this information and its relationship to the internal resource investments undertaken to cultivate these relationships like never before. Yet surprisingly, a sizable number of businesses that track sales do not track sales to whom.[7] Refined customer management cannot happen if this critical linkage is not made, which is why the emergence of customer scoring techniques is fertile ground.

Managing Loyalty as an Asset

Customer loyalty, the persistence and intensity of commitment to a product or service, is itself viewed as an intangible asset. More than one executive has boasted that the company has a loyal customer base, citing this as a reason for the company's vitality and assuming that, clearly, investors will consider the loyalty factor in the decision-making mix. Yet the analysis usually stops there.

As mentioned, it took the detailed work of Frederick Reichheld, a Bain & Company consultant, to explicate the hard economic implications of a loyal customer base, that loyalty as an intangible concept had quantifiable financial impacts. Loyal customers cost less to serve, tend to buy more over time, do not buy on price alone, and have proven themselves a good source of referrals. Loyalty is perceived as an asset within the larger domain of the customer asset that requires management no less than a financial or real-estate portfolio. Since the publication of Reichheld's book *The Loyalty Effect*, the race has been on to apply effort and resources to extract value out of this intangible phenomenon—in other words, to keep people loyal.

The loyalty of customers, and therefore high contribution margins, is a powerful asset because it is hard to achieve. Our jungle economy is chockablock with choices in everything from colleges to breakfast cereals. Vast consumer choices contribute to fickleness, an inclination to try something new, and the power of novelty to move customer segments from one competing product or service to the next. This is great for consumers but lousy for businesses hoping to win their business.

Arguably an alarming proxy for this phenomenon is the eroding power of brand loyalty in consumer packaged goods. The big guys are getting eaten alive by the private house labels, like Costco's Kirkland line. The quality is as good if not better, and the prices are demonstrably lower. Loyalty is not an asset requiring its depreciation on financial statements, but it might as well be because loyalty in some product categories is depreciating measurably, such as for Procter & Gamble,

Unilever, and Kraft. Wal-Mart's Ol' Roy dog food has surpassed Nestle's Purina as the biggest selling, for instance.[8]

Types of Loyalty

In the context of building a customer strategy around profitability, it is important to understand that loyalty comes in several flavors. For example, *synthetic* loyalty is the persistent relationship between customer and a business because the business offers inducements to stay. Frequent-flier miles are an obvious example. So is a buy ten, get one free card from your local espresso stand. Had the inducement not existed, would the customer stick around? Maybe. Synthetic loyalty is really just another way of competing on price packaged under another guise. Say your latte costs $2. If you buy ten and the eleventh is free, the unit cost is $1.82 ($20 ÷ 11). Price-based loyalty has value, but is it lasting?

Another type of synthetic loyalty is created when a customer is ready to bolt for a competitor and the business offers plenty of reasons to stay. This is the Mafia approach to loyalty management; make him an offer he can't refuse. Predictive analytics software has emerged to help businesses identify which customers are candidates for departure. Using sophisticated algorithms that parse hundreds of customer data points, this software is supposed to forecast the likelihood that a customer will flee so the business can enact some intervention to prevent the defection. SPSS claims that in using its software, one of its insurance customers predicted the departure of its automobile policyholders 60 percent of the time.[9]

A second kind of loyalty is the *lock-in* variety. Microsoft enjoys this kind. Loyalty is built because there is practically nowhere else to go for personal computer operating systems and productivity software. Local phone companies have historically enjoyed this kind of monopolistic lock-in. Monopoly is not the only kind of lock-in loyalty, however. Cellular phone companies have loyal customers because legally binding service contracts make them loyal: leave us before the contract is up and suffer financial penalties as well as potential legal ramifications, these contracts say. (Remember, service contracts are an intangible asset, and this is why.) The more competitive the marketplace, the longer the carrier seeks to lock in customers. Two-year contracts are increasingly common.

The most powerful loyalty is *organic*. Customers are loyal because they want to do business here—they get excellent products and services, helpful and knowledgeable customer service, and so on. You could argue that Apple fits into this category because of its fanatical user base, although lock-in and the related switching costs to migrate to Windows might be just as substantial as going the other way. But others abound. Amazon.com, L.L. Bean, Patagonia, Starbucks, Pepperidge Farm, and lots of others. Clearly, this is the most desirable kind of loyalty because it is genuine and arises out of a confluence of the creation of a number of other intangible assets, which collectively deliver loyal customers.

Satisfaction Is Not Loyalty

Another reason for loyalty's allure as an asset is that it is quantifiable and measurable. Customers are proven empirically either to be loyal or not. Contrast this with customer satisfaction, a squishy metric intensely followed by marketing people as an indication of product or service health. Customer satisfaction is often confused for loyalty when it clearly isn't, as there is no guarantee a happy customer will ever buy from a company again.

Customer satisfaction is captured through surveys and reflects attitudes about experiences in the recent past. Loyalty, conversely, captures what people do.[10] Customer satisfaction is backward-looking; loyalty is forward-looking. While taking the pulse of customers is important, satisfaction levels offer little probative value in determining loyalty and individual profitability.

Seeing the Linkage Between Loyalty and Lifetime Value

Given the increased consciousness of loyalty as an economic driver, how has clarity around the subject changed its management? It reaffirms the idea of including awareness of customer profitability into a comprehensive customer strategy, for one. High lifetime value customers are loyal customers, and it is persistence and intensity of commitment that drives LCV.

A deeper understanding of loyalty and its linkages to customer profitability also provokes managers into asking about the nature of the loyalty of its customer base. Is it synthetic, locked-in, or organic? Then managers should be able to answer with more clarity whether the cost associated with some kind of intervention to stem the tide of defections is really worth the effort. Within a company's most loyal cohort, what is the range from the highest to lowest LCV? How much more loyal are a company's highest lifetime value customers? In the end, is the synthetically loyal customer profitable for the organization? That is, would the organization give up too much to keep him or her? These questions are worth asking.

Customers and Human Capital

In all that we know about customers and how to serve them, what has remained a mystery is the direct linkage between how human capital management can influence customer behavior. How can innovations in the management of a company's workforce directly influence customer loyalty and customers' propensity to spend? The answer to this goes way beyond the obvious answer—friendly, helpful, and knowledgeable customer service employees. The question gets at the heart of managing people as an intangible asset class, given how primitive our understanding is of what strategic performance outcomes might occur to the business were this asset managed in a certain way.

Until recently, there has been little empirical evidence or causal data that have said that certain strategic impacts might happen if the organization were to manage its employees in a certain way. The Balanced Scorecard shed light on the causation between the management of people and strategic outcomes. Yet the causation is indirect. For many organizations, managing people has been fueled mostly by hunches and guesswork, which are frequently wrong.

Mercer Human Resource Consulting has developed a framework and set of tools for aligning human capital management with business strategy. A full analysis of this methodology is rolled out in Chapter 11, on human capital. Yet it is worth introducing the value of the approach here because the techniques add clarity into how human capital is deployed and managed for the greater management of customers.

Myths Behind the Employee-Customer Relationship

In making a case for its methodology, Mercer contends that its research blows out of the water popular misconceptions about employee behavior on customer satisfaction. One popular and seemingly obvious notion is that employee satisfaction and customer satisfaction are causally linked: happy employees equal happy customers. Mercer contends this clean causal linkage is not necessarily so for three reasons:[11]

1. Research indicates that employee satisfaction has little influence on job performance; happy employees may or may not do a good job day to day. Therefore, how does employee morale affect customer satisfaction?
2. The causation might be in the reverse; employee happiness does not influence customer happiness but rather the other way around.
3. Good business practices that have a positive effect on customer attitudes and behavior might have a similar effect on the employees surrounded and affected by these practices.

Mercer's point is that cause and effect with respect to employee attitudes and customer attitudes is more nuanced than conventional wisdom would have us believe. That's a keen insight, given that many businesses manage human capital dysfunctionally in the mistaken belief that if the company can keep employees pumped up, then sales are assured.

Mercer's contention is more refined. Its work has shown the following hypothesis to be true: employees who are knowledgeable about the company's products, services, and customers, who have the proper customer interaction skills (problem-solving and social skills), and who are in the right job can influence customer behavior positively.[12]

This is a careful parsing of words that on its face is little different from the original assertion: satisfied employees make for satisfied customers. What is different is the inclusion of the management system into which employees are placed. The inclusion of a broader management system in the equation is reflected in the idea that *knowledgeable* employees in the *proper job* can influence customer behavior. It's not enough that a satisfied employee makes for equally satisfied customers. It's that employees are placed into the proper human capital management system of processes and procedures that enhances the skills of employees, puts them into roles and responsibilities they are suited for, and supports them in their interactions with customers, thereby keeping up their morale.

This seems commonsensical to the extreme, but it is not. For Mercer, the centrality of the design of a proper management system into which human capital is placed is the cornerstone of its methodology. A company can hope to extract value out of its employees as the critical class of intangible asset only if the search for value is done within a well-designed system that fundamentally influences the performance of human capital.

The need to place human capital management in the context of a systemwide framework means that although people have been managed for years, it has not been optimal, and Mercer cites many examples to support this contention. Its research also reinforces the complementarity reality: although people can be managed as a discrete, stand-alone intangible asset, maximum value is realized through its interplay with other intangible assets. In this case, those other intangible assets are the elements of a management system in which people work. Again, this systemic approach to human capital management is covered at length in Chapter 11.

Driving Strategic, Customer-Oriented Outcomes

Mercer's methodology has been put to use in a number of business contexts. One situation clearly illustrates how an effective human capital strategy that considers people within a larger system improved customer relationships.

First Tennessee Bank is one of the fifty largest banks in the United States. Like many financial institutions, it possesses a highly focused, measurement-driven attitude toward customers and as a result tracks a number of dimensions constituting the customer profile, including retention figures, account size, and how much business the bank currently conducts with customers as a percentage of all financial services business each customer utilizes.[13] First Tennessee has also determined from market research that customer service quality is the foundation of its competitive position.[14] Because all important service quality turned on interactions between banking customers and its employees, the bank sought a much deeper understanding of the latter in order to maintain relationships with the former. Mercer contends that this desire showed First Tennessee as a far more forward-thinking company than many others, who would not bother to conduct rigorous analysis to determine such workforce impacts on customer behavior.

Using Mercer's statistical modeling tools, First Tennessee learned that branches with employees having the longest tenure at the bank were the highest performing in the organization in terms of retention, growth of premium accounts, net earnings, and market share.[15] Employees with deep knowledge of the company's products were measurably better equipped to drive customer satisfaction, the foundation of First Tennessee's competitive position.

In possession of this intelligence, the organization embarked on a human capital strategy that emphasized increasing retention of customer-facing employees who possessed not only knowledge of business in general but also the company-specific knowledge of its products and procedures that serve experienced employees well when dealing with the customers. First Tennessee estimated that increasing the years of service by only one year would boost revenue a total of $40 million through increases in revenue of 4 percent per existing customers and 2 percent in market share.[16] In other words, if First Tennessee could establish the proper human capital management system required to retain employees and increase their tenure, the company forecasted tangible and significant bottom-line results from the effort.

In order to refine its current human capital management system, First Tennessee returned to rigorous analysis with the aid of Mercer. Mining information across employee, financial, and customer data stores, Mercer learned that First Tennessee's human capital management system was not optimized to carry off this new goal. For one, as the bank expanded its offerings, it hired new employees who had business learning but not the company-specific knowledge needed to provide the best customer experience possible, which could only be obtained through years of service with the company. Because at the time of this analysis the labor market was tight, new hires were receiving top pay packages. An employee's lack of the company-specific knowledge valued so much by customers in their dealings with bank personnel was being rewarded as much as having that company-specific knowledge.[17] And at the end of the day, although compensation is not the only consideration in why people work where they do, it speaks volumes about what an organization values in its workforce. In First Tennessee's case, there was a fundamental misalignment between what management knew drove financial performance and what skills in its human capital it was rewarding.

The company reengineered its human capital management system to better align employee incentives with three goals in mind:

1. Establish a path for growth and advancement for high performers.
2. Include customer-facing employees in pay-for-performance compensation.
3. Invest more in training for employees.[18]

First-Order Linkages

For First Tennessee Bank, managing that intangible asset called customers effectively means managing its workforce more effectively. The linkage between one intangible asset and the other could never be clearer. While the issues in play and the tactics taken seem obvious and practical, they are obvious only to the extent that the company did the heavy lifting to determine with certainty that customer satisfaction was the fulcrum of its value proposition to the marketplace, that experienced, knowledgeable customer-facing employees drove that satisfaction, and that pieces of its human capital management system needed tweaking in order to support value extraction from that intangible asset.

As mentioned earlier in the book, while the Balanced Scorecard illustrates inferences of causality between people and strategic outcomes, it focuses on learning as the primary input from which human capital value is created, but then only indirectly. While learning and skills training are important in Mercer's methodology, this is only one component of a much broader and comprehensive human capital management system that influences employee performance. Mercer's approach makes a direct empirical link between human capital asset management within a holistic systemwide view and strategic outcomes. The ability to link human capital to strategic goals is new in our grab bag of intangible asset management techniques, which is why it is the focus of the next chapter.

Conclusions

Are managers provided any additional clarity into customer management in casting customers as a class of intangible asset? Probably not. Customers defy so many elements in the way intangible assets are defined that some would not consider their inclusion in the list, and they would have a good argument. Yet there are few managers today who would not claim that customers are assets in the broadest possible sense worth managing for value. So in the sense that customers are assets that bear little resemblance to physical assets, they get tossed into the intangible category. Suddenly, customers are relational capital.

Far more important than to what extent customers fit the definition of an intangible asset is what opportunities exist for their improved management? What unknowns surrounding this all-important asset exist that if better understood might provide value-creation opportunities for companies that have built relationships with them? What is intangible in our understanding of the customer today? It seems as if every dimension of the customer has been peered under and poked at. A hundred years of marketing and merchandising has delivered an endless stream of wisdom about customer behavior and how to manage customers along a number of dimensions, including race, age, gender, religion, affinity group, income bracket . . . the list goes on. For all our understanding of customers in the modern economy (since World War II), however, we are just learning about the implications of managing a customer's loyalty to a product or service as well as the cost structure the company assumes in that relationship. This is certainly fertile ground for further investigation.

If some readers choose not to conceive of customers as an intangible asset, keep in mind they are still very relevant to intangible asset management if for no other reason than this: lots of profitable customers that make a company successful are the result of great management of a number of intangible assets, such as information technology, intellectual property and innovation, brand, and the company culture. Think of customers as the exclamation point to an intangible asset management job well done. And it all begins with the one intangible asset that might confer a competitive advantage—human capital, the subject of the next chapter.

Chapter Takeaway

Companies that seek to better align internal resources with customers should consider the following:

- Childishly obvious though it is, companies must know who their customers are before contemplating this kind of strategy. It bears repeating because many who might benefit from such a strategy do not know.
- They should figure out what variable cost areas are candidates for closer reallocation to the realities of customer profitability: Customer service including the call center? Advertising?[19] The sales organization? Companies differ so much in their cost structures it is difficult to generalize, but a deep understanding of their variable cost structures is a necessary first step in executing this strategy because the idea is to shrink those costs for less-profitable customers.

- Industries whose variable costs across customers do not differ widely are not necessarily precluded from a profitability-resource alignment strategy. The reason for this is technology. For example, supermarkets are experimenting with a handheld device mounted on a shopping cart, which allows shoppers to scan in items as they are retrieved from the shelves. Customers pay at the cash register and then leave. The mounted device requires swiping a loyalty card so the merchant can gather purchasing habits and offer on-the-fly discounts. Those discounts can be easily tailored to a customer's loyalty score and LCV. This kind of technology solves some fundamental information problems for retailers—knowing who customers are and knowing their purchasing habits. These two data points are the foundation for any kind of targeted customer strategy.

- Because loyalty comes in many flavors, companies must understand what type of loyalty is driving customer behavior. The more artificial the loyalty of customers, the more difficult it is to implement a profitability alignment strategy. Consider the most spectacular example—the airline industry. Customer loyalty is predicated on the merchant giving away the service to such a degree that it is estimated that 10 percent of revenue-passenger miles—a measure of passenger traffic—is flown with redeemed frequent-flier miles. That represents $25 billion in lost revenue between 2000 and 2003.[20] If the freebies didn't exist, neither would the degree of customer loyalty. That's about as artificial as loyalty gets.

CHAPTER 11

MANAGING PEOPLE AS AN ASSET IS A CAPITAL IDEA

An organization's workforce is arguably the most important intangible asset in its portfolio. Without people, there are no other internally created intangibles. No IP, no knowledge, no innovation, no brand, and certainly no customers. As these intangible assets are the proven drivers of success, common sense tells us that a company's workforce is just as critically important an intangible asset class because the workers are directly or indirectly the creators of all other intangible assets.

Someone decided that the words *employees, workforce,* and *personnel* were inadequate in describing workers' influence in creating the value that contributes to marketplace and financial success. So a phrase was introduced into the lexicon of business and industry that more appropriately acknowledges the newfound importance of labor: *human capital.*

It is believed that this phrase entered our public consciousness in the 1950s and '60s, when labor economists began to look at issues around workforce quality when businesses spent money on training and education.[1] Companies developed an expectation that improvements in workforce quality through training would improve productivity as well as earnings. Therefore, these expenditures were considered investments by managers. Thus, the emergence of human capital, despite the differences that exist between this kind of capital and the financial and physical variety.

Moreover, though the concept of the workforce fails several dimensions of the definition of an intangible asset, it is considered one nevertheless. Perhaps the biggest reason for its intangibility is that our current financial reporting scheme does not treat workers as an asset at all. Employees are expensed and therefore treated as a hit to earnings and not a driver of value. The very existence of a workforce is a financial negative from a reporting perspective.

Does this mean employment costs should be shifted to the balance sheet and capitalized? No. What it does mean is that generally accepted accounting principles (GAAP) fail to communicate the nuance in the value of employees to the organization and, therefore, causes missed opportunities in their proper management. It is value that managers intuitively understand but have found difficult to leverage as an asset in the absence of any effective operational techniques. However, there is an attitudinal shift in some companies that recognize a much greater degree of sophistication is needed in the management of people as a critical factor of production in a company. Better management of labor as human capital might be one of the biggest sources of competitive advantage in the not too distant future.

The rhetorical flourish applied to the company workforce and the academic work of economists have belied the ability of organizations to manage it as the asset everyone in the business community believes it is. It is not that workers have not been managed. For better or worse, workers have always been managed, going back to the Egyptians, when slaves were organized and directed in moving large blocks of stone in the building of the pyramids. But they weren't managed as assets per se.

In reaching back to our definition of an asset as some entity that creates value for an organization, clearly if workers are conceived as an asset class, then logic dictates the following question be asked: have better management techniques emerged that support the belief that the company workforce is a source of value creation? The answer is yes.

A conceptual shift from the management of a workforce as a pure cost to management as an asset that is leveraged for value creation—financial and other strategic business objectives—can be clearly understood if current human capital and related methodologies are viewed from an evolutionary perspective. The three covered here are Human Capital Value Added and Human Capital ROI, the Balanced Scorecard, and Mercer Human Resource Consulting's methodologies (which we touched on briefly in Chapter 10). Through each example within each methodology type, you will see the emergence of value creation as increasingly the animating idea driving shifts in human capital strategy. In this way, the workforce evolves from a labor expense to a human capital asset.

Human Capital Value Added and Human Capital ROI

Human Capital Value Added (HCVA) and Human Capital ROI (HCROI) are two widely used analytical tools that help organizations make more cost-effective decisions around human capital investments. Invented by the Saratoga Institute, an organization specializing in the financial benchmarking of human resources, HCVA estimates the additional profits per employee if the company did not have to pay those employees salary and benefits—that is, if they worked for free— and is expressed in this simple equation:

$$\frac{(\text{Revenue} - (\text{Operating Expense} - (\text{Regular Compensation Cost} + \text{Benefit Costs EPTNW})))}{\text{Regular FTE}} = \$XXX$$

(EPTNW = excluding payments for time not worked)

The elements of the calculation are self-explanatory. Regular compensation includes all regular and overtime pay, commissions, and signing and referral bonuses. Benefit costs include medical and life insurance as well as retirement and savings plan payments. A regular FTE (full-time equivalent) is one regular employee working a total of 2,080 hours per year. The denominator of this calculation is the total number of employees in the organization. This calculation is commonly used to determine whether to outsource some workforce population to a third party.

HCROI is the pretax profit an organization generates for each dollar invested in employee pay and benefits. While HCVA is expressed as a dollar figure, HCROI is expressed as a ratio, as follows:

$$\frac{\text{Revenue} - (\text{Operating Expense} - (\text{Regular Compensation Cost} + \text{Benefit Costs EPTNW}))}{(\text{Regular Compensation Cost} + \text{Benefit Costs EPTNW})} = \text{X.XX}$$

As an example, an HCROI of 1.42 means that $1.42 of pretax profit is generated for every dollar invested in employee pay and benefits. This could also be expressed as a 42 percent return on investment. Following are real-world examples of how these calculations support workforce investment and policy decisions, both provided by Jeremy Gump, a senior manager with Ernst & Young's human capital practice.[2]

Scenario 1: Community Hospital

In this example, a community hospital asked E&Y to analyze cost reduction possibilities in its compensation and benefit expenditures. Table 11.1 illustrates the HCVA analysis. The hospital followed good recruitment and retention practices, yet E&Y pointed to places in the hospital's compensation practices in which $4 million could be saved—$1.6 million in compensation plus $2.4 million in benefit costs. Specific tactics implemented to reduce compensation and benefits included automating timekeeping to reduce errors in hourly wages paid, reductions in the amount of overtime the hospital was required by law to pay, and reworking policies around shift differential pay. Benefit cost reductions included increasing employee cost sharing of prescription drugs as well as negotiating better pricing terms from wholesalers.

Again, HCVA equals the dollar amount of additional profit per employee if no compensation or benefits were paid to the 1,817 employees at the hospital. You can see that before the cost reductions were implemented, HCVA at the hospital was $49,113. That is, the hospital would have earned an additional $49,113 per FTE had the hospital not had to pay its workforce wages and benefits. You can also see that after the $4 million in cost reductions, HCVA remained the same. This

Table 11.1 Human Capital Value Added—Community Hospital

	Before	After
Revenue	$186,501,901	$186,501,901
Operating Expense	$169,207,802	$165,207,802
Regular Compensation Cost	$58,133,484	$56,533,484
Benefit Costs EPTNW	$13,810,878	$11,410,878
Regular FTEs	1,817	1,817
HCVA	**$49,113**	**$49,113**

means that a $4 million cost reduction in compensation and benefit expenses by virtue of changes to management policy did not adversely affect the company's HCVA.

The hospital was able to reduce its investment in workforce compensation and benefits by $4 million yet still capture the same HCVA. This is so because there was no impact on company revenues. The compensation changes were revenue neutral, which is not always the case, as you will see. Had HCVA gone down after E&Y's compensation recommendations had been implemented, the hospital's cost-reduction decisions would have been suboptimal. Changes in compensation should always keep HCVA neutral or trending upward.

E&Y also performed an HCROI calculation for the hospital, depicted in Table 11.2. Before the compensation practices were changed, the hospital earned $1.24 of profit for every $1 invested in workforce compensation and benefits. After the compensation changes, the company could expect to earn $1.31 for every $1 invested in workforce compensation.

Both calculations present different positive impacts to the same budgeting decision—a $4 million reduction in compensation and benefits expenses.

Scenario 2: County-Owned Hospital

E&Y was called in to analyze the compensation structure for a county-owned hospital. Its size and workforce profile are similar to those of the

Table 11.2 Human Capital ROI—Community Hospital

	Before	After
Revenue	$186,501,901	$186,501,901
Operating Expense	$169,207,802	$165,207,802
Regular Compensation Cost	$58,133,484	$56,533,484
Benefit Costs EPTNW	$13,810,878	$11,410,878
HCROI	1.24	1.31

community hospital, yet you can see that the revenue performance is substantially lower (Table 11.3). This hospital serves a large low-income population, and many of the services it provides are never reimbursed. A lower-revenue performance with a similar compensation cost structure will logically translate into a lower HCVA.

Before E&Y's compensation reengineering, the county hospital earned approximately $9,000 less in HCVA than the community hospital, despite the fact that its compensation and benefit structure is actually several million less than the community hospital's. The reason for the county hospital's revenue being substantially lower is because of the patient profile it serves. This is depicted in Table 11.3. HCROI worked out to be no better than breakeven. As shown in Table 11.4, $1 in workforce investment delivered little beyond the investment.

While a low-income customer profile explained a portion of the hospital's relatively poorer HCVA and HCROI, upon investigation, E&Y found the real source of the problem was in staff turnover. The county hospital suffered chronic workforce turnover above benchmarked averages, and this meant substantial costs to the employer. To fill employment gaps between the departure of one worker and the recruitment of another, the hospital engaged the services of a temp agency, which charged between 50 and 100 percent above the cost of a full-time employee. Moreover, the inability to keep staff meant that four out of the facility's eight critical care beds went empty. Conceptually, the economics of a hospital are no different from a hotel's. You need a body—preferably a live one—in the room to earn any revenue. In the case of

Table 11.3 Human Capital Value Added—County Hospital

	Before	After
Revenue	$126,098,637	$129,298,637
Operating Expense	$125,956,276	$124,156,276
Regular Compensation Cost	$54,414,344	$59,214,344
Benefit Costs EPTNW	$12,364,922	$13,564,922
Regular FTEs	1,652	1,652
HCVA	**$40,509**	**$47,168**

Table 11.4 Human Capital ROI—County Hospital

	Before	After
Revenue	$126,098,637	$129,298,637
Operating Expense	$125,956,276	$124,156,276
Regular Compensation Cost	$54,414,344	$59,214,344
Benefit Costs EPTNW	$12,364,922	$13,564,922
HCROI	1.00	1.07

the hospital, 50 percent occupancy meant $800,000 in yearly revenue shortfall.

E&Y recommended that total workforce compensation and benefits be increased by roughly 10 percent. Keeping people working at the hospital through this compensation incentive would have the effect of reducing turnover costs, including contract labor expenses as well as the general low productivity of new hires as they acclimate themselves to a new employer. Reduced turnover would also allow for occupancy of unused beds now that additional staff was available to care for more patients.

Sure enough, an additional investment in workforce compensation and benefits delivered a $3 million revenue bump from the opening of the additional critical care beds and close to a 20 percent improvement in HCVA. HCROI also improved, albeit marginally.

E&Y's analysis of the hospital's turnover situation, the foundation of a shift in compensation strategy, uncovered the fact that nearly 70 percent of the 27 percent total turnover in the organization was from nurses who had been with the hospital for less than three years. That was not surprising, considering that starting pay at the county hospital was lower than at other hospitals. E&Y recommended that the additional expenditure in compensation not be spread evenly across the entire workforce. Rather, it should be targeted predominantly at this population of low-tenured staff who were more likely to leave for another employer but who were just as likely to stay if their pay became more competitive. Within pay ranges based upon years of service, lower paid (and lower tenured) nurses received a higher percentage increase in pay.

Comparison of Scenarios

HCVA and HCROI affirm labor's legitimacy as an asset that can be managed for value. The first scenario focused on compensation and benefit cost reductions only, yet ROI as an analytical concept is viable only as an asset investment tool. It doesn't work with expenses. There has to be some future value an organization can lay claim to for an ROI calculation to make any sense. HCROI showed a community hospital that incremental value could be extracted from its workforce were it to reduce its compensation and benefits practices. No additional capital was required to capture the incremental increase in returns, but it was won, rather, through cost reductions; this tactic raised the hospital's returns on human capital expenditures. Value was created from a shift in human capital management strategy.

The second scenario illustrated more explicitly how capital inputs can deliver additional returns, just like a physical asset. For an additional $4.8 million investment, a county-run hospital saw a 7 percent increase in HCROI as well as a more substantial lift in HCVA. When it comes to labor, gut instinct clearly tells the organization to cut, cut, cut because it is good for financial statements. Yet these calculations told the organization that cuts in compensation and benefit expenditures would have been a losing strategy. The specific circumstances dictated that more money for pay and benefits was required in order to capture additional value. That is what assets are all about: value.

The Balanced Scorecard

Just as it should be clear to managers that a workforce is the root of all other intangible assets, the Balanced Scorecard (BSC) reminds us that the workforce is the root of financial results in the organization. While it might be nearly impossible to isolate the unique contribution of one star employee to net income or earnings, the BSC demonstrates that the workforce collectively is the starting point in linking corporate strategy with actions and tactics that support that strategy, which is the whole point of the methodology. The BSC has been implemented widely, so it should be familiar to many readers.

Another important facet revealed by the BSC involves the interdependencies and equal importance of the customer, internal process, and learning (which means human capital) perspectives. Building performance measures within each of these perspectives is supposed to provide managers a road map for the decisions, projects, and activities that ultimately drive the financial goals of the company. Yet the internal logic of the BSC reinforces people as the root of all root intangibles. Table 11.5 depicts the relationships amongst the four perspectives.

The BSC does not favor one silo of measures over another; all measures linked to each specific perspective work together to deliver the financial outcomes a company seeks. However, the BSC says that breakthrough performance begins with people.

This becomes clear if we deconstruct the logic of this generic table. We'll assume a company is a stable organization in a mature industry. Therefore, it might choose return on capital as the ultimate financial outcome it seeks to measure. (A growth company, on the other hand, might choose revenue increases.) How is this accomplished? By delivering innovative products and services that will keep customers coming back. How is this accomplished? By putting the functions and

Table 11.5 The Balanced Scorecard: People at the Root of It All*

Financial Perspective	Return on capital
	Free cash flow
	Revenue
	Net income
	↑
Customer Perspective	Loyalty
	Satisfaction
	High lifetime value
	↑
Internal Business Processes Perspective	Manufacturing process quality
	Sophisticated marketing techniques
	Processes driving innovation
	Product development
	↑
Learning and Growth Perspective	Skills
	Retention

*Adapted from "The Balanced Scorecard," Robert S. Kaplan and David P. Norton.

processes in place across every facet of the company that will lead to the creation and delivery of great products and services. How is this accomplished? By equipping employees with the necessary skills to build and leverage the unique management processes on which they can unleash their creativity and insight to create great products and services that customers want.

The immutable logic of the BSC is a causal paradigm ending with financial performance and beginning with the performance and capabilities of people. It is an appealing set of causal linkages universally applicable to any moneymaking enterprise on the planet.

Figure 11.1 illustrates a financial services company that sought to reduce earnings volatility by broadening the sources of earnings through

Figure 11.1

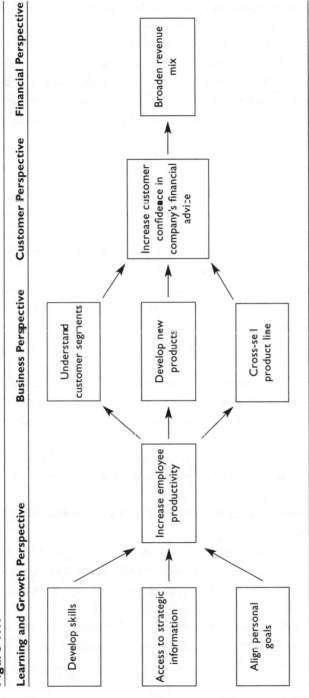

cross-sell and up-sell opportunities with existing customers.[3] The company realized that to accomplish this goal it would need to shift customers' understanding of what kind of financial institution it was. The bank needed to educate the public to the fact that it sold a broad array of financial products—it was a financial adviser and not just a check processor. Research dictated that if the bank wanted to broaden the revenue mix across its product portfolio amongst its existing customer base, educating this audience was key.

As part of its financial strategy (and the customer imperative driving that strategy in focus), the company identified the internal processes that required mastery in order to drive that customer goal. One of the new processes included reengineering the sales protocols from a passive order-taking function into a proactive relationship-building activity—that is, to cross-sell the product line. Two measures were implemented: cross-sell ratio (the average number of products sold to a household) and hours spent with customers. A relationship-oriented sales approach demanded that salespeople spend time with customers in order to better understand their financial needs and goals.[4]

Obviously, a new approach to selling requires a workforce equipped to execute it. In the causal logic of the BSC, the bank realized that increasing customers' confidence that it was a capable financial adviser and not just a check processor meant a wholesale change in sales force skills. This necessitated a number of human capital management changes:

- Employees needed to acquire deep understanding of the organization's product line as well as the new sales skills necessary to cross-sell.
- Employees needed integrated, detailed customer profiles to support their efforts.
- The company needed a new incentive program that aligned rewards with the goals it had set out to accomplish. This is the "align personal goals" dimension in the learning and growth perspective.

The Balanced Scorecard was never cast as a human capital asset management methodology, but in many ways it is. Here is why:

- **The BSC reveals complementarity:** Executing the three steps for its workforce the company identified in order to deliver the ultimate goal of a broadened revenue mix was not accomplished in a vacuum. Adjusting its human capital goals was just the first step in a multiplicity of initiatives across all perspectives that the company had to take. A broadened revenue mix requires human capital management within the context of a larger system of procedures and tactics; human capital must be fused with other intangible assets, such as new information systems and the new selling processes and supporting organizational arrangements, in order that it creates real value for the organization, value revealed in the financial perspective. The causal logic of the BSC shows complementarity clearly.

- **The BSC shows the way to new intangible asset creation:** For the bank to get a complete picture of the skills gap of its workforce required a redesign of its staff development process.[5] For instance, the bank embedded techniques and capabilities that would allow the capture of answers to such questions as: What are the required competencies needed to execute on the new strategy? What competencies exist already? What is the size and scope of the gap between the two? Answering these questions requires conducting value chain analysis, in which a detailed understanding of the critical processes across the creation of new markets (the creation of new products and services and the selling of those new products and services) is matched against the new job skills needed to execute those processes. The bank also needed to build competency profiles for its workforce, a detailed decomposition of the knowledge, skills, and behavioral and personality traits required to execute the new strategy. The causal logic of the BSC revealed to the bank the necessary skills upgrade if it were to achieve broadened revenue amongst existing customers. But once this was revealed, it became clear to the bank it needed the analytical framework to make sound decisions about workforce retraining and staff development. New processes and procedures around these activities that better equip the company to make workforce decisions in the face of a change in business strategy meant the company had created a new kind of organizational intangible asset.

- **The BSC reinforces value creation:** Building a road map that illustrates the path that must be taken to reach a strategic goal with human capital perched at the beginning of the journey shifts the organization's attention from managing people as a pure cost center to managing them as the critical first step in value creation. The leading key performance indicators (KPIs) found in each perspective of the Balanced Scorecard are collectively an integrated set of management goals that, if reached, deliver the ultimate outcome. The KPIs in the customer perspective for the bank include depth of relationship and satisfaction survey. The KPIs in the internal process perspective include product development cycles and time with each customer. And the KPIs in the learning and growth perspective (human capital) include information availability, goals alignment, and job coverage ratio (the skills gap analysis). The BSC methodology holds that reaching KPI goals in the customer and internal process perspectives is not possible unless the KPIs in the human capital perspective are realized first. While human capital management is three steps removed from the ultimate goal of a broadened revenue mix, its centrality in reaching that objective is clear and an affirmation of human capital's role in value creation.

The Mercer Way

Mercer Human Resource Consulting has developed a set of proprietary diagnostic tools that reflect fundamentally new ways of thinking about managing people for value. The company estimates the background research that informed its insights and consulting methodologies represents 450 person-years of study.[6] While an explanation as to how its methodologies work not only is beyond the scope of this text but also represents to the company a trade secret type of intangible asset in its own right, the rest of this chapter details the collective wisdom that shapes Mercer's human capital consulting practice and demonstrates in action the tools that support this new thinking.

The Three Pillars of Proper Human Capital Management

At a high-level perspective, Mercer contends that extracting value from human capital builds upon three principles of workforce management:

1. **System thinking:** Seldom is any workforce decision made that does not affect other elements of human capital performance. Yet managers continually make decisions in a vacuum with little regard as to how one policy directed at employees might affect another policy. For example, a company might believe that rewarding individual accomplishment fosters a meritocratic culture and motivates people to perform at their peak. Yet this kind of compensation system is in direct contradiction to another company policy, which seeks tight teamwork in the service of important business goals. A company misses the opportunity to maximize the performance out of its workforce when it does not consider human capital as a system of people, processes, and organizational design that collectively constitutes the complete asset. A system approach to human capital management acknowledges the complementarity of many different yet interrelated elements, with complementarity being at the root of an intangible asset's nature.

2. **Proper fact gathering:** Most human capital policy and strategy decisions are made using little more than guesswork, intuition, or perhaps even the wrong facts. This is a prescription for failure. Mercer points out rightly that organizations that would laugh at the suggestion of a million dollar capital investment without an ROI analysis will routinely spend as much money on workforce programs without any support for the decisions. Ernst & Young demonstrated clearly that the tools exist, yet many companies do not take advantage of them. In Mercer's estimation, faulty fact gathering that leads to poor human capital strategy results has three flavors. First are decisions based upon no facts but rather on conventional wisdom or "common sense," as in management's belief that worker productivity will rise

if workers have a stake in the profitability of the company. Second are decisions based upon unreliable facts, as in management's believing employees when they claim they are more likely to remain with the company if it were to offer profit sharing. And third are decisions based upon irrelevant facts, such as management's belief that copying the policies and practices of companies in other industries that reported good results will axiomatically deliver the same results at their company. As Mercer's work has shown, none of these contentions is necessarily true.[7]

3. **Focus on value:** Like any asset, human capital offers a stream of future economic returns. Regarding employees strictly in terms of the financial drain they represent to the income statement misses the opportunity for value creation the workforce represents if it is managed correctly. Employee costs, particularly in manufacturing, are a variable cost; that is, they can be ratcheted up or down depending upon production need (which is a function of sales). It is difficult for managers responsible for a P&L to break free of this kind of thinking and impossible for them to ignore the incentives built into decisions in which, on paper, labor is a cost that must be managed as tightly as possible. Yet Mercer believes a more enlightened approach that acknowledges the economic value employees can deliver net of costs is available and works.[8]

The following examples illustrate these three principles at work.

Principle 1: System Thinking

To see the human capital problems that beset one company when it failed to view discrete workforce decisions in the context of a larger human capital system, Mercer recounts its work for a manufacturer we will call Widget Express. The problems at the organization were threefold: new product introduction was running behind schedule, many products off the line were defective or experiencing quality problems, and customer satisfaction, not surprisingly, took a dive.[9] On paper, Widget Express should not have experienced these problems, given its strong management, consisting of experienced product development teams that were committed to developing employees' talents.

During an audit, Mercer discovered that the root cause of the company's problems was an inability of technical managers to lead critical areas of the business. It was not that the managers were inherently bad but that Widget Express had cultivated a rapid advancement promotion environment in which employees moved quickly from one job to the next within the organization, as rapidly as every two years or sooner. Not surprisingly, the frequency of job movement prevented workers from gaining sufficient grounding in the details of important work functions that would ensure success in product development and quality areas. Quite simply, many managers left one job for another before project completion. This ultimately led to Widget Express's operational problems.[10]

Further investigation revealed other company policies that undermined its operation. Widget Express had a built-in bias to hire from within. Many companies do, the logic being that promoting from within ensures that senior managers really understand the company and the business within which it competes. Of course, the underlying assumption to this policy is a belief that outside hires do not perform as well as employees who have moved up the ranks and gained all this firm-specific knowledge along the way. Mercer stuck a pin in this balloon, showing empirically that hires from outside performed almost as well, if not as well, as employees promoted from within.

Another contributor to Widget Express's operational problems was its reward and compensation structure. The pay bump employees got when moving up the career ladder made compensation for lateral moves seem puny by comparison. Managers were motivated to move up the ladder and not across the ladder to another position, where their talents might have been put to much better use but for which they were offered far less increase in pay. Paradoxically, employees also found that the path of advancement quickly developed into a choke point beyond which promotions seemed unlikely. Furthermore, employees knew that a lateral move quickly led to a hierarchical move up again. To summarize the situation: advancement up the ladder offered far more rewards than did a lateral move across the organization. But at a certain point, advancement became quite difficult. Employees who made lateral moves found that advancement up the ladder again happened fairly quickly. Therefore, employees moved laterally in order to move up in a kind of stair-case pattern. There was a lot of bouncing around amongst employees continually jockeying for position, which helped them develop exper-tise in a broad array of functions but not the deep experience in any of those that the company really needed.[11]

Finally, Mercer also found that the HR review boards (meant to iden-tify talent and help talented individuals advance) turned into lobbying agents for those employees who sought the department's help in evan-gelizing their cause for advancement.

The important point Mercer wants to hit home is that all of these management practices are reasonable when considered separately. When taken together, however, these human capital policies worked against the business goals of the organization. An optimized human capital strategy for this organization would have taken a system approach, in which all discrete policy and management elements fit together into a cohesive whole instead of working against each other. A system approach to analysis is common to many fields, including weather science, eco-nomic forecasting, and the social sciences. Why not the same with peo-ple strategies?

Principle 2: Proper Fact Gathering

As we saw in the system thinking concept example, management worked from erroneous assumptions in its belief that a hire-within policy is best. That anecdote is just as relevant to the second principle, which informs proper human capital management: base decisions on the facts and just the right facts. Widget Express took it on faith that cultivating people inside for bigger things provided it the quality of institutionalized wis-dom that could serve business goals in a way that hiring from outside could not. In the context of other workforce practices, however, this was not the case.

In Mercer's experience, the fact-based analysis dilemma has several dimensions. They include the following.

The "say-do" trap. Companies put a lot of faith in surveys and exit interviews to get a read on employee motivation and use these temperature-taking exercises as a basis for human capital policy making. The problem is that employees are human, and humans often say one thing to a pollster but act very differently. Heavy reliance on this type of "fact" gathering leads to poor results. Toyota relied on surveys to build a range of human capital management programs and was shocked to learn in feedback from employees through this mechanism that big investments in both pay for performance and training programs went unappreciated. Employees told the company that they did not believe pay and performance were tightly linked nor that training or movement within the organization provided any payoff either.[12]

Based upon these survey results, Toyota considered overhauling the whole effort. However, the survey results were faulty. Mercer found in a review of HR data that indeed higher pay and promotions went to star performers. The data also demonstrated that generally those who went through training and accepted moves throughout the company were promoted at a higher rate than those who did not. Toyota would obviously have made a grave mistake if it abandoned its human capital program simply because employees didn't believe in the professional rewards associated with its strategy. What Toyota had on its hands was a perception problem. Employees simply did not understand what the company valued from its workforce, the criteria used in promotions and pay raises, and what specific worker behaviors were translated into rewards. The problem was a relatively simple communications problem in which the record with employees could be set straight.[13]

Surveys have value, but oftentimes how questions designed to elicit answers are worded can have profound impact on what the survey target says. Surveys also tend to ask questions in a vacuum, with no regard for the real-world trade-offs people make in the course of their lives. For example, a company might ask workers to rate the importance of salary in their decision to stay or leave the organization. Mercer says that when no cost implication to the benefit is considered, people will generally answer "most important" or "highly important." The fact is, there is a cost to high pay—the trade-off of leisure time. Not everything can be "highly important" in the context of compromises and trade-offs people have to make all the time. Yet because surveys often overlook this kind of nuance, they can have limited human capital strategy diagnostic value.

Time perspective. Employee surveys elicit responses true at any point in time but subject to change as circumstances change. Mercer insists that a true understanding of the forces that influence employee behavior can happen only over time. Take compensation again. A worker's salary can be captured at any given time and compared against salaries fetched for comparable jobs. However, a more meaningful measurement might be the salary path or pay trajectory over time. Indeed, Mercer has found that for many workers, this pay trajectory is more important than salary level at any given time. Also, the rate of promotion is an important consideration for some employees. Mercer points out that these dimensions that influence employee behavior are all time-based.

To see the need for time-based fact analysis as the basis of proper human capital management, Mercer recounts its work with FleetBoston Financial several years ago, when the company was experiencing employee turnover of 40 percent, twice the industry average. The HR department used tried-and-true surveys to determine what forces were at play that caused people to either remain or leave the company. The surveys told the company that the culprits were excessive workloads and inadequate pay. So the company made adjustments it believed would reduce the rate of turnover. Despite approaches to relieve stress and adjust pay, turnover continued to rise.

The alternative path to enlightenment had Fleet examine turnover patterns over time as a means of capturing all the antecedents that would result in high turnover. The real story about turnover, Fleet learned, was at odds with what the surveys were saying. The analysis revealed that pay levels were a weak influence on turnover rates; a 10 percent increase in pay, according to the statistical modeling techniques Mercer used, would reduce turnover by 1 percent. If Fleet sought to reduce turnover using pay as a lever, the investment would be enormous and shareholders would likely approve. The true levers of retention turned out to be promotion, rate of pay growth, number of job assignments, and breadth of experience.[14] The specific, time series–based findings on retention included the following:

- The most powerful deterrent to employee departure was a recent promotion.
- The transition from hourly to salaried status motivated workers to remain with the company.
- Workers who were in the same position for more than the past two years had the highest probability of bolting Fleet.
- Workers were twice as likely to leave if their supervisors left, but only if the supervisor was a high performer so defined by Fleet.[15]

Informed with these empirically driven facts, Fleet embarked upon stemming the flow of people out of the company with the following strategy:

- Communicate clearly to high-performing managers the company's commitment to those elements of the compensation package that increase the likelihood they will stick around: advancement and career development. Keeping good supervisors also cuts down on overall turnover.
- Focus on those programs that help employees develop their skills and experience, and communicate career opportunities clearly.
- Focus on career paths that would move hourly to salaried employees, a retention tactic with a big impact to the bank.
- Do not allow valued employees to mire in a position for too long.
- Ensure that new hires were properly matched to their jobs and would have accurate expectations and understanding of the job requirements. "Quick quits"—new hires that bug out within a year or two of their hiring—always drag down retention ratios.[16]

The approach proved its worth. Fleet saw a 25 percent reduction in turnover of hourly employees and 40 percent for salaried employees. This result translated into annualized yearly savings of $50 million.[17]

Understanding of the magnitude of human capital strategy impacts. Historically, companies were satisfied to know that if certain human capital policies resulted in positive impacts, then the overall strategy was moving in the right direction. Mercer argues that the size of the impact must be considered, too, when embarking on a human capital strategy. Consider a manager who proposes a multimillion dollar investment because his projections show positive cash flows. Although enthused about the possibilities, his superiors might want to know the magnitude of those cash flows. Only then can they arrive at an informed decision. The logic holds for human capital investments. Workforce training proves itself an effective means to keep people working for the company. However, how many people remain and for what duration? Only when the magnitude of the policy impact is known can this question be answered with any confidence. And only when this question is answered can management grasp the full implications of the value of the strategy.

Marriott International has a policy of grooming property managers from within. As good managers are identified, they are moved into successively more complex and bigger operations to deepen their experience and extend the breadth of their skills. The company believes this approach is the most effective way to keep managers motivated to run along this fast track. The only concern Marriott had was whether a human capital strategy of moving good managers from one location to the next would cause profitability to suffer at properties they just left. The hotel chain was interested in knowing the negative implications of its retention and promotion strategy—that is, the full net impact of its preferred human capital development strategy. In the end, Mercer told them that no, there was no appreciable impact on property profitability resulting from the frequency of manager movement within the company. The research also confirmed what Marriott already believed—that manager movement up the chain contributed to retention. Yet Marriott would not have known the extent of the power of this human capital strategy had it not bothered to measure its magnitude.

The limitations of benchmarking. This is what Mercer calls striking the correct inside-outside balance in terms of where data are collected from to make a human capital strategy decision. Learning what the other guy is doing is a way of folding innovative procedures and techniques into the company. Benchmarking has a storied track record as an effective way for companies to adopt, in a number of operational contexts, best practices and the tried and true. But not human capital. Mercer finds that a benchmarking–best practice approach will simply not work in the human capital management arena the way it does for, say, running a call center or for manufacturing. There are so many unique interdependencies that collectively form a company's human capital strategy that simply forklifting what works elsewhere can be deadly.

A vivid example of this was a semiconductor manufacturer for consumer products and business equipment. Revenue growth and shareholder returns sagged in the mid-1990s, causing a top-down review that revealed rising turnover amongst the company's design engineers. Engineers with deep knowledge of chip designs were crucial to maintaining low design error rates and facilitating quick product launches, yet they were leaving the organization. While the chip company identified the immediate problem impacting financial statements—engineering turnover—it could not identify the cause of this turnover. With Mercer's assistance, the company got at the root of the problem, which included barriers to advancement and misaligned incentives in which variable pay and stock option compensation schemes clashed with a command-and-control culture that left little room for entrepreneurial performance.

The company solved the problems but not before attempting every workforce strategy known to the free world. It started to adopt best practices from other companies, including Intel and Apple. In fact, the stock option and variable pay tactics were established as a direct outgrowth of the company's desperation to find an answer to the attrition problem. Stock options became an important tactic in an attempt to emulate the swashbuckling culture of these more famous companies. This approach was doomed to failure, however, because the existing company culture did not support it. The chip company adopted a compensation structure that paid workers for risk taking and thinking outside the box, yet its reputation as a quality source for semiconductors was not for innovation but for process engineering managed with West Point–like discipline. A command-and-control management style left nothing to chance in the complex world of chip design. The company copied the management principles of others but discovered that human capital strategies are like snowflakes—no two are alike.

Principle 3: Focus on Value

The third broad principle of human capital management is a focus on value. At its most fundamental, this focus means a shift away from seeing human capital as labor and, therefore, as a cost that drags down financial performance rather than enhancing it. Easier said than done when financial reporting rules work against this philosophy. But it can be accomplished.

Mercer helped a health care company beset by rising operating costs and reduced insurance and government reimbursements see the light. Amongst other tactics it decided to employ to reduce costs, including overtime opportunities, the company chose to rely more on a part-time workforce whose cost structure was substantially lower than a full-time one. The company was obsessed with benchmarking, and in comparison with competitors, it had a low part-time to full-time ratio; increasing this ratio would cut costs and put the organization's labor cost structure more in line with others.[18]

The problems arose out of the fact that the health care company saw only half the story. Having more part-timers would reduce overall costs, but could such a workforce composition deliver the same value? The company soon learned the answer was no. Having a large part-time workforce killed productivity. In fact, Mercer pointed out that the composition of full-time workers needed to increase 15 percent from the level established after the increase in part-timers was implemented. Mercer believes there were several reasons why a dominant part-time workforce killed productivity: as the number of part-timers increased, the opportunities for promotions and pay increases for full-time employees decreased; part-timers did not have the firm-specific knowledge that allows employees to do their jobs more efficiently; reductions in overtime opportunities reduced costs, but the company did not realize that a 1 percent increase in overtime actually increased productivity 3 percent, completely missing the value-creating potential in increasing human capital expenditures.[19]

Recall the experience of First Tennessee National Bank from Chapter 10. The bank sought to find an optimal human capital strategy to fortify its competitive advantage in customer service. However, its aspirations also reflected the need to view labor as much more than simply a cost center. The bank discovered that long-tenured employees possessed the firm-specific knowledge that translated into high customer satisfaction with the bank. It also happens that traditionally experienced employees are more expensive than new hires. With the help of Mercer, the company was able to prove empirically the link between a higher workforce cost structure from utilizing more experienced employees and subsequent revenue increases; had the bank paid attention only to the cost implications of using experienced employees, it would have missed this value-creating opportunity.

Conclusions

As a phrase, *human capital* is not synonymous with people per se but rather describes the combination of skills, experience, and expertise of people in an organization. If human capital is an asset, then human capital strategy is a form of asset management; people and their various skills, experience, and expertise are managed in the name of some value-creating business goal. Conceptually, this construct works, but in the details, as we have seen, the idea breaks down in the context of value. Human capital assets bear little resemblance to assets as we have commonly understood them historically because unlike capital equipment, the way in which value is created out of human capital is far more subtle and less straightforward. Companies routinely calculate accurate ROI forecasts for capital equipment requirements to determine whether a physical asset makes sense for the organization. Calculating the ROI of a new hire receiving a total compensation of $80,000 yearly (the denominator of the calculation), as if he were like a new piece of machinery, simply won't work. Not because comparing a worker to a machine is crass but because so many elements bear upon this worker's value potential, including the mix of workforce policy practices as well as the company culture, that traditional economic value analysis tools do not include the inherent forces of complementarity in their calculations. Human capital is an asset, albeit a new kind of asset—one in which optimal management and measurement techniques are only now starting to be understood. It truly is an intangible asset because optimal value-extraction techniques are not stand-alone; they must take into account the complementary assets and elements that influence the overall effectiveness of any human capital strategy.

In Mercer's view, there are several elements that in sum represent human capital strategy, some of which we have seen at work in companies attempting to resolve some business crisis. These elements are universal to any business and are worth summarizing now.[20]

- **People:** It seems redundant, but people and their attributes represent the core of human capital strategy, whether they work in the boardroom or the mail room.
- **Work processes:** How work is organized and carried out is an important element of human capital strategy. An assembly line approach to work flow might require one set of talents, and a work team approach another set. Some argue that this is an intangible asset itself.
- **Managerial structure:** Command and control from on high or a more decentralized approach to managerial direction? We saw how one company's hierarchical managerial structure ran headfirst into an entrepreneurial compensation structure with disastrous results.
- **Information and knowledge:** How information flows throughout the organization affects productivity. Internal flows concern information moving up, down, and across the organization, and external flows concern information between customers, suppliers, partners, etc.
- **Decision making:** This element concerns the important decisions that affect strategy and operational areas, like sales, marketing, and finance.

Mercer also contends that human capital might be one of the few sources of competitive advantage left to companies. The immediate reaction is, yes, Mercer would say that because it earns hefty consulting fees helping companies with their human capital issues. The argument behind the assertion is nevertheless compelling; it was pointed out earlier in this book that physical assets have lost much of their differentiating potential. Financial capital is abundant or at least easier to come by, whereas in earlier days management struggled to acquire money needed to finance business goals. Machines in and of themselves are not only useful but essential to the proper running of a company, although in and of themselves they do not confer any special advantage. The same is true for much, but not all, information technology. Earlier pages in this text also pointed out that economies of scope and scale are no longer differentiators. In many industries, bigness is an impediment, as smaller competitors move more nimbly in a marketplace demanding agility and speed.

People, on the other hand, represent a vast uncharted territory for far better management, and companies that succeed in this venture can land competitive advantages for two reasons. One, human capital strategy is stable, persistent, and more enduring than other assets. And two, it is not easily copied by competitors.[21] This chapter demonstrated the limitations of a best practice approach to improved management. If some copied tactic happens to fit into the overall human capital mosaic in one organization, chances are it has found its way into other businesses as well. There goes competitive advantage.

In exploring issues and techniques for better intangible asset management, it is only fitting that this, the last chapter that takes a specific intangible asset and looks at the techniques around its improved management, should concern itself with human capital since an analysis of every other intangible asset leads back to one inescapable conclusion: if you cannot manage your human capital effectively, other intangible assets that serve as powerful sources of value are hard to come by. It all starts here.

Chapter Takeaway

Companies that seek to extract maximum value out of their human capital as an intangible asset should consider the following:

- Benchmarking will only get you so far. It should be limited to helping management gain clarity about potential human capital strategies but should not be used as the foundation upon which strategic decisions about this asset are made.
- Are you ready to spend potentially more money on human capital to maximize its value despite what the P&L might be saying? Both

Ernst & Young and Mercer prove vividly that leveraging human capital for its asset potential cannot simply focus on cost reductions because cost reductions alone miss the value-creating potential inherent in a company's workforce. Examples in this chapter using various methodologies from these two consulting firms demonstrate that a company might actually have to spend more money, not less, on human capital to arrive at the desired business goals. Companies focused relentlessly on cost reductions alone will not succeed in winning value out of human capital assets and should not bother trying.

- What are the drivers of competitive advantage in your organization? Engineering discipline? Great customer service? Ability to innovate? Human capital strategy can be executed only when company strengths are assessed and well understood first. Then the company is equipped to leverage that intangible asset—its human capital—by building those workforce practices that heighten those competitive strengths and turn them into measurable results.

- Go to the facts to understand the causal factors bearing upon human capital problems. The reason why E&Y and Mercer can arrive at what would seem counterintuitive but correct diagnoses is that their work is fact based. Reams of operational data available out of HR systems today are the starting place in understanding the constellation of workforce practices and policies that influence human capital performance issues. The problem for many organizations is making the proper interpretation of that data to arrive at the true problem. This is where the consultants make their money.

- Remember, Mercer stresses that its methodologies for improved human capital management have less to do with the specifics of the design or tactics deployed (training, new compensation structures, etc.) and more to do with the business context into which those tactics are introduced. This assertion should remind managers of the limited human capital management potential of any one tactic if not considered within that larger business context. This is why many human capital initiatives fail.

CHAPTER 12

ORGANIZING
FOR VALUE

Should managers do their jobs fundamentally differently if they are aware that, one, intangible assets drive enterprise performance and profitability and, two, many of those intangibles are created instead of acquired? It is unlikely that Jeff Bezos, the founder of Amazon.com, sat down one day with a vision to create a world-leading online bookstore and declared that such a vision required an intangible asset. And even when the leaders of the company knew it needed a world-class software platform to pull off the business plan, it is doubtful they cast the objective in terms of creating some stupendous intangible asset.

However, injecting clarity into what intangible assets really are does equip managers to do several things. For one, they can take stock of all the intangible assets in their own organizations: What are these assets? Why are they a source of value creation, the essence of any intangible asset? What value do they actually create? Managers might be encouraged to step back from their purview of direct control in the organization and ask in what way their domain of responsibility contributes to the creation and effective management of those enterprise intangible assets: What is the intangible asset or assets my functional area contributes to? Assets are fundamentally about value creation—how are the intangible assets within my domain contributing in this way? Are they well defined and discrete? Can these assets be measured? What are the complementary elements in the organization that add value to these assets? Would the management of these assets be better served were managers to have a direct communication link with other areas in the organization I barely interact with?

Asking these questions should make it concrete to the manager that although many intangible assets (like those we've discussed in these chapters) can be managed discretely, so many internal elements in other parts of the organization contribute to their creation and ultimate value creation that leveraging them for maximum value might mean the need for new organizational arrangements that acknowledge their fundamental complementarity. The implementation of new organizational structures to optimize not just the creation of intangible assets but also the creation of profits, which stem from the successful leverage of those assets once they are created, might prove to be as important as the management techniques themselves. What are the organizational implications for effective intangible asset management? We'll explore that issue in the pages that follow.

Information Technology

The organizational response for the more effective management of information technology, while perhaps not complete, is quite mature. Many organizations have embedded formal governance processes to include senior management in IT investment decision making in an effort to ensure any given project is better aligned with company strategy. This manifests itself in steering committees and prioritization boards as well as project offices in the IT organization itself, established to act as a kind of traffic cop that manages the work flow of projects from seed to completion. While the establishment of new institutional arrangements to better manage the value-creating potential of IT was not couched in the terms of intangible assets, these efforts nevertheless were motivated by a greater understanding of IT's complementary nature; its value is derived from the interplay with other elements in the organization, chiefly people and firm-specific business processes and procedures. Capturing technology's value meant ensuring that capital outlays took aim at the company's goals instead of focusing on unrelated targets, which has often been the case.

The CFO has engaged in a more collaborative role with the CIO as a move toward establishing greater accountability from the IT organization in response to its sometimes abysmal record in delivering value or at least delivering within budget. A debate within technology circles has raged for a number of years that speculates as to when the CIO will win a seat in the company boardroom as an explicit nod to this executive's influence in steering company direction. In some companies, CIOs have already done this, but in many they have not. Greg Hackett, founder of the Hackett Group, has noted that 70 percent of the CIOs still report to the CFO. Would that percentage decrease as technology chiefs acquire the financial literacy to articulate a vision of how technology can measurably drive strategic outcomes that end up on the bottom line?

As the types of IT that companies build or acquire moved beyond just support capabilities and data processing into business applications—ERP, CRM, supply chain—it has grown increasingly common to find that line-of-business employees take ownership of proposing IT projects and build detailed business cases. Departments are charged back for the cost of the project and are accountable for the results; that is, did IT deliver value reflected in the forecast? Again, these developments didn't emerge because IT was suddenly conceived as an intangible asset (even though for reporting purposes, IT is treated just like physical assets). These practices emerged in response to a management imperative that understood that technology assets must align if not drive business success. Empowering the employees with the greatest to gain from the investment with the ability to propose, advocate, and take ownership of those investments moved organizations closer to that objective.

Intellectual Property/Intellectual Assets

Because the customer organizations who come to QED and the yet2 .com exchange website occupy every niche of maturity on the intellectual asset management spectrum, the organizational changes to support open-market innovation will be as intense and comprehensive as is required to operationalize OMI practices. Certainly, OMI would feel right at home folded into the strategic planning process.

On the seller side, companies will need to establish an organizational and governance structure that embeds regular review of the company intellectual asset portfolio to determine a particular asset's candidacy for open-market licensing. That organizational response is necessary to answer questions, such as: Should the R&D budget increase, incrementally or substantially, in order to stretch the company goal of generating more income from IP/IA licensing because it embraces OMI? How have the company's goals shifted that might require it to reprioritize its portfolio so that an asset that was once viewed as strategic and deemed for internal use might now be licensed?

Consider also the opposite: Does the organization need to pull a patent or trade secret from the public marketplace because some managers discover its viability for product creation? Because the answer to these questions are cross-functional, touching finance, strategy, R&D, marketing, and maybe other areas, organizational design must also include open communication channels that support collaboration amongst any managers with a voice in deciding these OMI-based decisions.

The organizational response might be more structural on the buy side of the open-market exchange. An acquirer of intellectual property and intellectual assets is conceding that its future success is more likely to reside in ideas that originate elsewhere. Suddenly, a number of important issues come into focus as the company attempts to operationalize the acquisition instead of the creation of these intangible asset capabilities. Should the size and scope of the R&D function necessarily shrink? Is the most productive use of the cost savings from a reduced R&D function reinvestment in resources to manage OMI activities? The role of R&D engineers surely shifts from a mandate of idea generation into idea identification as they are rewarded more for a keen eye in recognizing others' IP or IA that fits company objectives and less their laboratory research skills. This, of course, requires reworking their entire compensation structure. But how much compensation should shift from the idea creation function to the idea identification and acquisition function? Are engineers possessing deep technical expertise suited to influence OMI policy given the need for a grasp of the strategic business implications around IP/IA acquisition? What kind of collaborative arrangement across job function and domain of responsibility best serves an OMI acquisition strategy? Who is at the table to decide specific acquisitions within a sanctioned acquisition prioritization model? These questions will be answered definitively as OMI matures and case studies of its implementation emerge.

Additional questions arise as more companies outsource the R&D function. A growing number of companies are not turning over R&D operations to outsiders as they might with certain IT operations in the pure sense of outsourcing. Yet they are building R&D capabilities in low-cost countries, such as India and China, where labor rates are far lower for comparably skilled technical professionals. Intel, for example, has shifted R&D of its next-generation mobile processor to Israel, and Nortel Networks is developing wireless Internet technology in India.[1] While the Internet and collaborative software have proven themselves up to the task of helping managers coordinate work flow from far-flung locations, what are the practical, everyday operational considerations in collaborating with colleagues twelve to fifteen hours in time away from headquarters? How big is the language barrier even when Indian and Chinese scientists speak fluent English? (One PC manufacturer issued a public mea culpa when, in response to customers' complaints that they simply could not understand what workers were saying, it stopped routing tech support calls to India.)

Is OMI on either side of the market exchange potentially compromised with this kind of operational arrangement? In terms of the complementarity of intangible assets, what is also fascinating about this trend is a company's belief that human capital is fungible; that is, one unit of human capital capability is easily replaceable with another—for example, substitution of an American scientist with an Indian or Chinese one in order to lower R&D costs. This core assumption undergirding efforts to establish R&D capability overseas is based upon the legitimate belief that science and technology are universal (physics, chemistry, and materials science are the same subjects in Indiana as they are in India) and that scientific activity is quantifiable (it is transcendent of direct organizational control in its creation and application).

Yet this view seems completely at odds with the reality of human capital, that it increases in value to the organization over time because of the accretion by employees of firm-specific knowledge. Mercer, for one, has proven this. Only time will tell if firm-specific knowledge is less important in R&D than in other areas for those companies that build that capability in foreign countries. Time should also determine whether a distant organizational relationship with that function undermines efforts to reap value from OMI.

Knowledge

The use of knowledge is inherently cross-functional, while knowledge creation is domain-specific. Is there an optimal organizational structure that resolves this tension? Proper knowledge management paradoxically might have its greatest value if considered in terms of antiorganization. A company can hire someone as its knowledge management director or chief knowledge officer to oversee a persistent, long-term KM strategy. They are likely more effective if their mission is to establish the conditions for knowledge sharing and creation rather than dictating those activities in autocratic fashion. Those conditions would include each of the following:

- Establishing a common understanding and buy-in across the organization of what knowledge management means and what the business objectives are in embedding this discipline
- Building the environment that encourages sharing, including a reward system for contributions as well as a compensation and job responsibility structure entailing explicit knowledge creation and sharing activities
- Facilitating knowledge sharing and creating with easy-to-use publishing tools—beyond Microsoft Office software like Word or Excel —and a robust search capability

Knowledge creation and sharing is almost an organic exercise, germinating from the ground up rather than the top down. Any organizational strategy that intends to support the management of this intangible asset is likely to fail if this fact is overlooked.

That a fluid rather than a rigid organizational structure serves knowledge management best has not stopped some from reaching into KM's organizational design pedigree in search of new techniques that advance its cause. One of the better-known techniques is social network analysis. The basis for SNA is rooted in the idea that social networks—known as social capital in intangible asset jargon—are essential to employee effectiveness and that understanding the topology of the networks between workers allows organizations to see where the nodes of greatest and least communication flows exist in the company and to reengineer the social topology to improve flows where needed. The idea goes that if communication flows are improved, knowledge sharing will improve as well. A simple SNA map is shown in Figure 12.1.[2]

A line between two teams indicates that a two-way social communication flow between project teams that collectively make up this mythical organization has been identified. This diagram does not represent

Figure 12.1

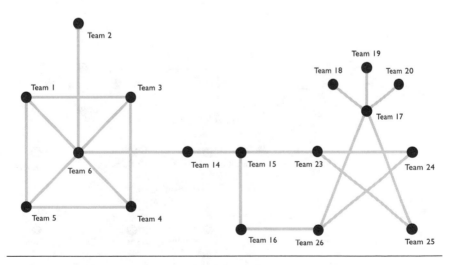

the physical connection between people (Ethernet) but the social connections that have developed organically. This social network topology reveals that Team 17 is at the center of a lot of communication, which includes knowledge sharing with other teams in the organization. Team 2, on the other hand, is relatively isolated. It has a direct connection with Team 6 only; however, it does have one degree–removed connections with Teams 1, 3, 4, 5, and 14.[3]

Analyzing this topology, SNA says that improving information flows across the organization might require the introduction of a direct connection between Teams 17 and 6, depicted in Figure 12.2.

That is an explicit directive requiring the interaction between the two teams. In doing so, the company cuts down the average path length by one degree while reducing the longest path from seven steps to four.[4] Or if the company decides that the sheer flow of information would overwhelm these already well-connected teams, another route in which to improve flows might be to implement a direct connection between teams 4 and 26. This alternative reaches the same objective by eliminating the bottleneck created at team nodes 14, 15, and 23.

Figure 12.2

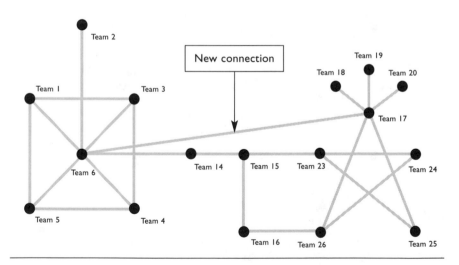

Many more indirect connections for information sharing are now available. The argument is that reducing the nodes into which information must flow throughout an organization hastens its delivery to the consumer and with less distortion than if it had taken a more circuitous path.

Although the use of SNA is not confined to knowledge management, it has been applied to this intangible asset management discipline because of a questionable insistence that organizational design principles are necessary to the task of extracting strategic value from knowledge. Companies might find SNA a useful high-level diagnostic to discern patterns of information flows across the organization and identify the choke points and floodgates.[5] For those who invested money and time in a portal to support the exchange of knowledge, such an analysis might reveal that knowledge might continue to flow through other channels. Employees build up informal networks with colleagues. Not all knowledge will flow necessarily through the portal, but it will be shared directly between the employee in need and the employee in possession of the expertise. Corporations are filled with subtle alliances and intrigues, and informal knowledge quid pro quos reflect this reality, no matter how loudly senior leaders espouse a one-for-all, all-for-one spirit of knowledge management efforts. In this way, SNA could help companies monitor the direction and intensity of information flows after an enterprise knowledge portal effort is launched. The most critical question managers need to ask is: Do information flows reflect that the portal is the driver of knowledge sharing?

SNA might have probative value if companies can drill down below just the flows of information SNA reveals and into the dynamics that explain why information is shared or not to begin with. Is the sharing incentive system working? What is the quality and relevance of knowledge being consumed by employees? How robust is the referral mechanism in which a knowledge seeker is directed by a colleague to a third party in the organization in possession of the needed knowledge when the portal fails to provide it? SNA might prove a useful diagnostic tool for organizations that take their knowledge management seriously, but it should not dictate strategy that attempts to link KM with business objectives.

Customers

If calculating LCV of customer cohorts for the purposes of differentiating service levels is implemented as a stand-alone technique, the organizational implications are not serious. However, if a deeper understanding of a customer's profitability is meant to inform a comprehensive strategy of individualized service and support, customized appeals to migrate customer classes, and, therefore, lift lifetime value and, hopefully, improve customer satisfaction, this is a whole other matter entirely.

For Peppers & Rogers Group, a pioneer in "one-to-one" customer relationship strategy and tactics, executing successfully on a vision exemplified by the experience of Convergys means axiomatically that companies must end their product and service orientation in addressing the marketplace and instead organize around customer classes. The idea makes eminent sense. The goal of the organization should not be to push products but to build personalized relationships with customers consciously tied to the value they represent to the business through which those products and services could be sold. An organization's products and services are assets to the extent that the public wants them. The real assets are the people who become customers. Organizing a business around customers rather than around what it sells is not inimical to building the capabilities a company needs to create products and services and innovate in the process, but it does clarify whether what it offers is what the marketplace wants. The mind-set shift is significant enough. The organizational implications are quite large.

One American automobile manufacturer was contemplating this new customer-oriented approach but apparently did not follow through completely. Had the company followed through, what would have been the organizational mandate to pull off this reengineering? The company would begin by acknowledging that unit sales of particular brands of cars were less important than ensuring that it sold a second car from any of its brands to the customer who already owned one from the company. It called this "share of garage." Brands would still be important in helping to influence buying decisions, but realigning internal resources around customer segments means not organizing around brands with the inevitable territorial prerogatives that ensue. Traditional marketing and branding functions themselves would remain intact, but the company's strategy would be directed toward supporting customer segments rather than supporting a goal to increase market share of cars under the brand: Are this brand and our marketing message relevant to the needs of identified customer cohorts? How can we manage the brand in such a way that customers will see the virtue in putting a second car from our company in their garages? Can brand and marketing management migrate an existing customer from a larger-margin automobile into a higher-margin car? This is a far different strategy from buying airtime during Saturday college football on ABC, informed by an educated guess that because men watch football, then the men who watch might like our ad for the new half-ton crew cab pickup.

As radical a concept as this is to the automobile industry, banks have taken small steps to organize around customer segments and break free of thinking that focuses purely on products. Just one small example of the organizational shift required is training of branch personnel.

Banks have changed their attitudes about the importance of branches in their sales network. The rise of the Internet and convenience of online banking had them believing branches were an anachronistic cost center, but they soon learned people liked dealing with people when it concerned their money. Suddenly, banks have caught branch fever, and those that embrace a customer strategy around profitability and growability are looking for ways to best support the vision. Historically, tellers who survive the turnover mill migrate into sales positions because they are good tellers. Good tellers balance every day and are operationally effective.[6]

This is exactly the wrong indication of their capacity to sell and service customers who come into the branch, but this has been standard operating procedure for career path trajectory in the industry. Banks that score customers and have a deep understanding of their existing financial situation and future potential business value are hiring entry-level people from retail; you can teach a natural salesperson financial service products more easily than you can teach sales technique to a banking clerk. This example is just one grain of sand on the shores of the manager's organizational reengineering agenda.

In fact, the organizational issues around executing a customer-centric strategy that acts upon an understanding of customer profitability are so large that deploying the techniques of the strategy persistently and consistently might prove less difficult than organizing the company to support the strategy.

For instance, the old MCI bought into this philosophy in possession of the knowledge that the top 5 percent of its customers represented 40 percent of its business.[7] Analyzing call patterns, it identified three needs-based groups and assigned managers for each group to drive business based on those identified needs. Managers would be evaluated on both the amount of increased business and loyalty they could capture from these customer classes.

The whole thing collapsed soon after launch. Customer management crossed too many boundaries, and senior leaders did not anticipate the organizational changes required to bring off the initiative.[8]

For this reason, experts advise a go-slow, quick-win approach to implementation. For example, Peppers & Rogers Group recommends first identifying the highest-value customers and the customers with high potential future value to the business and then implementing the strategy around these cohorts only. As the company succeeds in reaching business goals around the strategy and, therefore, validating its value, it can build out to successive customer groups accordingly.

Incrementalism or not, the change for some is wrenching. 3M's implementation of this customer strategy required a new kind of marketing executive entirely. No longer did it need product experts. It needed customer experts. Energy was redirected from figuring how to get customers to buy what it offered to figuring out how to deliver what customers articulated they wanted to buy. The new marketing managers act as intermediaries between the marketplace and product-oriented marketing people to ensure alignment between what the customer needs and what the company is capable of packaging. This organizational alignment is at the heart of proper management of the customer intangible asset.

Human Capital

Increased interest in the management of human capital is front and center on the CFO's agenda, and any time the CFO is interested in the management of some asset, changes (organizational and otherwise) are sure to follow. Ask any CIO who reports to a CFO.

The CFO's evolving interest is captured in a research study that was conducted by *CFO Magazine*'s research arm and sponsored by Mercer Human Resource Consulting.[9] Two percent of respondents knew with any confidence what return their aggregate expenditure on human capital was returning to the organization. Seventy percent knew the answer to a minimal or moderate extent.[10] Yet respondents say 36 percent of revenues are spent on human capital. It should surprise no one that, given the extent of the uncertainty of the value of people investments despite the sizeable amount of money those investments represent, CFOs have become keenly interested in human capital value issues.

This circumstance is not unlike a CFO being provoked into a more direct role in IT organization capital investment. The change in CFOs' attitudes toward people investment is captured in Table 12.1.[11] As you can see, the evolution in how the CFO as a proxy for the most senior

Table 12.1

Old Way	New Way
• Employee expenses are a cost.	• Employee expenditures are an investment and a source of value.
• HR function is a cost center.	• HR is a strategic business partner.
• Finance is involved in setting the compensation budget.	• Finance is involved in HR budgeting, too.
• HR creates and maintains metrics.	• Finance contributes to metrics design and use.
• Minimal effort is needed to understand HC spending returns.	• There is huge interest in measuring returns and value-creation cause and effect.
• HC is sometimes factored into M&A pricing.	• HC is frequently factored into M&A pricing.

of management in the organization views human capital issues touches a broad swath of operational and strategic activities.

The organizational implications from this new thinking might be largest in the HR organization. While the survey illustrates that 9 percent of CFOs view HR as a cost center only, a low strategic value administrative function, 28 percent view HR as somewhat strategic, and 11 percent view this function as highly strategic. The same survey found that more than 60 percent of CFOs believe they should play a leadership role in human capital strategy.

Clearly, CFOs believe that HR is positioned to drive enormous value through improved management of human capital, and they want to be a part of it. How their direct and regular involvement would look is unclear, however, because human capital management strategies that link labor to business strategy outcomes, looking beyond labor as a pure cost, are just emerging. The experiences of a couple of companies, however, illustrate how the greater role of finance in HR decision making might look.

At Unilever's Home and Personal Care business, the processes of design, manufacturing, distribution, and marketing are so tightly integrated that human capital management is an integral part of iterative steps in value creation.[12] Finance plays a large role in shaping HR strategy in terms of guiding HR's use of development, measurement, and compensation methodologies to make more informed human capital decisions. Finance is ideally equipped to inject analytical rigor into human capital practices that might be missing from HR's traditional support and administrative function.

The Dow Chemical Company is developing a model for quantifying the present and future contributions of employees to corporate financial goals by measuring specific contributions to specific projects they participate in. The idea will be to make better human capital allocation decisions as future projects arise. The method is being developed by a special team within HR with input from finance and business management.[13]

Notice that in both examples, the point of entry for finance into HR's domain is where the need exists to construct a measurement system that at least attempts to link causally human capital expenditure decisions with business outcomes. HR and finance are simply not coordinated organizationally this deeply at many companies. Yet it is probable that a much closer working relationship between finance and HR will similarly unfold in other organizations where human capital management is a top priority of senior executives.

Having a clearer understanding of the strategic value impact of a company's workforce beyond just gut feeling is a prerequisite for improved management of this intangible asset class. It is not surprising that cross-functional projects between HR and finance would emerge to quantify those linkages and embed accurate measurement methodologies to support future human capital management decisions. The good news for HR is that its credibility and visibility are poised to rise dramatically if it can deliver approaches to human capital management that drive financially quantifiable outcomes. It is then that labor will be confirmed as truly an asset rather than just a cost.

Brand

It was a calculated judgment call not to include an entire chapter on brand. Not for lack of importance but, rather, for lack of any new meaningful techniques that would add to our understanding of how brands should be managed.

The recognition that brands are an important company intangible asset goes back many years. Valuation techniques have matured, a direct result of heightened mergers and acquisition activity that began in the 1980s, in which brands played a prominent role.[14] In terms of management, brand audits and scorecards are two advances well documented in the literature. Yet some new thinking about how brands should be managed has emerged recently, and it is worth review. This chapter is the perfect place to introduce the idea because its underpinnings call for fundamental organizational changes.

First, a definition of brand. While a product, service, or company brand comprises many elements, the commonly accepted definition is that a brand is a promise of value delivered. This definition can be applied universally to any product or service in the marketplace.

In order to understand this new conception of how a brand should be managed, consider first that, historically, brand management had a product orientation. To manage a brand was to manage products and the communication about those products. Communication was key. The American economy evolved from strong local relationships between merchants and the customers who trusted them into a more distant relationship fueled by mass manufacturing and distribution. As physical and emotional distance separated customer from merchant, mass communication attempted to support and nurture what a brand became—a surrogate for the strong local relationship between the two that was lost after the industrial revolution.[15]

The Sears catalog is an example of this distance communication. For Sears the retailer, its brand came to mean a trusted, convenient, and personalized source for an array of goods. The brand stood in for the local shopkeeper no longer asserting the quality of the product directly and helping the customer make buying decisions: because Sears is selling it, it must have value and is worth buying. Brand management became communications management, and voilà—you have the rise of modern marketing.

The tectonic plate shift occurred, of course, with the rise of the Internet. Suddenly, the distance between product and service and the consumer was drastically reduced again, not physically but certainly informationally. It is information that contributes to brand awareness and perception. New intermediaries arose to serve a role not unlike the shopkeeper, who in another generation had been the trusted information source about a particular product sold in his store.

Google is an example of an intermediary that makes it easy for people to gather independent opinions about products and services from a variety of sources, like magazine reviews and blogs. Other information technologies under the direct control of the organization, such as customer relationship management, bridge that distance gap as well.

The work that advertising had done in a traditional branding context is more and more supplanted by IT in the form of software meant to cultivate direct relationships with customers coupled with a direct communications infrastructure that makes those direct interactions possible.[16]

The implication of this shift is straightforward, and the prescription for future success in this new world provocative. For all intents and purposes, the CIO is becoming the new brand manager of the organization despite the fact that he or she is not cast in this role at all and should have a say in brand management going forward. Casting the CIO as the new brand leader—or at minimum as a key actor in a brand's success—makes even more sense if you consider that it is not just customer-facing technology that drives brand value but all IT in the organization, which includes but is not limited to software controlling manufacturing efficiency and quality, logistics, inventory, supply chain, and billing.

These critical back-office applications are heavy contributors to a brand's success, and if you don't believe it, watch what happens to a brand over time when product quality goes down (and lawsuits go up), wrong or damaged goods end up on a customer's doorstep, or customers are constantly disappointed by stock outs, rain checks, and back orders. All the business conditions cited are influenced, sometimes heavily, by the management of IT. If a brand is a promise delivered to a customer, IT either indirectly or directly supports that promise. Figure 12.3 illustrates this point.[17]

Figure 12.3

Every interlocked sphere is either a function, department, or resource that contributes to the brand promise. Not one of these spheres falls outside the influence of information technology.

What does this all mean? Most important, the function of brand management must shift from a product orientation to a holistic systems orientation. The brand manager must no longer be concerned only with the traditional functions of deciding how much advertising, in which channel, and in which style should be directed at the public. To limit brand management to these functions ignores the critical contribution of technology to a brand's success. This argument holds that squeezing value out of this valuable intangible asset is a coordinated activity in which brand managers and the CIO work jointly to plan strategies and tactics for company products and services and execute on them.

How would such an arrangement look? The core of a coordinated management effort might have brand executives and the CIO, in conjunction with line and operational managers, design a measurement system that tracks key performance indicators (KPIs) at specific points through the value chain, which can affect the brand. Figure 12.4 depicts this.

To simplify the illustration, the value chain here comprises three broad, high-level activities. Admittedly, these categories are arbitrary but nevertheless illustrative of the role IT plays in brand value creation. For each of the three categories in the value chain are the associated technologies. In the interlocking boxes to the lower right of each of these technology categories are the relevant KPIs, which reflect the possible goals targeted by line and operations managers. These are just a few. At the end of the value chain is the brand intangible asset that companies build for themselves, a brand created through the qualities, attributes, and features of the products and services they sell powered by that technology.

It is unlikely the CIO would ever become the new formal brand manager of a company, given the crushing weight of the responsibility a CIO already bears. He or she is certainly poised, however, to act as a kind of translator and muse for the brand manager, an educator as to how technologies influence the goals that managers who toil in each of those three categories seek to fulfill. CIOs are increasingly capable of filling this role because of the mandate to increase their business literacy to better align IT investment with company strategy.

Figure 12.4

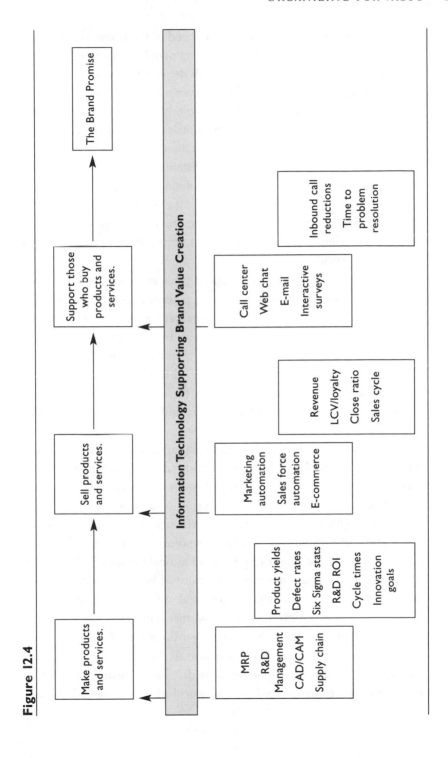

The brand manager, conversely, is in need of the translation because there is at least a perception that marketing people have punted in gaining a deep technical understanding of all the capabilities customer-facing technologies have to offer. They either are deathly intimidated by the technical complexity or believe, wrongly, it is not important that they understand all these capabilities in order to use them effectively.

Technical illiteracy and a lack of understanding as to how IT directly influences brand value mean the brand manager may be increasingly marginalized as more and more brand-influencing technologies emerge. The CIO is the natural domain expert to fill the void. He or she is smart about IT and could quite easily acquire the knowledge about brand management that would make him or her an effective intermediary between the world of IT and the world of brands.

Yet the brand manager who accepts a broader intangible asset management mandate should be as interested as line or operations managers in those goals because these KPIs telegraph the brand promise for a particular product or service. While the brand manager's scope of responsibility will not suddenly include manufacturing, R&D, or customer service, it could definitely increase if his or her role evolved from managing the communications function to helping manage and guide the brand as an intangible asset influenced and powered by information technology.

For instance, the brand manager's understanding of a customer's unmet needs would be highly useful information for product development, a place where KPIs might reveal room for improvement. Lower-than-expected revenue for a target period or a sales cycle that is not improving might, upon investigation by the brand manager, reveal customer confusion about a new product's points of differentiation from competitors. All this might require is additional education of the sales force or better marketing communications. The brand manager, in a broadened role, diagnoses the problem and assists in the remedy.

If the idea of repositioning the brand manager's role seems bizarre, could Ford Motor Company's experience make it seem less so? In 2000, Ford announced the return of $10 billion to shareholders because that was capital the company no longer needed.[18] The company made a conscious decision to divest itself of old-world physical assets, like parts manufacturing, and invest in intangible assets, such as the acquisition of the Volvo, Jaguar, and Land Rover brands of automobiles. It did not acquire much in the way of physical assets, such as manufacturing machinery, when it made the purchase.

Ford did acquire the brand equity of several kinds of well-regarded luxury automobiles. The idea was that the company could earn vastly better returns on capital because it had less of it and more of the value-creating kind of asset—brands. Whether Ford ever pulls off this business model shift—and it might take years to find out—what is the implication for brand management?

One of the reasons why Ford embarked on this strategy is the Internet. The company has the ability to outsource manufacturing, replacing manufacturing know-how with supply chain know-how and shedding physical assets along the way. The company also has the ability to communicate with consumers in new ways that can enhance the value of these brands.[19]

A shift in business strategy that emphasizes far more value creation from a brand rather than physical assets is a profound shift. It would hardly be surprising should the brand manager's scope of responsibility increase; if brands become the foundation upon which strategy turns, the importance of understanding all the complementary elements that contribute to brand value—elements that otherwise might have never been considered seriously—is suddenly in everyone's sights. It would hardly be surprising if new organizational structures were needed to maximize the value-creating potential of these new intangible assets.

Is all this a conceptual breakthrough in brand management? We will know only if and when organizations buy into it. The lack of empirical data means there is no definitive answer. The underpinnings of the argument are compelling, however. New technologies will continue to be introduced, which incrementally or fundamentally influence a company's brand through more direct, interactive communication. The latest might be RFID tags, which are poised to replace bar coding in the retail industry. RFID tags are positioned as IT that will add transparency to supply chains and inventory. Some speculate their use will move quickly to customer interactions; the day might not be far off when a customer standing before a product in a grocery store aisle will pass a smart card or some electronic device near an RFID tag in order to receive a customized offer or dynamic pricing on that item because the RFID tag and the device can synch.

A second, more urgent question arises: what risk does a company run if its brand is simply managed in the future the way it has been in the past? The answer might be less about hurting the brand than what the opportunity cost is of remaining faithful to the tried and true. That is, what value creation might the organization leave on the table if it fails to view a brand as the sum of many complementary and interdependent elements, which in concert deliver consistently that unique promise to the consumer but which require new organizational arrangements and new competencies in brand managers? It's worth thinking about.

Organizational Arrangements Are Assets Themselves

New organizational arrangements required to optimally manage a range of intangible assets can themselves become intangible assets—organizational capital. Organizational capital describes the unique business arrangements and managerial structures that give a company the distinctive capacity to compete. Cheap, reliable (compared with Electronic Data Interchange [EDI]), and ubiquitous Internet connectivity encourages these structures. Wal-Mart's supply chain, Cisco's Web-based maintenance and support environment, and Dell's build-to-order over the Internet capability are all examples of organizational capital.

Organizational capital might be the purest of all intangible assets. You can't see it, there is no market for it because it cannot be forklifted out of the company or sold as discrete entities, and its contribution to financial performance does not appear explicitly on financial statements. Yet organizational capital contributes significant value to organizations that create it. Following is an example.

Toy companies traditionally place entire orders for new toys with manufacturers in January and February—just after they have wrapped up the previous holiday season. By Christmas, the toy company experiences either shortages of hit toys or stockpiles of toys that bombed.[20]

Supply and demand are hugely out of synch because information flows between points in the supply chain are small, slow, or nonexistent.

One toy designer, LeapFrog Enterprises, married specialized modeling software with new supply chain relationships with its retailers to improve decisions around the production of its LittleTouch LeapPad toy, a gadget that makes noises when a toddler touches illustrations in a book. Historically, sales information on a monthly basis—let alone in real time—was difficult to come by because retailers simply would not part with sales statistics. Employees of Mattel, where a LeapFrog executive had once worked, for instance, would be sent to retailers to count the number of units on store shelves, even though they had no idea how many had moved out of the storeroom.[21] This was state of the art in supply chain management.

The emergence of the Internet caused retailers to pry open their databases, and now LeapFrog has real-time hooks into sales data. Any LittleTouch sales at Wal-Mart appear in LeapFrog's database overnight.[22] The company also invested in specialized software that analyzes sales data to enable better understanding of aberrant sales spikes, which might be caused by discounts, advertising and promotion, or toy placement in the store. Understanding such sales anomalies allows LeapFrog to understand true demand for LittleTouch LeapPads.

As it turned out, the software told the company it had a hit. Powerful IT in combination with new supply chain relationships informed LeapFrog that it should produce twice as many toys as were planned and allowed it to place an order in August, when standard operating procedure would have said the company was six months too late. The manufacturer (based in Zhongshan, China) with whom LeapFrog struck a deal to make the LeapPads would respond to this request by turning out as many toys in four months as it had in twelve from the first order.[23] Design and supply chain efficiencies at the manufacturer made the ramped-up production possible.

Refined organizational arrangements across the entire value chain create additional revenue for all participants. Everyone would be hard pressed to know the dollar value of these arrangements. They could not be sold as stand-alone assets, nor are they visible to the eye; yet they drive huge value for companies that can assemble the pieces that create these organizational structures. This is why organizational capital has emerged as more valuable than most physical assets today.

Conclusions

The greatest innovation may be the modern American company. Not the modern American company of Dilbert fame, but the corporation that proves itself up to the job of designing, manufacturing, distributing, and selling stuff that people want and for which, in turn, value is delivered to shareholders. You have to marvel at companies that build semiconductors or airplanes, sports cars or power generation turbines, exceedingly complex products, and do it well, because so many companies make simple things but not as well. Companies that succeed in this way demonstrate their ability to effectively allocate financial resources and leverage the skills and talents of thousands of employees to seize sometimes fleeting market opportunities. They are managing their organizational capital well.

EPILOGUE

The critic Northrop Frye once said that a change in metaphor is a fundamental change. No longer do companies have employees—they have human capital. No longer do companies have customers—they have relational capital. No longer do organizations possess oceans of information—they have knowledge capital. Capital. Capital. Capital. For a long while, the metaphors got ahead of our ability to completely understand the meaning behind them. As has been demonstrated in these pages, this is no longer the case, despite the fact that intangible assets defy neat and easy categorizations and definitions.

Managers now have tools to help them more effectively manage all the intangible assets in their domain, techniques sure to one day lose their lofty perch within the state of the art. New tools and techniques will certainly emerge as the processes of creativity and innovation meet a continuous need to refine our understanding of the forces behind the value-creating potential of intangible assets. This need will survive well into the twenty-first century because intangible asset contribution to economic value will only increase in scope and importance. It is hoped that the techniques and methodologies illuminated within these pages will add light to the sum of light.

As the illumination intensifies on the entire range of issues surrounding intangible asset management, the fun is in seeing what is next. What business need will arise that an intangible asset can satisfy and through that asset creation become a source of ferocious competitive advantage? Competitive advantage should be one of the higher aspirations of an intangible asset management strategy because physical assets have proven themselves exhausted in their ability today to provide it. An answer to this question has actually come into focus, and it bears watching.

It was Harvard Professor Clayton Christensen, author of *The Innovator's Dilemma* (1997), who illustrated that leading firms in innovation-intensive industries are often doomed to failure because their very success blinds them to the introduction of innovations by upstart competitors that are seemingly of no interest to the established firm's customers but wind up feeding the next wave of industry growth. The perversity of the argument is scary. Companies don't fail because of bad management but because of good management.[1] Christensen asserts, "By doing what they must do to keep their margins strong and their stock price healthy, every company paves the way for its own disruption."[2] Did he mean to say "destruction"?

While Christensen painted a picture worthy of hanging in the Night Gallery, he has turned his attention from the problem of the innovator's dilemma to the solution. This is where intangible asset management enters the stage.

Because good management sows the seeds of failure, good management alone is unlikely the answer, although the mission is clear; businesses should build the capacity to endure and disrupt, disrupt and endure. This yin and yang of a business model has never been tried, but Christensen believes some version of it must because it might end up as the salvation for many well-managed companies whipsawed by disruptive innovations. Many companies have successfully disrupted once or even a few times, including IBM, Intel, and Intuit.

The key question is whether disruption can be embedded into an organization as standard operating procedure. Can companies regularly blow themselves up with sabotaging innovations that nevertheless represent the next tier in opportunity and profitability? Can a company create a *disruption engine*? Posed another way, can a company create an intangible asset combining the necessary organizational, human capital strategic, and other elements that collectively enable a company to successfully, deliberately disrupt its business in the name of self-preservation? Christensen did not frame the issue explicitly as an intangible asset management imperative, but that is what it is nevertheless.

Christensen has formed a consulting firm to sell a new growth strategy methodology. It is far too early to tell whether this methodology is sustainable in the long term, but given his track record it probably will be. A business model strategy that balances managing for growth with deliberate disruption begs such questions as these:

- What will this asset, this highly unique organizational capability, look like?
- What is the nature of its complementarity?
- What tactics were deployed to implement it?
- What organizational rearrangements were required to accommodate it?
- Will the effectiveness of this asset be predicated upon near-zero marginal costs, network effects, and positive feedback? What unique risks will such a strategy entail?

Because we have enhanced our understanding of the nature of intangible assets, these will not be foreign questions. Hopefully, this book provides the foundations to the answers.

NOTES

Chapter 1

1. Margaret M. Blair and Steven M. H. Wallman, *Unseen Wealth: Report of the Brookings Task Force on Intangibles* (Washington, D.C.: Brookings Institution Press, 2001), p. 10.
2. Ibid., p. 51.
3. "Service Parts Management—Unlocking Value and Profits in the Service Chain," Aberdeen research report (September 2003), p. 8.
4. Adapted from Alvin J. Silk, "Brand Valuation Methodology: A Simple Example," *Harvard Business Review* (January 26, 1996), p. 3.
5. Ibid., p. 2.
6. *Statement of Financial Accounting Standards* No. 141, Financial Accounting Series (Norwalk, CT: Financial Accounting Standards Board, June 2001).

Chapter 2

1. Margaret M. Blair and Steven M. H. Wallman, *Unseen Wealth: Report of the Brookings Task Force on Intangibles* (Washington, D.C.: Brookings Institution Press, 2001), p. 52.
2. Steve Barth, "Defining Knowledge Management," *KM Magazine*, destinationkm.com/articles/default.asp? ArticleID=949.

3. Andrew Osterland, "Decoding Intangibles," *CFO Magazine* (April 1, 2001).

4. Ibid., as well as the Brookings report.

5. Baruch Lev, *Intangibles: Management, Measurement, and Reporting* (Washington, D.C.: Brookings Institution Press, 2001), p. 21.

6. Ibid., p. 22.

7. If you don't think a reservation system is a discrete intangible asset, consider the experience of AMR, the parent of American Airlines, in the sale of an equity stake in Sabre, American's reservation system. AMR sold an 18 percent stake in October 1996. The market immediately valued Sabre at $3.3 billion. The market cap of AMR as a whole was $6.5 billion. In other words, half the value of an airline resided in a reservation system. See Lev, p. 24.

8. Lev, p. 26.

9. Ibid., p. 29.

10. Ibid., p. 32.

11. Ibid., p. 32.

12. Ibid., pp. 38–39.

Chapter 3

1. Robert Holman and Daniel Kahn, "Intangibles: The Measures That Matter," Ernst & Young *Cross Currents*, http://www.ey.com /global/download.nsf/Bermuda/Cross_Currents_-_Fall_2000 /$file/Cross%20Currents%20-%20Fall%202000.pdf.

2. Greg Ip, "The Rise and Fall of Intangible Assets Leads to Shorter Company Life Spans," *Wall Street Journal* (April 4, 2002).

3. Leonard Nakamura, "Intangibles: What Put the *New* in the New Economy?," Federal Reserve Bank of Philadelphia *Business Review* (July 1999), p. 9.

4. Lester C. Thurow, *The Future of Capitalism* (New York City: Penguin Books, 1996), p. 66.

5. None of these concepts is new to students of our evolving economy. These realities are the only real defense of the much-

maligned phrase *new economy*. See Paul Romer, paulromer.com; Carl Shapiro and Hal R. Varian, *Information Rules: A Strategic Guide to the Network Economy* (Boston: Harvard Business School Press, 1999); and the work of George Gilder concerning the ideas of scarcity and abundance in an intangible asset-driven economy. Classical economics is turned upside down.

6. Joel Kurtzman, "An Interview with Paul Romer," *strategy + business* (1997).

7. Charles Leadbeater, "Time to Let the Bean Counters Go," *New Statesman* (April 17, 1998).

8. Margaret M. Blair and Steven M. H. Wallman, *Unseen Wealth: Report of the Brookings Task Force on Intangibles* (Washington, D.C.: Brookings Institution Press, 2001), p. 11.

9. Nakamura, p. 4.

10. Robert Buderi, "In Search of Innovation," MIT *Technology Review* (November–December 1999).

11. Robert G. Eccles, et al., *The ValueReporting Revolution: Moving Beyond the Earnings Game* (New York City: John Wiley & Sons, 2001). Abstract as reported at getabstract.com.

12. Andrew Osterland, "Decoding Intangibles," *CFO Magazine* (April 1, 2001).

13. pwcglobal.com/Extweb/service.nsf/docid/EDB9BDD35FE9 1E37CA256BB20011AB2A.

14. www.skandia.com/en/ir/financialgoals.shtml.

15. "Customer Relationships and Growth in Value," supplement to Skandia's 1996 annual report, p. 14.

16. Ibid., p. 17.

17. Osterland, "Decoding Intangibles."

18. www.skandia.com/en/ir/skandiashare.jsp

19. There is an exception to this, as Watts of CBIZ Valuation Group points out, per FASB 141. If, in an acquisition, these expenditures result in a "completed" R&D asset, they will be capitalized. If the elements being acquired have not reached "completion," it could be considered an in-process research and development and expensed during the acquisition accounting.

20. AKR Capital Research, akrcapitalresearch.com.

21. Andrew Osterland, "Knowledge Capital Scorecard: Treasures Revealed," *CFO Magazine* (April 1, 2001).
22. Ibid.
23. E-mail from Baruch Lev (December 15, 2002).
24. Ibid.
25. Ibid.
26. This is an adaptation of the Knowledge Capital Scorecard published in *CFO Magazine*. Two dimensions of value that were deliberately left out of the original are industry Market Value to Comprehensive Value and Market Value.
27. "Customer Relationships and Growth in Value," p. 5.
28. There are exceptions to this. Although goodwill impairment testing was not required previously, companies were still required to conduct a qualitative assessment about how well business was going. If the company concluded a positive assessment, it might put a memo in the file documenting the exercise in order to satisfy SFAS 121. If some negative event or business condition did not occur, the presumption was that an impairment test was not required. Now it is. Interview with Greg Watts, director, CBIZ Valuation Group (March 6, 2003).
29. "Understand SFAS 141 & 142," PowerPoint presentation, Greg Watts, director of CBIZ Valuation Group, 2001.
30. Amortizable intangible assets need only be tested for an impairment on an as-needed basis. For instance, some customers will return to continue doing business with an organization while others will leave. Those who leave constitute an impairment event where intangible value adjustments—such as the dilution of the value of a customer contract—require reporting. Another example would be the end of a customer relationship if the customer is bought by another company that chooses to take its business elsewhere. Nonamortizable impairment testing would arise if a company decided to retire a certain brand within a specific time frame. The asset's life has been impaired because it will no longer deliver any economic benefits to the organization after the time period has elapsed. Not only is the asset impaired, it is now categorized as an

amortizable intangible asset because the company knows its
economic life will end two years (or whatever time period)
hence. Another impairment to nonamortizable intangible assets
is damage to the reputation of a product line—the Tylenol scare
of the early 1980s is a vivid example. Interview with Greg
Watts, director, CBIZ Valuation Group (March 6, 2003).

31. The formal rule for the two-step impairment test is as follows:
(1) Determine whether the book value of acquired assets of the
reporting unit exceeds the unit's so-called fair value, defined as
the value the assets would fetch on the market. (2) If fair value is
lower than book value, the company then must determine
whether the fair value of the unit's goodwill is less than the
goodwill's book value. If yes, an impairment loss has to be
recorded. The point of this exercise is not to understand the
impairment test but rather to see the implications in the fact
that an impairment test must be conducted. The impairment test
requirement forces managers to analyze intangible sources of
value in an acquired company with greater clarity and rigor,
which may result in a greater comprehension of what those
unidentifiable intangible sources of value really are. See Craig
Schneider, "Pool's Closed," *CFO Magazine* (July 1, 2001).

32. Ben & Jerry's had Wavy Gravy. Anything is possible!

33. Henry Sender, "Study Sees Hundreds of Companies Writing
Down Goodwill This Year," *Wall Street Journal* (April 24,
2002).

34. Stephen Taub, "Reverse Charge: Qwest Takes $41 Billion
Impairment Hit," *CFO.com* (October 29, 2002).

Chapter 4

1. While reporting standards treat technology this way, only
recently has the government changed its attitude. In 1999 the
Bureau of Economic Analysis, a unit in the U.S. Department of
Commerce, changed the way it calculated software
expenditures. It now categorizes such purchases as investments
rather as an input to production for the purposes of calculating
aggregate economic output, such as national income and gross

domestic product. Recategorization, the BEA estimates, added 0.2 percent to average annual growth rate to real GDP from 1959 to 1998, the years the recategorization was applied to—a sizable amount in dollar terms. See Eugene P. Seskin, "Improved Estimates of the National Income and Product Accounts for 1959–98, Results of the Comprehensive Revision," *Survey of Current Business* (December 1999). This upward adjustment in economic output reflects evolved thinking about the sources of wealth inside companies and how that wealth generates increases in economic output. This simple shift in thinking acknowledges implicitly if not explicitly that IT is a powerful driver of wealth creation inside organizations that use it shrewdly. Consigning such expenditures to a simple factor of production input understates software's importance in this wealth creation. See Brent R. Moulton, Robert P. Parker, and Eugene P. Seskin, "A Preview of the 1999 Comprehensive Revision of the National Income and Product Accounts, Definitional and Classificational Changes," *Survey of Current Business* (August 1999).

2. Erik Brynjolfsson and Shinkyu Yang, "The Intangible Costs and Benefits of Computer Investments: Evidence from the Financial Markets," Sloan School of Management, MIT, (May 1997), p. 26.

3. Standish Group press release (March 25, 2003).

4. Interview with Barbara Gomolski, research director at Gartner (January 13, 2003). The irony is that many IS (information systems) organization budgets are confined to utility services kinds of projects—maintenance and scheduled upgrades—even though many chief information officers have felt compelled to get economic value religion by improving their business and financial literacy as a way to ensure alignment of IT (information technology) project execution with tactical and strategic goals of the company.

5. Sometimes managers confuse the two, payback and ROI. Keen interest in economic value depiction of IT has turned ROI into a buzzword for all the different ways this value can be expressed

numerically. Yet ROI has a strict definition in finance, just as payback, internal rate of return, and net present value do.

6. Interview with Prasanna Dhore, vice president, Dreyfus (February 20, 2003).

7. "Customer-Centric Technology Investments: Where's the ROI?," Saugatuck Technology and CFO Research Services white paper (December 5, 2002). This study also found, against popular wisdom, that smaller companies were more inclined to embrace nonfinancial techniques to the depiction of the economic value of IT. The false assumption is that smaller companies, which tend to have less discretionary capital available for riskier technology initiatives, would cling to hard numbers as a way to mitigate uncertainty of returns. In fact, smaller companies, having less complicated business models and organizational structures, come across as freer thinkers on the subject due to looser and less formal procurement and budgeting procedures.

8. As a side note, MAP is useful as a project prioritization arrangement, too. A level 1 IT investment might very well require a level 4 investment first. As a measurement technique, Real Options is applicable here. See Henry Lucas, *Information Technology and the Productivity Paradox* (New York City: Oxford University Press, 1999).

9. Conceptually, this triage approach was introduced by Lucas in *Information Technology and the Productivity Paradox*. He did not use a pyramid concept but rather a pipeline stylization to make essentially the same point. Some technology is a precondition to other technology, and understanding the relationship between the two is the start in comprehension of IT's economic value. It is an astonishingly simple observation, but many important observations that inject clarity into discussions are.

10. Oracle opt-in e-mail marketing message from *BusinessWeek* magazine subscription.

11. At first blush, mentioning the hardware in the mix of value-creation elements seems reductio ad absurdum, but it is not. All

you have to do to see this is ask a CIO about the required
incremental hardware costs associated with deployment of new
enterprise software. It might include data warehouses, more
network capacity, or storage area networks as the proliferation
of data arising out of these investments balloons. New level 3 or
4 investment to support level 1 or 2 investment can be
substantial. Insofar as hardware investment is required in
advance of strategic software investment, it must be
acknowledged in the mix as a driver of value creation because it
is certainly a cost that ends up in the denominator of an ROI
calculation.

12. Jon E. Hilsenrath, "Behind Surging Productivity: The Service
    Sector Delivers," *Wall Street Journal* (November 7, 2003), p. 1.
13. John Berry, "The E-Learning Factor," *InternetWeek* (November
    6, 2000).
14. Ibid.

Chapter 5

1. *Intellectual Asset Management* magazine was launched in May
   2003 by Globe White Page Ltd., London. The magazine's sales
   pitch is: "*IAM* is unique because it treats IP as a business asset."
   This confirms that the attitudinal shift in which IP is something
   to be managed just like machines and real estate is still
   emerging.
2. The Intangible Asset Market Index, PLX Systems.
3. "Current Issues and Trends in the Economics of Patents," UC
   Berkeley and National Bureau of Economic Research, Bronwyn
   Hall (September 2002), p. 11.
4. David Wessel, "Capital Exchange" column, *Wall Street Journal*
   (December 16, 2003).
5. Greg Watts, "Valuing Intellectual Property," presentation,
   CBIZ Valuation Group (July 11, 2002), p. 7.
6. Ibid.
7. Lev, p. 34. Some of the most fervent innovation activity has
   taken place in countries that did not have patent laws. For
   example, Swiss inventors tended to concentrate their efforts in

watchmaking and specialized steelmaking for scientific and optical instruments. Their innovations were almost impossible to reverse-engineer and, therefore, were well suited to trade secret as opposed to patent protection. The English attempted to crack these innovations but failed. See Teresa Riordan, "A Stroll Through Patent History," *New York Times* (September 29, 2003).

8. Joel Mokyr, *The Lever of Riches: Technological Creativity and Economic Progress* (New York City: Oxford University Press, 1990), p. 79.

9. Alexander Poltorak and Paul Lerner, *Essentials of Intellectual Property* (New York City: John Wiley and Sons, 2002), p. 5.

10. Interview with Phil Stern, chief operating officer, QED (November 5, 2003).

11. Darrell Rigby and Chris Zook, "Open-Market Innovation," *Harvard Business Review* (October 2002), p. 5.

12. Interview with Phil Stern, chief operating officer, yet2.com (February 3, 2003).

13. Bill Roberts, "Rediscovering Corporate Treasures," *Knowledge Management* (May 2001).

14. Claudia H. Deutsch, "Industry Expertise Has Itself Become a Product," *New York Times* (May 13, 2002).

15. Susan Biagi, "Not Invented Here," *Telephony* (June 5, 2000).

16. Ibid.

17. While Lucent opted to acquire Chromatis instead of renting its IP, the conditions that drive OMI were clearly visible here: the need to get into a new market with innovative products and serious time-to-market issues. IT companies often buy their way into new markets, the voracious Cisco Systems being a good example.

18. "Open-Market Innovation," p. 3.

19. Ibid., p. 4.

20. pb.com/cgi-bin/pb.dll/ourcompany/pb_group_company_detail .jsp?groupCatName=Our+Company&groupOID=8003&locale= US&language=ENG.

21. Ibid.

22. Ibid.

23. Pharmaceutical Research and Manufacturers of America, phrma.org.

24. National Science Foundation, as published by the Aerospace Industries Association, aia-aerospace.org/stats/facts_figures /ff_99_00/Ff99p143.pdf.

25. Dennis K. Berman, "At Bell Labs Hard Times Take Toll on Pure Research," *Wall Street Journal* (May 23, 2003).

26. Ibid.

27. Interview with Tim Bernstein, vice president of operations, yet2.com (May 27, 2003).

28. "Open-Market Innovation," p. 4.

29. "The DKPTO/CBS Lecture on Intellectual Property Strategy, 2002/2003," Bronwyn Hall, Copenhagen (September 17, 2002).

30. Interview with Darrell Rigby, director and retail industry practice leader, Bain & Company (August 8, 2003).

31. "Open-Market Innovation," p. 8.

32. Big Idea Group information gleaned from its website, bigideagroup.net.

Chapter 6

1. Interview with Tim Bernstein, vice president of operations, yet2.com (July 22, 2003).

2. Ibid.

3. The experience of the Wright brothers might have been the first example of buy-side open-market innovation that, alas, failed. The year before their historic flight in December of 1903, the brothers proved the airworthiness of their engineless airplane design. In that off-season, the brothers queried about ten engine manufacturers in search of a workable propeller engine design that could be applied to their innovation for a powered flight. Many of the manufacturers built engines for steamships. To the brothers' dismay, not one of the engine designs proved applicable to their needs. An employee at the brothers' bicycle shop in Dayton, Ohio, was given the responsibility of building the engine that would usher in the century of flight.

4. Interview with Tim Bernstein, vice president of operations, yet2.com (July 29, 2003).
5. Timothy Aeppel, "Brothers of Invention: Design-Arounds Surge as More Companies Imitate Rivals' Patented Products," *Wall Street Journal* (April 19, 2004).
6. Ibid.
7. Ibid.
8. Lev, p. 14.
9. Michael Porter and Scott Stern, *The New Challenge to America's Prosperity: Findings from the Innovation Index* (Washington, D.C.: Council on Competitiveness, 1999), p. 3.
10. Ibid., p. 5.
11. Ibid., p. 13.
12. Ibid., p. 61.
13. Carl Shapiro and Hal R. Varian, *Information Rules: A Strategic Guide to the Network Economy* (Boston: Harvard Business School Press, 1999), p. 179.
14. Lev, p. 12.

Chapter 7
1. As of August 29, 2003.
2. From Michael Bloch's *Ribbentrop* (1992), as reported in *The Atlantic Monthly* (September 2003), p. 138.
3. brint.com/km/whatis.htm
4. cio.com/research/knowledge/edit/kmabcs.html
5. km-forum.org/what_is.htm
6. Artificial Intelligence Applications Institute at the University of Edinburgh, www.aiai.ed.ac.uk/technology/knowledge management.html. Might as well get a global perspective of how many definitions there are.
7. destinationkm.com/articles/default.asp?ArticleID=949
8. As you can tell, I like using search results illustratively. They happen to be very accurate proxies for a variety of circumstances and realities to support particular arguments.
9. A chronic misuse of a word really meaning that which is subject to a lawsuit.

10. "Moving Beyond Information Technology to Knowledge Management," Xerox advertising supplement (2000).

11. Leigh P. Donoghue, Jeanne G. Harris, and Bruce A. Weitzman, "Knowledge Management Strategies That Create Value," Accenture Institute white paper (1999).

12. I first wrote about the Hill & Knowlton story for *InternetWeek* in a piece titled "Employees Cash in on KM" (May 22, 2000). I followed up with Ted Graham in a series of interviews on the same subject in early September 2003.

13. James Surowiecki, "Decisions, Decisions," *The New Yorker* (March 24, 2003), p. 33.

14. Ibid.

15. Norm Alster, "It's Just a Game, but Hollywood Is Paying Attention," *New York Times* (November 23, 2003).

16. Ibid.

Chapter 8

1. Providing individual notes for every idea originated in the work behind Knowledge Object Theory would be far too cumbersome for me and no more useful for readers in search of further detail about the methodology. With permission from Michael Cahill, the inventor of KOT, this note serves as a global blanket note for all the ideas behind the theory. Readers are directed to futureknowledge.biz, where they can find a wealth of white papers, backgrounders, and technical documentation about the methodology.

2. Michael Cahill, "Using Knowledge Objects for Analysis," The Future Knowledge Group Inc. white paper (2002).

3. http://abstracts.aspb.org/pb2003/public/H06/0584.html

4. One brief side note to clear up any confusion. The KOM creator does not have to be an eyewitness to some phenomenon in order to declare its accuracy. Reasonableness in collecting information in order to validate KOMs is the standard I am trying to get across. If a set of KOMs expresses a competitor's position in the marketplace and these were based upon a report from a competitive intelligence-gathering consultant, they could

still be wrong. But they won't be inaccurate because the creator failed to follow due diligence in verifying their accuracy. She bought the expensive report and based the KOMs constructed around this information in the expectation it was accurate. If it wasn't, then the police might want to get involved. The police will not be interested in the perpetration of bad KOMs but rather with fraud.

5. A related issue to validity is survivability. Knowledge Object Theory holds that in order for a KOM to be valid, then some element of the input in the Triad must survive so that the element is part of the output as well. For example, cool water → heater → hot water is a KOM that survives because some attributes of cool water survive in the output of hot water, and that attribute is water. In cool water → heater → explosion, this KOM survives because the result is water on the floor where the heater is located. In crude oil → refinery → gasoline, this KOM survives because some chemical elements or properties in crude oil remain in gasoline. In crude oil → refinery → ice cream cone, this KOM does not survive if the intent of the KOM is to show the process involved in the making of gasoline. It might survive if the intent of the KOM is to show how terrorists are smuggling bombs into a refinery plant in an ice cream truck that visits workers on their lunch break. Survivability is inextricably linked to the intent of the knowledge. What is the KOM attempting to demonstrate?

Chapter 9

1. This is an adaptation of two columns I wrote for *InternetWeek* in May and June of 2001. I joined the best of both into a brief tutorial about what LCV is and what it is designed to measure. Thanks should be extended to Julian Chu, at the time a director at the consulting firm Mainspring, who vetted the calculations. Mainspring has since been acquired by IBM.
2. Ibid.
3. Marcia Stepanek, "Weblining," *BusinessWeek e.Biz*, cover story (April 3, 2000).

4. They ought to try. House brands and private labels, such as Costco's Kirkland line, are eating alive the name brands from consumer packaged goods companies. See Matthew Boyle, "Brand Killers," *Fortune* (July 21, 2003).

5. Lynn Russo, "It Really Is All About Value," *1to1 Magazine* (May/June 2003), p. 4.

6. This scenario is adapted from a piece I wrote for *InternetWeek*, "Marketing Automation Gives CRM a Lift" (March 20, 2001).

7. Ibid.

8. Don Peppers and Martha Rogers, *One to One, B2B: Customer Development Strategies for the Business-to-Business World*, draft version (New York City: Currency Books/Doubleday, 2001).

9. Ibid., p. 17.

Chapter 10

1. The Convergys experience is based upon a series of interviews I conducted with various executives for a piece I wrote in *InternetWeek*, "Reorganize Around CRM," for the June 2001 issue. Interviews also included Peppers & Rogers Group, which Convergys hired to develop this lifetime value strategy.

2. *One to One, B2B: Customer Development Strategies for the Business-to-Business World*, p. 18. This happens to be exactly the approach of Amazon.com. It established customer relationships with books. Now it leverages those relationships across a number of product categories that current and new customers would be interested in. Who thought a few years ago that Amazon would sell clothes and medical supplies?

3. Geoffrey Moore and Paul Wiefels, "Keeping the Competitive Edge," *Optimize*, issue 13 (November 2002).

4. Convergys 2002 annual report, PDF version, p. 2. (http://www.convergys.com/2002_annual_report.html)

5. Ibid., p. 15.

6. Ibid., p. 8.

7. "The Customer Profitability Conundrum: When to Love 'Em or Leave 'Em," Booz Allen Hamilton and knowledge@wharton white paper, *strategy + business* (2002).

8. Matthew Boyle, "Brand Killers," *Fortune* (August 11, 2003), p. 89.

9. "Winterthur Insurance," SPSS brief, 2000, p. 1.

10. Mark Klein and Arthur Einstein, "The Myth of Customer Satisfaction," Booz Allen Hamilton brief (no date), p. 1.

11. Haig R. Nalbantian et al., *Play to Your Strengths: Managing Your Internal Labor Markets for Lasting Competitive Advantage* (New York City: McGraw-Hill, 2003), p. 152. It is propitious timing that this book was published so recently, as it deals exclusively with the management of people as an intangible asset. I footnote liberally from this text here and in Chapter 11, on human capital.

12. Ibid., p. 155.

13. Ibid., p. 64.

14. Ibid., p. 64.

15. Ibid., p. 65.

16. Ibid., p. 65.

17. Ibid., p. 66.

18. Ibid., p. 66.

19. Advertising has the character of being both a fixed and a variable cost. Historically, advertising campaign costs were not dependent upon sales, but the Internet is changing that. The business models of certain sites depend upon visitors clicking through an ad or promotion for their compensation. Beyond the cost of creating the ads, actual advertising costs are tied directly to sales performance.

20. Scott McCartney, "Why Your Free Trip to Maui Is Hobbling the Airline Industry," Middle Seat column, *Wall Street Journal* (February 4, 2004).

Chapter 11

1. Nalbantian et al., p. 187.

2. Interview with Jeremy Gump, senior manager, Ernst & Young's human capital practice (December 10, 2003).

3. Robert S. Kaplan and David P. Norton, *The Balanced Scorecard: Translating Strategy into Action* (Boston: Harvard Business

School Press, 1996), p. 151. Figure 11.1 is an adaptation of a figure on p. 152.

4. Ibid., p. 153.
5. Ibid., p. 154.
6. Nalbantian et al., p. 236.
7. Ibid., p. 34.
8. Ibid., p. 57.
9. Ibid., p. 17.
10. Ibid., p.18.
11. Ibid., p. 20.
12. Ibid., p. 37.
13. Ibid., p. 39.
14. Ibid., p. 46.
15. Ibid., p. 46.
16. Ibid., p. 47.
17. Ibid., p. 48.
18. Ibid., p. 60.
19. Ibid., p. 62.
20. Ibid., p. 4.
21. Ibid., p. 6.

Chapter 12

1. Abe De Ramos, "The China Syndrome," *CFO Magazine* (October 2003), p. 74.
2. Both Figures 12.1 and 12.2 are from Valdis E. Krebs, "Managing the Connected Organization," white paper, orgnet.com/MCO.html.
3. Krebs asserts that empirical research shows that a mix of direct and indirect (one degree–removed) connections is the optimal mix to create greatest social capital. The research showed that too many direct connections slowed workers down because they spent too much time managing relationships and communicating with their peers. Conversely, indirect connections are just as valuable a source of knowledge as a direct connection is. In

Figure 12.1, Team 15 has the optimal social capital, according to the precepts of social network analysis, because although it has limited direct connections to other teams, it has a combination of direct and indirect connections to a significant number of teams in the network.

4. Krebs.

5. Knowledge Object Theory might provide similar flow-mapping benefits. Think back to the example of BestGrow and the scientists behind the construction of a knowledge base using Knowledge Object Machines to analyze R&D of a new fertilizer product. When it was time for the marketing executive to plan the product launch, she explored the KOMs created by the research scientist, which expressed the results of lab trials. This was the basis for product launch planning. The first KOM she accessed that was directly relevant to her information needs we could view as the transition point into her domain of expertise. The research scientist's KOM expressing test results became the launch pad for the knowledge base the marketing executive would build for BestGrow's introduction into the marketplace. These transition points from one subject matter domain into another can be considered nodes, or connectors, which link various employees in the organization around expertise. Given that these KOMs can easily be hyperlinked in authoring software, these nodes would not be hard to map visually, and such a visualization would give a KM manager a high-level view of how successful KOT is as a tool for both knowledge sharing and reuse. A visualization might show that the R&D knowledge base is the source of many other knowledge bases from other areas in the organization, while HR's knowledge base has not been leveraged by any other functional area or line of business. Is this a problem or a reflection of the limited usefulness of HR domain expertise in other parts of the organization? That depends upon the specific situation in the company. Just as important, a visualization will give managers a high-level view of

knowledge diffusion across the enterprise. Their happiest suspicions might be confirmed: the universality of KOT as a way to express any knowledge drives knowledge reuse and sharing across the entire company in ways not imagined. A map will reveal these paths.

6. Interview with Jim Eckenrode, vice president, TowerGroup, a financial services research firm (August 2003).

7. Don Peppers, Martha Rogers, and Bob Dorf, *The One to One Fieldbook* (New York City: Currency Doubleday, 1999), p. 207.

8. Ibid.

9. "Human Capital Management: The CFO's Perspective," CFO Research Services and Mercer Human Resource Management (2003). The survey yielded 180 responses, 51 percent of which were from CFO or senior vice presidents of finance. Sixty-nine percent of companies in which these executives worked had $1 billion or more in sales.

10. "Human Capital Management," executive summary, p. 2.

11. Adapted from "Human Capital Management," executive summary, p. 2.

12. "Human Capital Management," p. 19.

13. Ibid., p. 20.

14. "Brand Valuation Methodology," p. 1.

15. Interview with Andrew Zolli, founder, Z + Partners (November 11, 2003).

16. Ibid.

17. From "Brand and Deliver: IT's Role in Creating Killer Brands," slide show presented at Computerworld's Premier 100 IT Leaders Conference, Scottsdale, Arizona (February 23–25, 2003).

18. Lev, p. 10.

19. Ibid.

20. Geoffrey A. Fowler and Joseph Pereira, "Behind Hit Toys: A Race to Tap Seasonal Surge," *Wall Street Journal* (December 18, 2003).

21. Ibid.
22. Ibid.
23. Ibid.

Epilogue

1. Polly LaBarre, "The Industrialized Revolution," *Fast Company*, issue 76 (November 2003), p. 114.
2. Ibid.

INDEX